GOVERNMENT INFORMATION MANAGEMENT
A Primer and Casebook

D1571884

David F. Andersen
Nelson A. Rockefeller College of Public Affairs
and Policy
University at Albany
State University of New York

Sharon S. Dawes
Nelson A. Rockefeller Institute of Government
State University of New York

Prentice Hall, Englewood Cliffs, New Jersey 07632

Library of Congress Cataloging-in-Publication Data

ANDERSEN, DAVID F. (David Fadum)
  Government information management : a primer and casebook / DAVID
F. ANDERSEN, SHARON S. DAWES.
    p.   cm.
  Includes bibliographical references.
  ISBN 0-13-361866-8
    1. Public administration—Data processing—Management.
    2. Government information—Management.   I. Dawes, Sharon S.
  II. Title.
JF1525.A8A53   1991
350′.00028′5—dc20   90-35453

For
Matt and Robbie
Katie, Beth, and Meg

Editorial/production supervision: *Edith Riker/Bea Marcks*
Cover design: *Patricia Kelly*
Manufacturing buyer: *Mary Ann Gloriande*
Prepress buyer: *Debra Kesar*

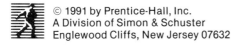

© 1991 by Prentice-Hall, Inc.
A Division of Simon & Schuster
Englewood Cliffs, New Jersey 07632

Printed in the United States of America
10 9 8 7 6 5 4 3 2 1

ISBN   0-13-361866-8

Prentice-Hall International (UK) Limited, *London*
Prentice-Hall of Australia Pty. Limited, *Sydney*
Prentice-Hall Canada Inc., *Toronto*
Prentice-Hall Hispanoamericana, S. A., *Mexico*
Prentice-Hall of India Private Limited, *New Delhi*
Prentice-Hall of Japan, Inc., *Tokyo*
Simon & Schuster Asia Pte. Ltd., *Singapore*
Editora Prentice-Hall do Brasil, Ltda., *Rio de Janeiro*

CONTENTS

iii

PREFACE

This text, *Government Information Management: A Primer and Casebook,* has been designed to teach students of public administration, policy, and management the basic principles of information management in the public sector. The past two decades have witnessed explosive growth in computing technologies, yet most of today's public managers rose to positions of responsibility before computers were widely used within government. It seems likely that tomorrow's managers will be using information technologies that have not even been invented today. These rapid technological changes challenge our modern curriculum. As a result, information management has joined the list of core skills for effective public management, along with such topics as human resource administration, budgeting and finance, administrative law, and principles of organization and management.

The book is predicated on the observation that a growing portion of public resources is being spent on information. Government is, itself, an information processing and distributing mechanism. The text discusses how to use information resources to manage government operations and hinges on several key perspectives and theoretical points of view.

Perspectives and Theoretical Lenses. We hold the view that effective information resource managers must understand three managerial perspectives—that of the data processing professional, the agency program manager, and the government policy maker. The field of public information management requires skill in all three areas. This basic concept is discussed briefly in Chapter 1 and then reinforced throughout the book.

A second organizing premise, introduced in Chapter 2, involves the four theoretical lenses of technology, economics, organization, and politics. Important decisions regarding information resources and management involve application of all four lenses to the enterprise of public management. The ability to look at problems from these four vantage points will be a key to effective use of information resources.

The text uses these three perspectives and four theoretical lenses to analyze a wide range of material under the broad term *government information management*. We use both discursive essaylike chapters and case studies to teach its lessons. Readers are encouraged to travel back and forth between these two complementary ways of approaching both teaching and learning. They allow the book to be used equally effectively in case-based courses, in concept-based courses, or as a supplemental text in academic or professional programs on managerial computing, research design and computing, management information systems, decision support systems, or information resource management.

Using the Text in a Concept-based Course. For courses involving pre-service students or a mixture of pre-service and in-service students, we prefer to begin with concepts—reading and discussing the issues in the five chapters first and then moving into the case studies. This gives all students a common conceptual framework in which to approach the cases. Exercise at the end of each chapter are explicitly keyed in to one or more of the cases, allowing instructors and students to "cross-walk" from the chapters directly into the cases studies.

Using the Text in a Case-based Course. For more advanced in-service students with significant work experience, instructors may wish to orient the course more exclusively around the case studies. In this instance, we recommend that class exercises and homework assignments refer to the concepts covered in the chapters. "Further Reflection" exercises have been included at the end of each case study to facilitate this approach. They refer students to selected portions of the earlier chapters. However, we do recommend that the first two chapters be assigned before beginning the first case study. These two chapters summarize the major perspectives that run through all the cases.

Using the Text as Supplemental Material or in Training. While this book can be used as the basis for a full semester of classes, it is also designed for use as a supplemental text in courses on managerial computing, research design and computing, management information systems, or information resource management. It is also effective in professional development programs. In these instances, instructors will probably prefer to focus on selected case studies to accomplish specific purposes. Again, Chapters 1 and 2 should be used to provide a common conceptual foundation for approaching the case studies.

A Note on the Case Studies. With the exception of two cases—"Managing the Introduction of a Voice-oriented Clinical Data System in a Psychiatric Facility" and "Where to Draw the Line: Public, Private, and Illicit Uses of Personal Information"—the situations depicted in the cases represent actual administrative situations with which one or more of the authors have had firsthand knowledge or experience. However, a hypothetical element has been added to each experience-based case to create a situation that can help focus class discussion. For example, in the Hazard County case, a fictional fire was added to the authors' experiences and knowledge of disaster recovery systems in real social services agencies. In the Forensic Mental Health Database case, the suicide in the Highmountain facility provides a point of focus for investigating cross-agency information systems. While all the characters are fictional, the information systems and the underlying issues are not.

How This text Came to Be. The motivation for writing this book came from our collective experiences, totaling more than thirty years, working with information systems exclusively in the public sector. Our joint backgrounds combine designing, installing, and managing information systems with programs of teaching and research. These academic and practical threads were woven together in 1986 by several events. First, the National Association of Schools of Public Affairs and Administration (NASPAA) required all graduate schools of public affairs wishing to offer an accredited professional master's degree to teach their students the rudiments of government information systems. Presumably this new requirement would extend beyond the technical training in computing and information systems most schools then offered.

At the same time, a coalition of experienced public managers in New York State asked the Rockefeller Institute of Government to assemble a curriculum to teach mid-career professionals basic principles for managing information systems and technology in the public sector. The members of the coalition foreshadowed the structure of this book. They included data processing professionals, program administrators, and representatives of the state's control agencies.

It seemed to us that the academic world and the world of practice were saying the same thing—good training material was needed to teach preservice and mid-career professionals alike the principles that underlie the interaction between information and government. Much good material already existed about the unique nature of public sector management—that is the stuff of good public administration programs. Even more covered the technical concepts of information systems. What seemed to be missing was material that spanned the two domains without duplicating either.

The cases in this text were developed first and used initially with a sophisticated audience—senior data processing managers, program administrators, and policy makers. They were first used in "Managing Information in New York State Government," a 1986–87 seminar series sponsored by

New York State, Digital Equipment Corporation, AT&T, IBM, and Unisys. This initial group had extensive technical, managerial, and public policy background.

The essay chapters were subsequently written to provide less-skilled students with some of the insight the original audience had gained by experience. The full text has been pilot taught with pre-service first- and second-year MPA students. These students had prior coursework in computer concepts and techniques as well as background in statistics and research design such as is found in almost any good core curriculum. Aside from this common coursework, their backgrounds and career aspirations varied. The text assumes, then, that students have basic computer literacy and some hands-on experience, usually with a microcomputer.

ACKNOWLEDGEMENTS

No book is ever written solely by its authors. Like most human enterprises, the end product represents contributions beyond counting. We gratefully acknowledge the support, talent, and enthusiasm of the many friends and colleagues who played a part.

Jane Zacek took our original executive seminar series under the umbrella of the Management Resources Project at Rockefeller Institute and Catherine Gerard and Ramon Rodriguez of the NYS Governor's Office of Employee Relations secured funds for us to proceed. Warren Ilchman, then Director of the Rockefeller Institute, saw the project as an example of the fruitful convergence of ideas and action that has been our philosophy throughout. Ron Mason of AT&T, Lucia Clemente of Digital Equipment Corporation, Tom Brun of IBM, and Frank Burnett of Unisys Corporation brought the considerable resources of their companies into what then became a public-private-academic partnership. The most important ingredient, however, was the group of forty senior New York State executives who stayed the course through five sessions over six months and who taught us more about the synergy of perspectives and ideas than we can ever say.

Pete Seagle of the University at Albany Business School worked with us on every seminar and made a special contribution to the book through authorship of the Hazard County and State Treasurer cases. Catherine Couse of the NYS Council on Children and Families was one of the original seminar participants and later turned her professional expertise and writing talents into the case on Services to People with Disabilities.

Still, the book would have remained an unrealized idea were it not for David Andersen's sabbatical at the Norwegian School of Management where Jørgen Randers and Fred Wenstøp made it possible for the first draft to be written. Many transatlantic exchanges and versions later, the material was pilot tested with a group of able and willing graduate students in the MPA program at the University at Albany.

In the meantime the original seminar participants, working with Sharon Dawes, created the NYS Forum for Information Resource Management capturing in a systematic way, the cross-agency, multi-perspective, intersectoral exchanges that inspired us in the first place. At the risk of omitting the names of many other active supporters, special thanks must go to Paul Fisk, Thomas Donovan, Charles Blunt, Jacqueline Del Rossi, George Mitchell, and Lorraine Noval for exceptional insight, energy, and dedication.

Good ideas, talented colleagues, and a completed manuscript, however, do not make a book. We thank Karen Horton and Delores Mars of the Prentice Hall College Division for taking on our project, Professor Gregory Streif of Georgia Tech and Professor John Charles Kresslein of Orangeburg-Calhoun Technical College for their perceptive reviews of the text, production editors Edie Riker and Bea Marcks of East End Publishing for both talent and patience with our last minute ideas, Marie Lines and Deborah Andersen for careful editing and review of the entire manuscript, and Karen Geffert for turning out picture-perfect artwork with our inexpert guidance and impossible deadlines.

To these and all the others who worked with us in the seminar series, the Forum, and the University, we extend sincere thanks. Only their good ideas are here—all the mistakes are ours.

David F. Andersen
Sharon S. Dawes
Albany, New York

SUGGESTED READINGS

Kiel, L. Douglas. Information Systems Education in Masters Programs in Public Affairs and Administration. *Public Administration Review* 46(SI): 590–94, November 1986.
National Association of Schools of Public Affairs and Administration, Ad Hoc Committee on Computers in Public Management Education. Curriculum Recommendations for Public Management Education. *Public Administration Review* 46(SI):595–602, November 1986.
Simmons, Al. New York's Info Forum. *Government Technology Magazine*, 1(4), July–August 1988.

CHAPTER 1

INTRODUCTION: THE NEED TO MANAGE INFORMATION IN THE PUBLIC SECTOR

On a blustery day in October 1986, a small bundle of two thousand microfiche cards mysteriously vanished from Canada's federal tax office. No larger than a lunchbox, the packet contained names, addresses, birth dates, Social Security numbers, spouses' names, and confidential income data for all of Canada's citizens. Investigators for the Royal Canadian Mounted Police suspected the worst. Criminal or terrorist elements might have stolen the data for illegal purposes—falsification of passports or birth certificates or fraudulent pension and welfare claims.

In Parliament, Prime Minister Mulroney's Conservative government faced a crisis. Opposition leaders called for the resignation of Tax Minister Elmer Mackay, insisting all taxpayers be informed that their Social Security numbers might no longer be confidential. Mackay suspected the theft was a politically motivated attempt to discredit the government. But how had all of this vital information come to be collected in one place? Why were internal management and security procedures so lax as to allow the data to be stolen? Had any real damage been done?

Mackay ordered an immediate investigation of his department's information management policies.[1]

---

[1]For more details on this vignette, see the case study "Where to Draw the Line: Public, Private, and Illicit Uses of Personal Information."

THE CONCEPT OF GOVERNMENT INFORMATION MANAGEMENT

Mackay's problems dramatically illustrate the critical role that information management and policy play in all modern governments. Governments maintain records about virtually all citizens with details of their health, finances, or personal and household characteristics. Specialized information centers for research and instruction in state university systems, those serving the many related needs of criminal justice agencies, and the specialized programs of scores of other public organizations create a massive storehouse of government-held data. While government information is stored and manipulated by the same technology as corporate information bases, Mackay's problems with the Canada's tax files demonstrate the unique issues that stem from government's powers to act in the broad public interest.

At all levels, governments are actively managing information in electronic form, but at the same time the basic technology of electronic information systems is rapidly changing. Virtually all of today's top-level managers received their formal education and much of their informal on-the-job training before wide use and heavy reliance on electronic information processing came on the scene. The information technology we will deal with ten or fifteen years from now will be substantially different in design, operation, cost, and capability than anything we can reasonably expect today.

Those who manage information technology in the public sector are like ships' captains moving toward port through strong currents and shifting winds. A wise and lucky captain chooses a course that takes advantage of those forces. Another, less knowledgeable or fortunate, is forced on a longer, more costly voyage. Those costs show up in poorly invested resources of three kinds: technology, people, and information itself.

The new breed of information managers must have skills traditionally defined in three separate domains of expertise. Figure 1.1 illustrates the intersection of these domains. They are technical data processing management; traditional management skills such as substantive expertise, organizational skills, and administrative abilities; and specialized knowledge of the policy context of government operations. Unfortunately, few are truly skilled in all three areas. The traditional organization of jobs and functions within government means that few managers have acquired skills in all three domains, but it is precisely this mix of skills that will be necessary if governments are to manage their information futures wisely.

The contours of government information management are not well understood. Perhaps in ten years we will have definitive answers to how the large and complex public sector organizations should approach the information management frontier. For now, we must be content with moving forward slowly, hoping we can at least ask the right questions and frame some interesting alternative answers. This problem is ubiquitous at all levels

Technical Data Processing Skills

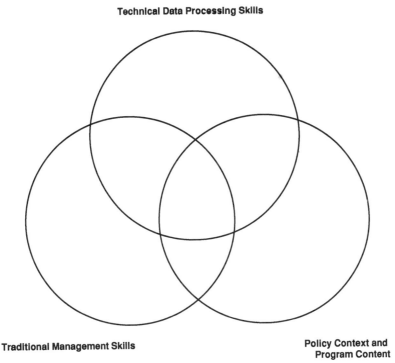

Traditional Management Skills   **Policy Context and
                                                      Program Content**

Figure 1.1   Government Information Management as the Intersection of Three Domains
             of Knowledge

and branches of government. Most organizations, both public and private, face similar issues requiring integrated expertise from all three domains. What seems most needed now are forums and opportunities for professionals to exchange views and craft new strategies that synthesize the diversity of skills and insights that arise from their separate perspectives.

WHERE GOVERNMENT INFORMATION MANAGEMENT HAS BEEN

Most large, complex organizations in both the public and private sectors have been through roughly three phases in their responses to the challenges and opportunities of rapidly emerging information technology.

The first phase in the late 1950s and early 1960s was characterized by experimentation with the newly developed digital computing technology. Operating in a batch processing mode initially, large repetitive jobs were automated to support public programs like motor vehicle registration and tax processing as well as internal operations like payrolls. The success of those early applications coupled with the rapid growth of the computer industry as a whole led to the second phase spanning the mid-1960s and much of the 1970s. This phase—the mainframe era—saw a steady increase in the number of large organizations that successfully demanded their own mainframe systems. Smaller agencies purchased services from larger central systems that had excess capacity or from time-sharing systems set up specifically to provide computing services to smaller or more specialized users. The problems associated with acquisition of these large and expensive mainframe systems centered for the most part on their cost and the justification of potential uses. Governments responded by creating oversight units, usually within budget offices, to review and approve computer acquisitions throughout the jurisdiction. An appropriate and useful policy response for the second phase of information technology expansion, these units have tended to dissolve as another phase emerged.

The third phase, spanning the last years of the 1970s and the 1980s, has been driven by dramatic technological change—micro-electronic circuitry. As the price of computing devices plummeted, first minicomputers and then microcomputers made the acquisition of data processing equipment more like the purchase of a typewriter than a major capital expenditure. In the early years of microcomputing, both the hardware and software markets were chaotic, inundated with new products and unlimited promises for ever greater and "friendlier" computing power. Experience, however, often fell short of promise, and the specter of massive expenditures for incompatible devices and technologies was, and remains, a significant cause for concern. Contracting procedures and consulting services established within central service agencies were among the policy responses developed in this phase. Their goal, of course, was to rationalize and stabilize responses to a turbulent marketplace.

With the relatively late entry of IBM into the microcomputer market, an informal industry standard emerged around IBM compatibility and the MS–DOS operating system. As a result, some of the confusion was cleared away. The highly competitive information technology market has taken its toll. Today, there are fewer choices but also more compatibility. Unfortunately, the next generation of hardware now under development in vendor labs on both sides of the Pacific may promise another hectic transition to the more powerful technologies of the future.

The third phase has also seen the public workforce become increasingly sophisticated in its knowledge and use of microcomputers. Advanced by specialized training offered by government itself as well as by virtually every university and computer vendor in the nation, more and more nontechnical professionals are demanding, and getting, desktop technology often unrelated to their agencies' mainframe systems.

While this third phase of development is still under way and requires continued attention, the public sector now stands poised on the brink of a fourth wave of technological challenges. With a massive sunk cost in both computing and human capital, those responsible for the public's information resources are beginning to look for ways to integrate hardware, software, people, and data. Communications systems, huge networks that span the globe and small ones that connect the workers in your office, herald a change in information power like nothing that has come before. As this fourth phase unfolds, mainframe specialists, micro users, telecommunications experts, program managers, agency executives, and central control organizations will collectively determine the future of government information management.

WHERE GOVERNMENT INFORMATION MANAGEMENT IS GOING

While the exact nature of this fourth phase of development is not fully clear to anyone, some trends can already be discerned. Government is in its second decade of "doing more with less." This has commonly meant less money. In this new era, however, what we will have relatively less of is human resources. As government is increasingly understood to be in the information processing business, computing will play an ever more crucial role in its white-collar productivity. The cost of computer hardware has fallen to the point where we now invest in slack equipment that rests idle on a worker's desk most of the day in order to boost the productivity of information-intensive hours. It is only a matter of time before our machines will handle information transmission and manipulation regardless of its form—voice, data, or image. And the nature of work itself is changing. Professionals interact directly with text-creating and text-generating machines, and the traditional boundaries separating clerical from professional work are beginning to blur. We are becoming aware of a new set of hazards to office workers, and ergonomics gives us a way to understand the puzzling interfaces that are developing between workers and their machines. No longer confined to locked, climate-controlled rooms, these new electronic machines are everywhere in the office. They are beginning to take voice commands from human operators, and some even talk back to us. The mail room is giving way to electronically transmitted documents, and local area networks are connecting offices into what may someday become the paperless workplace.

In general, the fourth phase is one of ambiguous boundaries and uncertain distinctions. Information technology is spilling out of the computer room and seeping into nearly everyone's job description. Some compare its impact with the mechanization of blue-collar work in the nineteenth century. Clearly these trends pose immense managerial challenges. They demand skills beyond traditional competence in data processing (but in-

npetencies), demand insight beyond the traditional fields of
but include a deep knowledge of those subjects), and chal-
tional views of how public policy does and ought to work (but
_ ...ust work within them).

THE NEED TO MANAGE OUR INFORMATION FUTURE

The command to do more with less, and the potential for electronic information processing to help us do just that, present a virtual mandate to public
managers. That mandate requires us—technicians, program managers, and
decision makers alike—to pool our expertise, to shape a collaborative response to government's information future.

In the Chinese character set, the concept of "crisis" is represented by
the dual characters representing "danger" and "opportunity." The crisis we
face today is unprecedented technological change. Our challenge is to make
the right investments in computing and human capital while at the same
time seizing the opportunities that these new technologies offer. The im-
plied premise behind this book is that we will collectively manage best if we
can learn to view information systems from the viewpoints of the three
domains: technology, management, and policy. Our goal is a more productive government earning full value for its investments in human, technological, and information resources.

APPROACHES TO LEARNING ABOUT GOVERNMENT
INFORMATION MANAGEMENT

We can approach government information management by several paths.
Each emphasizes a different blend of the technical, managerial, and policy
aspects of the field. Each differs in the amount of attention given to the
uniquely public aspects of the field versus more generic approaches that
stress similarities between information technology and management issues
in the public, private, and not-for-profit sectors.

This book emphasizes the uniquely public aspects of government information management and policy issues. Our treatment of the technical aspects of the field is intentionally brief. Since most of the technical issues
surrounding information management and policy in government are, in
fact, mostly generic, we have not attempted to duplicate the number of very
good books that exist on computer science and data processing techniques,
management information systems, and decision support systems. Here our
emphasis is on the organizational and political aspects of information management and policy that are unique to the public sector.

This approach complements many others and can be used to supplement material in a number of academic courses and professional development programs. Fundamental courses in managerial computing, for example, stress topics such as basic programming, spreadsheet and database packages, and statistical applications. They provide baseline knowledge of computing applications for managers. Material in this volume builds on that technical knowledge and explores the organizational and political implications of computing systems in the public sector. Courses in management information systems (MIS) and decision support systems (DSS) explore the flow of information through an organization. They use modeling and other analytic techniques to enhance information use as a basis for making choices. Several cases in this book look at the installation of MIS and DSS applications, stressing their organizational and political nature. The cases provide context and background for a better understanding of how generic MIS and DSS concepts are applied in government settings. Finally, full-blown courses in information resource management (IRM) take a much broader view of the full range of resources brought to bear and policies needed to manage information in organizations. The material here emphasizes government-specific issues such as freedom of information or personal privacy.

HOW TO USE THIS BOOK

This book contains two rather different types of materials—regular chapters that discuss concepts and issues, and case studies designed to knit these concepts together in the context of live managerial situations. Exercise material, study questions, and bibliographic references at the end of each chapter and case serve to weave these two strands together. You would be well advised to work back and forth between these two quite different ways of looking at the field of government information management.

Chapter 2 surveys the field through four conceptual lenses: technological, economic, organizational, and political. Reading this chapter first will give you an overview of much of what is to follow. Chapter 3 provides a framework for looking at the organizational impacts of information management, drawing on the concept of organizational effectiveness in the public sector. Chapter 4 explores the distinctly public nature of information management within government. A series of operating constraints and issues unique to government are outlined and discussed in some detail. Finally, Chapter 5 outlines the often tangled issues of privacy and public access to government records, exploring them from both the administrator's and the citizen's point of view.

One good way to use this book is to read the first five chapters in order and then proceed to the case studies. Exercises and suggested readings at the end of each chapter provide opportunities to deepen understanding and sharpen analysis of the concepts developed in the chapters. All the case studies cut across the issues raised in the chapters. That is, in live management situations all the various dimensions are co-mingled into a complex nexus of decision and choice. For the most part, the cases are built as decision-forcing situations, requiring that you come to conclusions and make choices, often looking at a given situation from the three perspectives of technology, management, and policy.

An equally useful way to approach this book is to begin with one or several of the cases. Each case is essentially self-contained and can be treated at several levels of sophistication. In our experience, first-year students of public administration and policy can vigorously engage the issues raised in the cases. Similarly, seasoned professionals with several decades of experience can address the issues with equal energy, but of course at a deeper level of awareness. Discussions that mingle all of these various levels of background can be lively and interesting all around. If you begin with the cases, you may wish to use the "Further Reflections" section at the end of each case to deepen your understanding of the material presented. These sections will refer you to the chapters as well as to relevant readings in the field as a whole.

No matter which path you choose, we hope one central point stands out. Effective management of the public's information resources requires understanding and cooperation between the three domains of technology, management, and policy. Learning to appreciate these three perspectives and their essential interactions is the key to becoming a more effective public information manager.

EXERCISES

1. Government data on individual citizens are located in many places. You might be astounded at the number.

   a. Make a list of the government records you believe might personally identify you. Of the government records on your list, which do you believe are in machine-readable form?

   b. Reexamine the list you have just made. Which of the records do you believe are actually cross-indexed with others? For example, the record of your driver's license might be cross-indexed with the record that registers your car. Which other records could, in principle, be cross-indexed?

   c. In Japan, many of the prefecturate governments (roughly equivalent to our states) are actively constructing a single citizen record file to unify the disparate personal records that are now kept in different locations. In your opinion, what are the relative advantages and disadvantages of this more centralized record-keeping system versus the more decentralized pattern that we maintain in the United States?

2. Computer-based information systems are rapidly being implemented in most government agencies. Think of an agency or unit of local government with which you are familiar.

   a. Briefly describe the function and organization of the jurisdiction or agency you have chosen.

   b. Beginning with 1950, for every ten years thereafter up to the present (1960, 1970, 1980, etc.) estimate the number of full-time employees of the agency or jurisdiction you have chosen. For the same points in time, estimate the number of central processing units (CPUs) that have been purchased, leased, or installed in that same agency or jurisdiction. (Count the CPU of a mainframe and the CPU of a microcomputer each as just one CPU.)

   c. From your estimates in part b above, compute the ratio of CPUs per full-time employee for all the points in time that you have considered. What do you believe the ratio of CPUs to full-time employees will be ten, twenty, and thirty years from now? Why do you think the trend will go as you have predicted?

3. Some analysts roughly divide the costs associated with information technologies into hardware costs, software costs, and "orgware" costs. Orgware includes the personnel, training, and other labor- and organizational-intensive aspects of maintaining and using information systems.

   a. For the same unit of government you picked in Exercise 2 above, list the categories of hardware costs (such as purchase of microprocessors) that it probably bears.

   b. List the categories of software costs that pertain to the agency or jurisdiction.

   c. List the categories of orgware costs.

   d. Which of these three classes of cost do you believe to be the greatest? What would you guess is the ratio of hardware to software to orgware costs? What fraction of the budget for total agency operations do you believe is spent on information management?

4. In the State of Goodwill, county and municipal governments rely on property and sales taxes for the bulk of their income. The sales tax is administered by the county and distributed to municipal governments and special districts according to formulas. Both municipal and county governments levy and administer property taxes. Property assessment and evaluation is currently a function of municipal governments only.

   The state has recently been put under a court order to equalize its assessment practices more fully. In a surprise move, the legislature mandated that property tax administration be centralized at the county level, the same as the sales tax. This implies that a major new assessment and data processing operation will have to be installed within county governments.

   a. Discuss the advantages and disadvantages of allowing data processing professionals to take the lead in defining how the new tax functions will be integrated into the counties' operations.

b. Discuss the advantages and disadvantages of allowing program specialists in the counties' tax departments to take the lead in defining how the new tax functions will be integrated into the counties' operations.

c. What role, if any, should countywide control agencies such as the Budget Office, Personnel Office, and County Legislature play in deciding how to implement these new tax requirements?

PROJECTS AND CASE EXERCISES

1. Read carefully the case study "The Information History of the Office of the State Treasurer." Reed Jones, the current state treasurer, is faced with conflicting recommendations on how to modernize information processing operations in his department. The director of the Information Services Division, Peter Mann, has recommended an incremental approach. An external consultant has recommended a more drastic, far-reaching reorientation. Each option has apparent benefits and disadvantages.

   Taking the role of a staff analyst to Jones, draft a memo that analyzes for him the pluses and minuses of the two proposals. Detail for him what additional questions he might ask or what additional information he should be seeking. In your memo, explicitly analyze each proposal in terms of its technological feasibility and its impact on the management of the agency. Also discuss how each proposal might be received by the oversight agencies to which Jones must respond, including the State Budget Office and the Civil Service Commission.

2. Read the case study "Disaster Strikes the Hazard County Welfare Department." In this case, a fire destroys the Hazard County computing facility, requiring that an emergency backup system be put into operation. The incident raises questions about what would happen if the state's central computing center were to sustain a similar disaster. In this situation, Roberta Clemson, deputy commissioner for Information Systems, John Ross, deputy commissioner for Assistance Payments, and Ray Stack from the State Budget Office represent respectively the three perspectives of technical specialist, program manager, and policy maker.

   How should these three professionals work together to set policy for disaster recovery within the State Welfare Department?

   Who should be responsible for taking the lead in setting such policy? In practical terms, how should the staff from these three areas work together to set an overall disaster recovery policy?

SUGGESTED READINGS

Bozeman, Barry, and Stuart Bretschneider. Public Management Information Systems: Theory and Prescription. *Public Administration Review* 46(SI): 475–87, November 1986.

Cleveland, Harlan. Government Is Information (But Not Vice Versa). *Public Administration Review* 46(6): 605–7, November–December 1986.

Cleveland, Harlan. *The Knowledge Executive: Leadership in an Information Society.* New York: E. P. Dutton, 1985. Reviewed in *Public Administration Review* 46(6): 673–74, November–December 1986.

Dizard, Wilson. *The Coming Information Age.* Second Edition. New York: Longman, 1985.

Gorry, Anthony, and Michael S. Scott Morton. A Framework for Management Information Systems. *Sloan Management Review* 13: 55–70, Fall 1971.

Gurwitt, Rob. Computers: New Ways to Govern. *Governing* 1(8): 34–42, May 1988.

Horton, Forest W. *Information Resources Management.* Englewood Cliffs, NJ: Prentice Hall, 1985.

Horton, Forest W., and Donald A. Marchand, eds. *Information Management in Public Administration.* Arlington, VA: Information Resources Press, 1982.

Ives, Blake, Scott Hamilton, and Gordon Davis. A Framework for Research in Computer-based Management Information Systems. *Management Science* 39: 910–34, September 1980.

Keen, Peter G. W., and Michael S. Scott Morton. *Decision Support Systems: An Organizational Perspective.* Reading, MA: Addison-Wesley, 1978.

Kraemer, Kenneth L., and John Leslie King. Computing and Public Organizations. *Public Administration Review,* 46 (SI): 488–96, November 1986.

Kraemer, Kenneth L., et al. *The Management of Computers.* New York: Columbia University Press, 1981.

Perry, James, and Kenneth Kraemer, eds. *Public Management: Public and Private Perspectives.* Palo Alto: Mayfield Publishing Co., 1983.

Toregas, Costis. People, Services, and Technology. *State Government News,* 31(10): 8–9, October 1988.

CHAPTER 2

INFORMATION POLICY
IN THE PUBLIC SECTOR

His mind racing, Mike McGraw hung up the phone. The call was from the local fire department. The county data processing center was ablaze, apparently the result of a rupture in an underground gas line. It was 3:00 A.M.

As the coffee brewed, McGraw considered the future. As director of Data Processing for Hazard County, he would lead the response to this disaster. His first thoughts were the biweekly payroll, welfare, and Medicaid checks he was responsible for issuing. How could he get them out in time? A backup arrangement with Crane County had worked well last winter during a blizzard. But would his people be ready for a total and long-term loss of capacity? Were their procedures well-enough documented to be transported to a new site on such short notice? Could he rely on the state for some backup?

Repairing the damage would be an immensely costly job—McGraw replayed in his mind the bleak budget hearings he had attended just last week. Could the county afford to rebuild the center? This might be an opportunity, though. New telecommunications equipment would undoubtedly be needed. Perhaps they could finally get the system upgrade he had been arguing for all year long.

The morning was going to be a long one. The county had a disaster recovery plan and he had to implement it. Without breakfast, he drove downtown to inspect the damage.[1]

[1]For more details on this vignette, see the case study "Disaster Strikes the Hazard County Welfare Department."

McGraw had instinctively looked at his problems from four critical angles. He first saw the political implications of the disaster, scanning possible consequences of the county missing its statutory obligation to provide paychecks and transfer payments. Second, McGraw reviewed the capacity of his staff to respond effectively. Questions of inter-organizational cooperation with a neighboring county and the state immediately leapt to mind. McGraw thought next in economic terms. He understood that replacing a major capital investment would involve considerable cost and managerial attention. Last, constantly attuned to new advances in technology and always looking for opportunities, even those born of disaster, McGraw saw a chance to upgrade his department's technological base.

In sorting through these issues, McGraw will rely heavily on policies he and others have developed over the years—policies for work units within his department, a countywide disaster recovery plan, and statewide policies for the administration of public assistance and Medicaid. His ability to manage this disaster over the next few days will depend critically on the quality of those policies. No doubt he will learn a great deal, and those policies will eventually be improved for his experience.

The Hazard County fire sets the stage for this chapter. It illustrates some major perspectives, issues, and policy considerations that define the scope of government information management. The four perspectives that McGraw used are the ones we will also use—technological, economic, organizational, and political.

The chapter discusses some major issues that confront public sector information managers. They range from how and when to take risks in acquiring new technologies, to how to sustain a technically skilled workforce, to considerations of the Civil Service and collective bargaining processes. The chapter concludes with a discussion of the kinds of policies government information managers need to do their jobs well—policy at the work unit level, organizationwide policies, and policies for an entire jurisdiction.

THE CONCEPT OF PUBLIC INFORMATION POLICY

By *public information policies* we mean those strategies that allow us to use information well and adapt government organizations and information systems to a rapidly changing environment.

These policies may exist at the level of the work unit (such as a regional office or a bureau within a central office), at the level of a large organization (such as an entire executive agency), or at the level of the entire government. Obviously, these multilevel policies should form a coordinated hierarchy. The purpose of strategic policies is to provide organizations with the strength and resilience to withstand (but not be isolated from) shocks and rapid changes in the environment. Finding the correct balance between stability (often, and mistakenly, thought of as strong centralization) and flexibility (often, and again mistakenly, seen as laissez-faire autonomy) is difficult. Too much of the first implies rigidity and nonresponsiveness to change. Too much of the second leads to lack of direction and dissipation of energy.

The dual demands of rapidly changing technology and the need for organizational control and stability commonly lead to a desire for firm policies that can endure the storms of change—detailed hardware acquisition policies or fixed standards for data definitions or database structures. One is reminded, though, of the old story of the mighty oak and the slender reed. We long for the stability and strength of the oak when managing large and complex systems. But in high winds (and at times the external information environment appears to be a virtual typhoon), an oak can be uprooted in its entirety while the supple reed survives the blast. In real life, of course, we are neither oaks nor reeds but must search for a satisfactory compromise between stability and flexibility.

The importance of these issues can best be understood by an appeal to imagination. Think of what would happen to the operations of a modern government if it were to lose suddenly and completely all its information processing technologies. Surely, the first thing to be missed would be the telephone. Individual units of agencies would become fragmented, agencies would be isolated from one another, and the public would be virtually unable to contact the government except by mail or in person. Imagine the waiting lines outside every office. Massive restaffing would be required to handle face-to-face contact and mountains of letters. The design of work and operating procedures would need a complete overhaul.

Now imagine no computers. How would the government issue paychecks, track its own financial transactions, process taxes, and keep track of personnel movements, retirement benefits, or employee health insurance? In a word, the internal operations of the government would grind to a halt, and a major reorientation would be required before most agencies could become operational again.

Picture next how major sectors of the economy and the economic and physical well-being of individual citizens depend critically on government computing. Think of the billions of dollars flowing through the health-care system that are processed and tracked by government computers. Consider the senior citizens, dependent children, veterans, and others who rely on routine, reliable operations of government data centers for their basic subsistence. How about drivers, scholarship winners, property owners—virtually everyone else in society who must communicate or transact business with government?

Government runs on information. As the public sector has grown, so too have its stores of data and its ultimate reliance on information technology to process data. Information is a major input to government programs. Information is, in fact, a primary product of government activity. Collecting, housing, protecting, and using it well are fundamental responsibilities of the public sector.

FOUR PERSPECTIVES ON GOVERNMENT INFORMATION MANAGEMENT

The impact of change on government information management can be evaluated from four points of view: technological, economic, organizational, and political.

The Technology

The first and most obvious way to think about the changes in government information management is in terms of information technology per se. This evokes a familiar list of variables that are changing exponentially over time: applications, the sales of hardware, and the introduction and sale of new software products are all increasing, as shown in Figure 2.1. The time needed to complete a fixed number of computations is rapidly decreasing

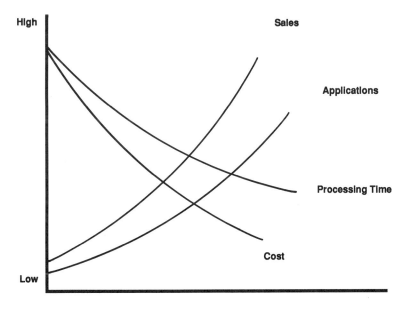

Time in Years

Figure 2.1   Trends in Major Variables Pertaining to Information Technology

(estimates cut it in half every three to five years). Similarly, the cost per executed instruction has been cut in half every three to five years for the past thirty years or more.

These often-cited statistics are impressive and these trends are likely to continue. They have broad structural causes and serious implications. As illustrated in Figure 2.2, they are fueled by three powerful interlocking cycles involving basic research, hardware development, software production, and realized applications. These four segments of the information processing industry interact in ever-widening cycles of growth. Basic research into such areas as circuit miniaturization and laser optics, for example, provided the breakthroughs that have fueled the hardware sector through one generation of machines after another. In turn, hardware sales generate a pool of seemingly unlimited research funds that fuel the basic research sector. This cycle will in all likelihood continue until basic research fails to yield fundamental advances in information technology. The end, however, is nowhere in sight. The second self-reinforcing cycle, between hardware and software, amplifies the hardware-research cycle. The availability of new hardware, like microcomputers in the early 1980s, feeds the demand for new kinds of software. Conversely, as new and better software attracts more users, hardware sales are stimulated. Finally, there is a reinforcing cycle between software development and applications. The availabil-

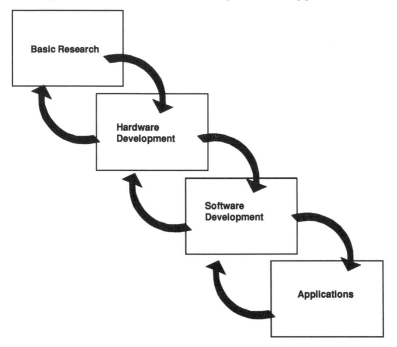

Figure 2.2   Interlocking Cycles Causing Exponential Trends in Information Technology

ity of new and often specialized software packages, such as micro-based spreadsheet and database packages, greatly increases the number of possible applications and hence users of the technology. In turn, as more applications and users enter the arena, the size of the total market expands, thereby encouraging even greater software development, hardware purchases, and research and development.

These three positive feedback loops are a powerful set of causal influences that over time create dramatic trends. They will slow or cease as the market for applications saturates or the marketability of new insights from basic research evaporates. Neither is soon likely. The key implication is that public information technology management will continue to be driven by rapid changes in hardware and software development as well as in applications. For the foreseeable future, technological change beyond the direct control and influence of the public sector will continue unabated.

Shifting Economics

A survey of the economic trends associated with information management casts the cool eye of dollars-and-cents calculations over the field. Macro-economic effects are perhaps cited most often in the popular press where attention is often drawn to the issue of job displacement due to the automation of work. The companion trend, redevelopment of a national or regional economy around the newly emerging information industries, is usually offered as a powerful antidote to the job displacement effect. The rapid redevelopment of the Massachusetts economy in the late 1970s and 1980s is often cited as one of the more dramatic success stories. Other macroeconomic effects center on the shifting structure of the workforce, the training and educational impacts, and the ability of national and regional economies to compete in a global market with strong players in Western Europe and the Pacific Rim.

Microeconomic implications center on the key concept of cost. This seems simple, yet the concept of cost itself is another of the things changed by information technology. Consider these distinctions. Information processing costs may be viewed as operating costs or as capital costs. That is, costs associated with information processing technologies can be factored into our budgets in one-year increments like the cost of fuel in heating our buildings or in multiyear funding schemes like the capital calculations associated with acquiring the buildings themselves. If we think of information technologies as capital expenditures, then the lifetime over which they are to be amortized becomes an important question. All three categories of operation—hardware, software, and "orgware"[2]—can be examined from the capi-

---

[2]We first heard the term *orgware* from Costis Toregas, president of Public Technologies, Inc., a Washington-based nonprofit consulting firm devoted to better use of information technology in local governments.

tal versus operating cost perspective. The clarity of this perspective changes, however, if the useful lifespan of a given technology is twenty years versus five years, if the cost of the product involved is five thousand dollars or five million, or if we are investing in human versus physical capital. These questions are of particular interest because they constitute policy issues that should be under the control of public managers.

The concept of cost is further complicated by the distinction made in both public and private sectors between cost and investment. The conceptual distinction here centers on whether one views computing and information processing as a necessary cost of doing business or as a strategic investment in the overall effectiveness of an organization. Many organizations do not look at information technology costs as expenses to be contained, but rather as investments to be increased for their powerful potential to enhance organizational effectiveness and, in the private sector, profit.

A third cost-related concept is the interplay of costs and benefits. Benefits from the introduction of new technologies may come in the form of direct (hard-dollar) savings, as when a faster and more reliable piece of equipment replaces an old expensive-to-maintain one. Indirect (soft-dollar) savings accrue from an automated record-keeping system that obviates the need to hire additional personnel to handle manual filing operations. Enhancements to effectiveness or productivity are another form of benefit, as when an automated system with quick response times provides better service and reduces waiting lines. While the distinctions between hard-dollar benefits, soft-dollar benefits, and productivity enhancements are often difficult to make, they do represent important conceptual differences in how we think about these technologies. Moreover, the way we treat these cost questions often depends on whether we are discussing hardware, software, or orgware. Most importantly, however, these financial management distinctions represent policy levers, under our control, that can yield more or less wise decisions in our attempts to manage public programs. We must learn to manipulate and control them.

These cost-related concepts all converge around the important policy area of procurement. Government procurement policies must match the time frame of the financial payout to the useful life of the equipment or software being purchased. It must distinguish between information costs and information investments. It must also be sensitive to the relationships between the costs and benefits of the acquisition.

Organizational Implications

The apparently clean conceptual distinction between the economic and the organizational aspects of information management usually breaks down in practice. As we have just seen, the initially bloodless calculations of dollars and cents often depend on an evaluation of concepts such as "organizational effectiveness" or "productivity." These concepts are claimed in common by economists, financial analysts, and organizational theorists. From a managerial perspective, the economic and organizational aspects of information management are closely linked.

Traditionally, organizational phenomena have been analyzed at three levels—the individual, the workgroup, and the organization. Administrators have looked at organizational phenomena in terms of functional categories such as design of work, procedures and practices, and organizational structures. Figure 2.3 combines these two taxonomies of organizational phenomena to create a nine-cell matrix that can be used to help understand the scope and diversity of the organizational impacts of the information revolution. The cell entries are illustrative only. They merely suggest the range of possible effects. As illustrated by the top row, the impacts on an individual's performance may be complex and varied. For example, the structure of the workday may be changed radically by the possibility of working at home. Today, executives and professionals in both the public and private sectors use microcomputers that allow them either to continue office work at home after hours or to substitute home time for office time during the normal workday. People with disabilities or caretaker responsibilities who may not have entered the workforce at all may now do so thanks to "telecommuting." The implications of easier access to information technologies are obviously substantial for both the individual and the office working group. Similarly, end-user-oriented software can significantly alter the work process of an individual professional. No longer dependent on the schedules and priorities of the data processing shop, he or she is free to approach the job in new ways, acquiring in the process skill and sophistication that are both personal and organizational assets.

Impacts on individual performance are not limited to professionals. Clerical support staff often witness a restructuring of their working environ-

FUNCTIONAL CATEGORIES

	Structure	Procedure	Job Design
Individual	Professional Work at Home vs. Office	Individual Work Changed by End User Software	Changed Nature of Clerical Functions
Workgroup	LANs Change Communications Flow	Computer-Assisted Group Decision Making	Blurring Distinctions between Clerical & Professional Work
Organization	Chief Information Officer Position	Automated Delivery of Public Services	Revised Job Titles for Data Processing Positions

Figure 2.3   Illustrative Impacts of Information Technology on Organizational Performance

ment when information technologies are introduced. These changes can be for better or for worse. Clerical positions can be enriched by word processing, accounting, electronic mail, automated scheduling, and other packages that can expand the traditional range of clerical responsibilities. On the other hand, it is possible to reduce some jobs to eight hours a day at a terminal screen, removing the interpersonal contact and variety of assignments formerly associated with the position.

At the work unit level, information technologies can similarly redefine office structures, procedures, and the essential features of job design. For example, a local area network (LAN) can change patterns of information sharing and exchange. Electronic scheduling can alter the structure of interactions among staff. Computer-assisted group decision making can change the way formal and informal choices about resource allocation or work scheduling are made. The blurring distinctions between professional and clerical work (with professionals more involved with text creation and manipulation and clerical staff more involved in functions like accounting and spreadsheet analysis) redefine overall job responsibilities (and personal relationships) within the work unit.

While the organizational implications of information technology are considerable for individuals and their workgroups, the implications for entire organizations are even greater. Overall responsibility for managing information and information technology is moving out of data processing centers. In some organizations, a new position, chief information officer, is part of the organizational response to technological diffusion. This position, usually reporting to the CEO or agency head, is a structural innovation that recognizes the wide-ranging impacts that information and information technology have throughout an organization. From a procedural point of view, the advent of new information technologies can mean complete revision of the full range of organizational processes. Consider, for example, a public library that installs an automated catalog, a social service agency that develops an on-line client-oriented record-keeping system, or a department of labor whose job-matching functions are automated. The entire set of procedures for interacting with the public changes, as do the staff skills and working relationships within the organization. These changes are not easy to make. They are prone to difficulties and failures during implementation, and they require the explicit attention of the organization's management at the highest levels. Finally, these organizational, structural, and procedural changes often bring with them the need to create new job titles, revise old ones, and generally revamp the way an organization describes work, hires personnel, and defines and rewards performance. Often these changes involve shifts in government wide policies that are beyond the control of any single organization but must be negotiated with Civil Service or with public employee unions where they exist and have influence.

One informal rule of thumb predicts that the dollar impact of new information technologies is distributed among hardware, software, and organizational considerations in the ratio of five cents hardware, ten cents software, and eighty-five cents orgware.[3] This of course implies that the cost of revising organizational structures, procedures, and job design will far outweigh the costs of acquiring the hardware and software systems. Surely, effects of this magnitude demand our full attention. Fortunately, the level of organizational impacts is exactly where managers can make a difference. Unlike trends in the technology itself and, to some degree, in the economics of the technology, organizational factors can be almost entirely within our influence. We say "can be" rather than "are" because managing these impacts requires close cooperation and understanding between technical professionals, information users, line managers, policy makers, and external control agencies—no trivial task.

Political Dimensions

Political and organizational theorists distinguish clearly between the "BIG-P-Politics" of elective office and "small-p-politics" that characterize bureaucratic relationships. The field of information management influences and is shaped by political forces of both kinds. Information managers would be not only ineffective but foolish if they failed to recognize these political impacts and manage them carefully. A few examples will help to make this point.

A new information system is to be installed in the regional offices of a social service agency. A number of apparently technical decisions must be made: how the basic data elements are to be defined, in what form summary reports and query screens are to be formatted, who has access to what portions of the database, what types of microcomputers should be purchased, what database software should be used, and so on. Perhaps the most important lesson of the growing literature on information technology management in both the public and private sectors is that these apparently technical decisions are shaped by the give-and-take of bureaucratic politics. The best government information managers know how to read and work with the political dynamics touched off by seemingly technical decisions.

Information systems play a role at the level of electoral politics as well. Consider, for example, programs in which responsibility is shared across several levels of government (public assistance, for example, often involves federal, state, and local contributions to program funding and administration). The installation of an information system in an intergovernmental setting can subtly affect who actually controls the program, and it determines what information is available to whom. Clearly, political considerations will often (and with good cause) enter into the design of these systems.

[3]Costis Toregas is also the source of this idea.

At another level, large-scale information systems can considerably expand the range of information available to support legislative decision making. Take, for example, the recent introduction of Generally Accepted Accounting Procedures (GAAP) in New York State. Sold as an information system that promoted "good government" practices, GAAP also made executive accounting information more available and open to direct inspection by legislative staff and committees. Similarly, the availability of on-line databases with interactive decision support modeling capabilities can substantially alter the dynamics of the legislative compromises that determine allocation formulas. Legislators interested in who wins and who loses from proposed changes in local school aid can interactively explore a large number of possible allocations using microcomputer databases and decision support modeling systems. The availability of these tools in the legislature, as well as in executive offices, affects the balance of power in the political negotiations that surround these decisions.

Finally, a series of controversial political issues have emerged around new uses of information itself. For example, the ability of government agencies to match records from multiple sources (such as wage records with unemployment insurance or welfare files to identify ineligibles) raises thorny questions concerning privacy, security, and the right of government to collect and use information about individuals. All of these activities, exacerbated if not brought about by modern information technology, are also hotly debated political issues.

In brief, government information management is not a field of neutral competence the implications of which can be understood solely in terms of technical expertise, benefit-cost analyses, or break-even points on investment. Nor is it a field in the sole domain of managers, affecting people, processes, and organizations. Powerful information technologies are increasingly reaching into the essential nature of our democratic institutions. In turn, the ways in which we acquire, deploy, and manage those resources are shaped and limited by the manifold political processes that define our form of government. Public sector information managers must remain sensitive and responsive to these political realities.

Melding the Four Perspectives

All four of these angles of vision are necessary for understanding the complex issues facing public information managers. Each gives a valid, but partial, picture of the many interacting forces that together produce sound information management. What one perspective tends to highlight, another glosses over or obscures. The challenge is to meld these sometimes complementary and often competing views into a comprehensive vision to guide design, implementation, and management.

EMERGING ISSUES IN GOVERNMENT
INFORMATION MANAGEMENT

A series of specific information management topics emerge from this broad background of technological, economic, organizational, and political perspectives. Several are discussed below.

Risk

The level of risk—taking appropriate for government operations is an important issue. At what point in its life cycle should government managers "buy into" a new technology? Early acquisition of state-of-the-art technologies could allow an agency to realize earlier and longer-lasting benefits. For example, buying an expert system based on artificial intelligence (AI) to assist in management of tax audits could be an excellent early application of that technology. Alternatively, waiting would allow a new technology to be refined and made more effective and less costly by competition, thereby saving the government from premature and costly experiments with new ideas.

As another small example of this dilemma, consider the purchase of microcomputers during the first few years after their introduction. At that time, manufacturers offered many options with a plethora of operating systems, hardware, and software. Eventually, a consensus began to emerge around CPM as a standard operating system. Just when the market appeared to be agreeing on this standard, IBM, the industry giant, introduced its PC. Its DOS operating system quickly became the de facto standard. An agency that bought the CPM technology then had a considerable investment in equipment and technology that was no longer widely supported in the software market. Multiply each micro purchase by thousands of units and hundreds of organizations, and the dollar implications of having unknowingly bought into a dead-ended system are immense. On the other hand, waiting for a resolution of the market can lead to continued indecision, leaving an organization with unsolved information problems and further and further behind the state-of-the-art.

Another version of the risk question centers on entrepreneurial activity among government employees. For example, should government agencies have access to a pool of funds that would allow their employees to develop new applications, or should government depend on the market to produce in standard form the products and services it needs? Private sector organizations make deliberate decisions concerning basic investment in research and development functions; government rarely does. Yet, public sector information problems are often unique and are solved by innovative applications that, in other settings, would be considered the result of R&D work. Perhaps government information managers should invest more in their own problems and their solutions, relying less on vendor-imported solutions to public problems.

We need to appreciate that public sector decisions can be quite complicated. Citizens expect government to be a source of stability, and although they want good, businesslike service, they don't want it at the cost of untried techniques that may fail, causing inconvenience at best and social disaster at worst. This reinforces the tendency of governments to make conservative technological decisions, even when the payback from slightly riskier investments could bring significantly improved public services.

Managing the Costs of Information

As we have already discussed, our way of thinking about and measuring the costs of information management presents some challenging conceptual and technical problems. The three distinctions made earlier—operating costs vs. capital costs, cost vs. investment, and cost vs. benefits—more or less define the conceptual space. A simple example may help show their effect:

A large department in the State University acquires five microcomputers, linked to each other in a local area network, to support the production of course materials, manuscripts, and correspondence by the faculty. Two machines are deployed on the desks of the two department secretaries and three are available for direct use by faculty. The total cost is $15,000.

By all reports, the new system will increase secretarial productivity by the equivalent of one additional position. Since the annual salary of another secretary would be close to $15,000, the payback period of this investment would appear to be just one year. But, no fewer secretaries are on the staff after the purchase than before. That is, by all accounts productivity went up by the equivalent of one clerical position, but a budget examiner would not observe any savings in personnel services. An argument could be made that the new system has just increased overall cost.

Another factor complicates this analysis. Faculty are using the machines for direct data entry as they draft course materials or manuscripts at the keyboard. (In fact, some of the faculty bought their own machines to complement those owned by the department.) Department managers, of course, need to measure the benefits of the new equipment in order to justify its purchase. Should they count as a cost or as a benefit the fact that faculty are now spending their time sitting at a keyboard in addition to meeting with students or being otherwise involved in their research?

Moreover, department managers calculate that the cost of paper, disks, printer supplies, and maintenance is running $3,000 per year, or about 20 percent annually of the base purchase price. As time goes by, the machines are becoming older and are depreciating, not to mention the fact that in three to five years they will be obsolete and will in all likelihood be replaced by a new generation of hardware. The cost of converting old files to a new system must be taken into account. Finally, they must factor in the costs of training and retraining staff and faculty. Most experts would agree that these are critical investments in human capital, but they show up now as forgone productivity this year, not as enhanced productivity in future years. We often submit budget requests for funds to support a new system that we expect will save money and increase productivity. But in the end productivity-improving and cost-saving measures somehow always appear to cost more.

This simple example illustrates some of the problems that managers face when they must define and then measure the operating costs and investment costs, as well as the benefits, of technology. These issues become magnified when one is discussing the acquisition of a multimillion-dollar mainframe or a government wide telecommunications facility. The questions vary depending on where you stand in the system. A program manager (in our example the department chair) may pay most attention to the satisfaction and productivity improvements of his staff. A budget examiner may look skeptically at the "bottom line," noting that in the final analysis the system just point blank costs more money. There are no easy resolutions to these contradictions. They arise from fundamentally different points of view.

Managing the Pace of Technological Change

Managing change is always difficult. Managing technological change is even more problematic because technology itself is changing so rapidly. As a result, the preferred technological goal at the beginning of a large project will often be obsolete by its completion. Consequently, most projects will either end up with technology that is well behind the state-of-the-art or, worse, needs to be replaced almost as soon as it is fully installed. Managing new technologies is like painting the Golden Gate Bridge—once you have finished the job you immediately have to begin again because things have changed so much in the meanwhile.

Figure 2.4 illustrates the wide variety of lifespans that government information managers encounter. The shortest cycle is the duration of the annual budget. Lasting only one year, it provides the most definitive (and perhaps least useful) planning horizon available to public managers. Constitutional or statutory provisions often preclude making firm commitments beyond the limits of currently authorized funding levels.

However, most agencies sustain a "long-range" program planning cycle of from three to five years. Notice that the lifespan of "state-of-the-art" technology is about as long. Within this time we can expect the market to introduce a cheaper and more efficient technology for performing the same functions provided by this year's so-called state-of-the-art. Unfortunately, the lifespan of a major systems development project (from initial system design

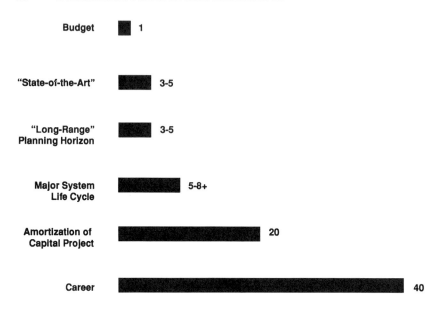

Time in Years

Figure 2.4   Mismatching Time Frames That Cause Problems in Managing the Pace of Technological Change

to installation, shakedown, staff training, and implementation) will run from
five to eight years or more. Agencies often expect a useful life of at least ten
years. Taken together these facts more or less ensure that systems designed
today will be applied to program needs that are beyond the current planning
horizon of the agency and they will rely on technology that will predictably
be obsolete. As a result, we are always repainting our technological bridges.

Furthermore, the life cycle of most major capital projects (highways,
buildings, or other public facilities) is about twenty years or more as measured by typical amortization periods associated with capital financing. If we
were to view the largest system development projects, easily costing millions
of dollars, as traditional capital projects, new investments made today would
be obsolete four times over before we could repay the bonds that financed
them. Finally, a person's working life is roughly forty years. If we planned to
retrain staff to stay up to date, we should plan to train and retrain our entire
workforce eight times within the span of a single worker's career.

Government information managers juggle these conflicting senses of
time, all made more troublesome by the pace at which the base technology is
changing. Moreover, that pace shows no sign of abatement in the near
future, certainly not in this century. It should surprise no one that these

conflicting, compressed, and confused time frames often lead to critical management problems.

The three preceding issues—taking risks, managing the costs of information, and managing the pace of technological change—do not operate singly. The government procurement process is an example of how they interact. As discussed more fully in Chapter 4, technology-intensive acquisitions raise special issues. Competitive government procurement regulations are often aimed at low-price, low-risk investments, intangible products, or measurable services with relatively slow change rates. The technology for building roads, for example, does not change much from year to year and from vendor to vendor. Moreover, low-cost *equipment* bids may not always be appropriate, since an information technology can vary dramatically among vendors on several performance dimensions and since the actual hardware plus software costs entail only fifteen cents of each information dollar spent (remember the eighty-five cents that goes almost unheralded to orgware).

Sustaining a Technically Skilled Workforce

Surely, it will be impossible to manage an information-oriented public sector if the public workforce does not have the skills necessary to use information technology effectively. As suggested above, the typical worker will need to be retrained (on the job or otherwise) at least eight times during his or her career in order to stay abreast of new developments. The prospect is intimidating until we look separately at the various types of training that are needed. An effectively prepared workforce will need to have at least three basic kinds of knowledge—technical skills, technical concepts, and technology-managing concepts. The training requirements for each are different, but cumulative.

Technical skills change rapidly and will probably require fairly complete retraining with each new generation of hardware or software. For example, an operator skilled in running one word processing program using a specific operating system will require some retraining in order to use another word processing program embedded in a different operating system running on a new generation of machines. Similarly, programmers skilled in languages such as FORTRAN or COBOL will require retraining to convert to one of the new fourth-generation languages. Fortunately, skill training can be accomplished fairly rapidly, often on the job, provided workers have received conceptual groundwork adequate to deal with the changes. Of course, to be effective, skill training must be accompanied by a positive attitude toward the new technology. More will be said on this problem later. The reason skill training can proceed rapidly is that the underlying concepts do not change as rapidly as their applications. That is, each new generation of hardware and software builds on the past, and at a conceptual level, one has only to learn about changes inherent in the enhancements rather than unlearn and then relearn the technology "from scratch."

Consider, for example, the case of a technically skilled professional, educated in computer concepts in 1970, who had to learn to use a micro-based spreadsheet package introduced in 1982. Several generations of main-frames, minis, and microcomputers had come and gone in that twelve-year period. However, the number of truly innovative conceptual advances is small. Figure 2.5 displays basic conceptual innovations, from 1970 through 1982, against a time scale representing the lifespan of a career (1970 through 2020). In 1970, this worker would have been trained in the basic concepts underlying the operation of a fundamental von Neumann computing ma-chine (such as the IBM series 360), the concept of programmability, and the dual concepts of higher-level languages (e.g., FORTRAN or BASIC) and operating system principles. Finally, the student of 1970 would have learned about basic matrix operations.

Between 1970 and 1982, only three or four conceptual advances were introduced to produce spreadsheet applications. In hardware, on-line graphics and full-screen editing became a reality circa 1975, both brought about by the advent of pixel-oriented memory to drive the screen. In the late 1970s, floppy disks were introduced and miniaturization of circuits led to low-cost microcomputers. These few conceptual ingredients, coupled with the creative insights of the first developers of packages like VISICALC and

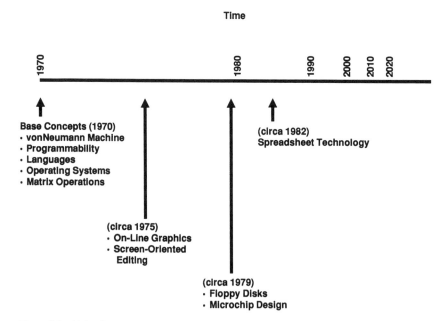

Figure 2.5   Major Conceptual Advances Contributing to Spreadsheet Programs (1970-82)

subsequently expanded versions like LOTUS 1-2-3, set the stage for the wide array of applications now possible using spreadsheets. The point is that professionals grounded in the basic concepts of computing can adapt to new tools with relatively little skill-oriented training. Today, the major task facing information managers (as well as educators in schools of management) is not only to provide the basic conceptual training our hypothetical technical professional received in 1970 but also to train a diverse workforce in many stages of career development. This helps explain the immense rush of computer-oriented training during the late 1970s and 1980s. Once the inventory of conceptual knowledge within a workforce reaches a threshold level, a lesser program of updates and skills training will be sufficient. This assumes, of course, that those entering the workforce today are receiving adequate conceptual education in high school, at the university, in graduate school, and elsewhere.

The third category of educational needs—technology management concepts—can be met by case studies and related material that show the broad context within which technologies function. Managers with little prior technical background can still come to grips with the special issues inherent in managing technology-based innovations. Similarly, those with strong backgrounds in technical skills and concepts can become familiar with the special management-oriented issues inherent in government information use.

As a final note, not everyone either needs or wants to become a member of the technically literate workforce. Workers' willingness to engage new technologies will vary considerably. It is often useful to think of this range of enthusiasm in terms of a simple taxonomy—those who might be classified as experts, those who are technology leaders, and those who are technology followers. Strategies designed to provide technical training to a diverse workforce will generally work better if these types are recognized and treated accordingly.

Experts are the ones who open the crates, hook up the peripheral equipment, and install the various software systems when new equipment arrives. It seems that every office has at least one. Often thought of as the "computer hackers," experts are relied on to provide much of the on-the-job training for others. Training strategies appropriate for experts (such as advanced coursework or release time to experiment with new systems) may not be appropriate for others.

Technology leaders peer over the experts' shoulders as they are unpacking and installing the equipment. They are naturally curious about technology and want to learn more. Perhaps they see learning the new technology as a path to job advancement, professional enrichment, or just as a stimulating intellectual adventure. Leaders should be identified early in the training cycle and given special encouragement and opportunities. Coursework and experiences appropriate for the experts may not be right for the leaders at first, but eventually they might be encouraged to take over part of the expert's role. This group is likely to have the best balanced view of the technology, seeing in it the means to accomplish organizational goals. Technology followers are not particularly interested (at least initially and perhaps forever). At one extreme are those who might be characterized as "cyberphobic," exhibiting complex avoidance behaviors so as not to engage a computer, or any new form of technology, hands-on. In the early phases of any implementation, problems occur that frustrate even the most experienced and enthusiastic users. So it seems wisest not to try to engage followers in new technology before it is well tested. As the new technology becomes more fully understood, followers will usually show some interest—provided the organization as a whole has had a generally positive experience. In any case, technology followers should gradually be encouraged to "warm up" to a new way of doing business.

New Organizational Forms

New information technologies will spawn new structures, procedures, and descriptions of work at the level of individual performance, in the local workplace, and for the entire organization. By implication, similar structural and procedural changes occur governmentwide—changes in Civil Service, in acquisition processes, in technical standards and protocols, and in the definition of standard data items for common use. Both public and private organizations are experiencing an evolution in organizational structures accompanied by revised procedures and descriptions of work. For example, many organizations are defining a new top-level management position—a chief information officer. The CIO's functions vary from one organization to the next, but in general the office is conceived of more broadly than that of a director of a data processing center (no matter how large) and often includes broad responsibility for end-user services, telecommunications, integration of mini and micro systems with mainframe systems, and broad policy considerations such as public access, physical security, and the overall cost equation for managing information-based resources. The information resource center is emerging as an organizational structure designed to have more open boundaries than the traditionally defined data processing center. Here, skilled users and data processing professionals define new working relationships. Sometimes, the revised job titles give formal recognition to the new skills. More frequently, however, staff working with these new technologies find themselves working in technically "out-of-title" situations, waiting for the formal description of work to catch up with reality. These structural issues are treated in more depth in Chapter 3.

Civil Service and Collective Bargaining Considerations

Most of our organizational analysis and discussion thus far has focused on entire organizations and their constituent smaller units. Political and organizational theorists disagree on whether an entire level of government, a state for instance, can or should be viewed as an organization per se or rather as a loose conglomerate of sometimes competing, sometimes cooperating, but always distinct organizational units. It is hard to see, for example, how the goals, control mechanisms, decision-making structures, and standard operating procedures of a department of transportation, a department of social services, and a department of taxation are enough alike to characterize them as belonging to the same organization. Perhaps it is better to think of each as an independent organization with its own leadership, decision-making structures, goals, and objectives. Regardless of the resolution of this academic debate, a number of common procedures tie these organizations together—those centering on budgeting, personnel management, expenditure control, and auditing, to mention a few. Changes in information technologies affect these common procedures and therefore influence the broader "organization" of government. One critical common feature is the Civil Service system and related collective bargaining processes. Together they circumscribe how work is defined, how performance is rewarded (or censured), and how advancement is structured across all units of government.

The issues discussed here are really broader than the term *Civil Service* traditionally implies. In today's labor relations environment, many items have come to the collective bargaining table and therefore involve the public sector labor unions and the offices of employee relations, as well as the institutional structures that normally oversee the public workforce. All the issues discussed above regarding the creation and maintenance of a technically skilled workforce fall under the broad heading of training, a key component of the staffing function.

Information technology complicates the definition of job titles as well. There are specialized titles directly related to information technologies (such as programmers, systems analysts, and word processing specialists). But there is also a need to redefine other titles that now have an important information processing component (for example, program analysts need an ability to manipulate and interpret data sets and other forms of computerized information), and there are other occupational titles comprised of skills and abilities that are half in a substantive area and half related to expertise in some form of information technology. For example, a program specialist working in the energy conservation office may design and implement an excellent microcomputing operation to help manage weatherization projects. But he or she may be blocked from advancement. The experience gained is broad, varied, and valuable to the organization, but it is neither wholly data processing nor wholly program analysis, and promotion exams will tend to test for either, but not both sets of skills. Ironically, while we are especially interested in creating these amphibians—persons who can live comfortably both in a program and in a data processing world—a system that emphasizes sharply defined occupations can block them from direct lines of career advancement. Promotion, then, is a final category of work-force considerations. We must decide if technology skills should be properly viewed as broad prerequisites for all titles (like reading and writing) or as specialized skills (like those that result in a Coast Guard license or a medical degree). On some career ladders, persons with technological skills seek promotion in broad management titles, while on other ladders these skills are confined to specific functional areas. When technological skills are viewed as broad prerequisites for promotion, we risk losing important distinctions between occupations. But if specific technical skills are the only basis for promotion, then we may be creating increasingly narrow job definitions doomed to become obsolete after only a few years.

Setting Standards and Maintaining Stability

This capstone issue is a broad and cross-cutting one, touching upon all the others. It sets the stage for a discussion of how public organizations can respond at a policy level to the challenges of technological innovation. Perhaps the key to understanding government information management centers on a paradox. Public information managers must comprehend, strive for, and achieve two opposing purposes at once—stability and flexibility. These opposites are represented in the workplace by centralized and laissez-faire policies. Both approaches are based on fundamentally sound premises but when taken to extremes lead respectively to rigidity or to chaos. The best policy responses are constantly adjusted, subtle blends of these two pure types.

To illustrate these most important points, we begin with a quick look at the premises that underlie each of these positions. We then look at how each can go wrong. Finally, several examples of "blended" policies combining both laissez-faire and centralized control are presented.

In its absolute form, the centralist position is founded on the premise that the market for new and emerging technologies is a plethora of diverse and competing hardware, software, and services. Left to their own devices, well-intended professionals and unit managers will make choices that are rational from an individual or "local" point of view. However, when these many small decisions are summed, the result is a melange of uncoordinated stand-alone systems without standardized hardware, software, or support procedures. The centralist solution is to define and enforce as completely and explicitly as possible standards that guide equipment acquisition, system development, implementation, and operations. Of course, the inevitable problem is that central system designers are never able to anticipate all the eventualities that surround the implementation and operation of a real system. Since design, development, and implementation usually take several years, the centralized decisions made at the start are seldom useful guides for dealing with problems later on. Moreover, the technology available to solve those problems is sure to have changed. The result is an overspecified and inflexible system unresponsive to local needs. End users are likely to be more than annoyed at a central office that ignores their preferences and needs and bars them from the decision-making process.

The absolute form of the laissez-faire policy begins with the major weakness of the centralized policy position. In a rapidly changing technological environment, this line of reasoning goes, it makes no sense to freeze in advance overall system specifications. By allowing "many flowers to bloom," new and better ideas spring from the system development process. By maintaining an open and flexible attitude toward change, optimal and flexible systems will emerge.

Of course, this strategy, taken literally, leads almost inevitably to the sort of chaos most feared by those who favor centralization. Uncoordinated and incompatible hardware systems arrive on the scene supporting an array of software systems with a confusing overlap of applications and data definitions. The resultant system may make sense in a very local context, but if the organization is to function as a whole, such policies can be costly and counterproductive in the long run.

Obviously, good policy blends these two extremes. Let's look at several simple examples of how this can occur. An agency with a large mainframe operation is moving into the era of distributed microprocessors. Astute managers recognize that their purchase represents not only a financial decision but policy choices. The advocate of centralization would urge the agency (or some central committee of technical professionals and users) to survey the available options and then select a standard set of hardware and software for use throughout the organization. All purchases out of agency funds would conform to these standards. The proponent of laissez-faire policy would simply let individual professionals and local managers purchase whatever they think best. The fallacy of the laissez-faire policy, of course, is that as soon as a variety of uncoordinated systems arises, mainframe personnel are besieged by unending requests to support every sort of microcomputer and software package under the sun, and no one is able to communicate with his or her neighbor. Over time, the centralized policy collapses as well because users with important and valid needs for alternative machines or services are denied those tools, or have to go through considerable red tape to get them, or have to learn to end run the system entirely. None of these approaches makes for organizational harmony and none serves the organization's underlying information needs.

Certainly, many good compromises between the two extreme types can be found. The agency could specify that uploading and downloading to and from the mainframe will be supported only on one or two selected machines or that the agency would underwrite the maintenance costs of one or several types of micros by establishing a qualified in-house repair shop. These two carrots toward standardization might be combined with small sticks such as requiring an extra step in the authorization process to purchase other than the one or two authorized brands. Clearly, considerable middle ground exists between strictly centralized and purely laissez-faire approaches.

Consider a second example where an agency must maintain a statewide client database used for several purposes in both regional and central offices. A policy oriented toward centralization would require strict adherence to an agencywide data dictionary of client-oriented information. In the long run, new uses for the data will come up which do not fit within the constraints of the dictionary. Unless it is easy to revise or expand the dictionary, users will eventually ignore it and its value will quickly deteriorate. Laissez-faire policies, on the other hand, will generate pandemonium because conflicting data definitions will ultimately make it impossible to collect any statewide data from information systems that have been allowed to develop without appropriate coordination. The compromise positions once again involve a combination of carrot-and-stick tactics. Interactions with the mainframe files can be mandated as to format (otherwise corruption of the statewide files would result). But local variations on the statewide standard could be permitted with the addition of data items or clarification of existing items (by adding sub-codes for example) so long as a clear and explicit mapping between standard items and the localized systems can be maintained. Incentives might include making useful comparative data from the state or from other localities available to those sites that make consistent use of the standard definitions. Policies must be firm to protect the integrity of centralized data sources, but at the same time flexible enough to meet the needs of local users as they themselves define them.

Creative policies walk the sometimes thin line between overly structured, rigid, and nonresponsive systems and the potential chaos of completely uncontrolled development. This brings us to the central issue of how governments can deliberately set policies that enhance rather than impede performance.

Three Levels of Policy for Government Information Management

As we have just seen, the management of information in the public sector is characterized by striking innovations in hardware and software, many ways to look at the same problem, a host of technology-specific issues, and rapid change in the environment. And it seems that every axiom or rule of thumb is tied to its antithesis. The result is paradox. We strive for stability, but once attained, stability can become rigidity and an inability to respond to change. Centralized policies yield overall consistency, but they stifle initiative at local points in the system. Training is an expensive investment in the future, but expensive skills imparted today will predictably be obsolete within three to five years. We use computer matches to crack down on fraud and misuse of government funds, but we end up also creating a crisis in preserving individual civil liberties. This web of contradictions is more complex in the public sector than elsewhere. We serve multiple, and often conflicting, goals. We are constrained by law and by public expectation in ways no private organization experiences. When we fail, the public often has nowhere else to turn for the services it needs—public services are often crucial monopolies.

A successful technological future for the public sector comes from skillfully crafting understandable and sustainable policies that balance competing forces. Figure 2.6 summarizes a partial taxonomy of the kinds of issues that must be considered in policies for work units, agencies, and entire jurisdictions. As Figure 2.6 illustrates, formal policy statements promulgated by work units, organizations, and entire systems of government may deal with a wide variety of topics ranging from hardware and software considerations, to data definitions and standards, to organizational procedures and structures. Of course, not every unit needs explicit written policies about all of these items (and conversely, some may need to develop policy in areas omitted from the list). Necessary and appropriate policy guidelines will vary from setting to setting and from one application to the next. However, Figure 2.6 does serve to illustrate the wide variety of possible policy levers that managers can use in a strategic response to information issues. Each of the general categories is briefly discussed and illustrated below.

Work Unit Policies

Work units within government agencies operate information systems ranging from one or two word processors to support clerical functions to large mainframe or telecommunications systems maintained by a data processing or communications unit. Here *work unit* is defined as a local or regional office or as a subdivision within a bureau, department, or laboratory. At the very least, work unit managers must make decisions concerning what information to collect; what its uses are; what equipment to purchase; how to allow access to it; what software to acquire and run; how to back up, provide access to and security for the system; how to prioritize hardware capacity and staff time; and who will be in overall charge of the technology. Often, many of these decisions have already been made elsewhere in the hierarchy (such as when all local offices are required to use a system chosen by the central office), or full freedom of choice has been circumscribed by centralized decisions (as in our earlier example where the agency's mainframe only supports uploading and downloading on a certain machine or class of machines). Even in these cases, however, decisions about equipment location, staff access, and staff training (both formal and informal) often fall to the unit manager. Active involvement of these managers in the definition

HARDWARE
      -Acquisition
      -Equipment Maintenance
      -Physical Location
      -Security and Disaster Recovery
      -Standards

SOFTWARE
      -Acquisition
      -Build versus Buy
      -Code Maintenance
      -Code Standards
      -Documentation
      -Security and Disaster Recovery

DATA CONSIDERATIONS
      -Access
      -Accuracy
      -Data Dictionaries
      -Definition of Record Hierarchies
      -File and Record Disposition and Archives
      -Information Sharing and Exchange
      -Personal Privacy
      -Report Types and Formats
      -Sources and Ownership

PROCEDURES
      -Backup
      -Confidentiality
      -User Access
      -Data Entry, Uploading & Downloading Protocols
      -Hardware Use Priorities
      -Job Priorities
      -Operations
      -Security
      -Public Access
      -Records Management
      -Stimulating and Rewarding Innovation
      -Training and Professional Development

STRUCTURES
      -Role of Users and Advisory Groups
      -User Support
      -Who Controls Operations?
      -Who Makes Policy?

Figure 2.6   Partial List of Subjects for Information Policies

of local and central policies is a key component in successful system performance.

Developing Policy for the Organization as a Whole

The development of coherent policies to shape an entire organization's information strategy is much more complicated than developing these policies at the work unit level. While the taxonomy of issues sketched in Figure 2.6 still applies, policy development becomes more and more complicated as the size of the organization, the complexity of its data processing and telecommunications functions, and the number of competing interests and points of view within it increase. Who should be in charge of the policy development process? This is one of the most difficult questions associated with policy development at the organizational level. Historically, information policies have been set and controlled by a data processing shop or an office responsible for phones and telecommunications. In the past, these units controlled the lion's share of information technology functions in most organizations. However, as information technologies move out from behind locked doors and spread through the organization, the number of users and managers who believe they have a stake in information policy grows substantially.

The most common, and certainly the usual initial, solution is to have no center for information policy at all. Since all these technologies are fairly recent inventions, in most organizations a center for information policy decisions would be the exception rather than the rule. However, in the long run this solution is structurally unstable. Some problems migrate up the organization to land on the commissioner's desk, some drift down to be resolved by junior systems analysts, and many just cycle through the organization never receiving adequate attention—until a crisis occurs. The creation of a more formal policy structure can arise from many sources—an operational crisis, departure of a person performing a key informal policy role, or organizational leadership attuned to the need for organizational policy.

One formal solution (usually a temporary one) is to have questions of information policy handled directly by the agency's chief executive or his or her executive staff. Usually born of crisis, this solution quickly becomes untenable. The organization's chief operating officer cannot afford to give sustained, detailed attention to such issues. Another formal solution makes the director of data processing the center of information policy. Often preferred as a first step in organizational evolution, this strategy has some advantages. The DP director is often "up to speed" on many issues and has the necessary technical skills. However, good information policy rests more on information use than on information technology, and in issues that involve a dispute between user groups and data processing staff, the director of data processing has a built-in conflict of interest. A third approach involves elevating the position of director of data processing operations to something like "director of information technologies." Additional functions would be "tucked in" under this new expanded position, and typically a deputy director of information technologies would take over day-to-day operations of the computing center. This strategy works well when promoting a particularly qualified director of data processing who is widely respected within the organization. But again, this solution brings with it built-in conflicts of interest. A "chief information officer" may be a solution in some organizations. Reporting to the chief executive, the CIO is expected to have a good grasp of the technology, but more importantly, keen insight into how information resources support the agency's mission. The CIO as an organizational entity is discussed further in Chapter 3.

No discussion of formal structures for handling information policies would be complete without at least a brief look at advisory committees. Nearly every organization makes use of both standing and ad hoc advisory committees comprising both users and technicians. The exact membership, formal authority, and substructures of the advisory committees will vary considerably from situation to situation. In some organizations, advisory committees are given formal power to approve or disapprove deviations from stated organizational policy (such as the purchase of a "nonstandard" microprocessor). In other organizations, they are literally "advisory." Often the committee's own organizational structure can reinforce established interests within the agency, both good and bad. Committees can be structured with more or less formal authority within the organization, ranging from fully active and collaborative professional decision-making bodies to powerless "rubber stamps." Quite obviously, these important issues of committee organization, formal authority, and operating procedures will be of great interest to committee members themselves, to upper management within the organization, and to key user groups. Committees, after all, operate by the time-honored rules of organizational politics.

As we have seen, the range and complexity of organizationwide policy positions vary considerably from one agency to the next. All share a common problem, however. It is all too easy to develop policies around the technological tools and to ignore the value of information itself. Information policy should primarily be concerned with how the organization uses information. Without an explicit understanding of what information is important to the organization—and why—attention to the technology will be at least somewhat beside the point.

Creating Appropriate Governmentwide Policies

The fundamental question about governmentwide policies, especially for large jurisdictions, is not how they should be set but whether they should exist at all. Theoreticians and practitioners differ sharply on whether a government is a unified enough entity that it can or should issue policies at the operational level. Many argue that jurisdictionwide policies must be drawn at a level of abstraction that cannot take into account the detailed realities of "street level" operations. They contend that centralized operating policies lead to rigidity and actually impede operations and stifle initiative and innovation. At a different level, however, governmentwide policies can be positive forces. For example, the Freedom of Information Act gives overarching guidance about the release of information by public agencies.

Grounded both in constitutional principles and in a normative vision of how a democratic government ought to function, FOIA and other statutes-as-policies offer broad principles to guide agency decisions.

Groups of agencies that share substantive concerns can often benefit from jointly developed information policies. For example, the courts, police, corrections, parole, probation, and other law enforcement agencies (state, local, and national) all need to share information within the criminal justice system. Hence, the development of standard definitions and processes (e.g., how to track arrests, convicts, and parolees) can serve the joint interests of the participating agencies and, by extension, the public. Similar opportunities exist in the social services and health-care systems where several agencies have relationships with overlapping client populations and service providers. Note, however, that none of these applications lay claim to a need for policies that span the full range of government operations.

Finally, virtually all agencies within a single jurisdiction share a limited set of common functions. For example, Civil Service and labor relations procedures, budgeting, and accounting are common to all. These common functions are often cited as an appropriate area for governmentwide data standards. They might prevent the unhappy situation where agencies repeatedly "reinvent the wheel" with their agency-specific versions of expenditure control or personnel systems. Another benefit would be an ability to aggregate key data items giving greater support to those few important areas where the jurisdiction in its entirety is the subject of analysis.

The foregoing discussion raises questions about whether the full range of possible policy areas listed in Figure 2.6 can apply to an entire government. This is certainly open to debate. However, a consensus seems to be developing that in carefully defined substantive and functional areas a legitimate need does exist for policies established at the level of the government as a whole.

As with organizationwide policy statements, the idea of governmentwide policies entails questions of how and by whom such policies should be established. Several models exist. The first and perhaps most common model for governmentwide policy development is a do-nothing or do-little model. It is a policy of default usually involving several agencies, each taking on a piece of the overall policy problem. Budgeting agencies take the lead on questions of procurement; Civil Service on training, promotion, and career ladders. Questions relating to telephones and telecommunications are often taken up by a central services agency, and those on records management, disposition, and archives are handled by yet another. Of course, the problem is that these areas of subpolicy interact. Operating agencies find themselves caught in a tangle of conflicting central edicts, finding it difficult to create holistic agency policies that harmonize with these uncoordinated cross-directives.

A common alternative to the do-nothing approach is a strong, independent, governmentwide policy agency—perhaps an office for information management. Such organizations are created to provide a single central locus for policy development and control. While attractive in theory, they also present practical problems. A major one is that the directives of the information policy and planning agency can conflict with directives of other control agencies. For example, what should be the appropriate relationship between an agency's information technology plan and its budget request? A related problem is one that all control agencies share. They are not well positioned to anticipate, plan for, and be responsive to the needs of all units within a large and complex government. For example, a governmentwide telecommunications network may adequately serve the needs of most agencies, but a university center may need special access to supercomputers requiring unusual bandwidths, or a police agency may need access to criminal files with exceptional security requirements. Centrally controlled policies can be unresponsive to these special needs.

Sometimes a major data processing center within the government will evolve into a locus for policy making. Technical expertise is often located in such a unit and these arrangements can work well for a time, but eventually the scope and complexity of information functions across the government overwhelms the ability of a single center to serve all needs well. Moreover, setting governmentwide policy and maintaining the center's own operational responsibilities will inevitably conflict.

Still, the arguments favoring a central locus of governmentwide policy making are many and often powerful. For example, a centralized policy-making body could provide for hardware standards, shared software licensing agreements, shared telecommunications facilities, standardized data dictionaries for data items that cross individual agencies, technical assistance to smaller and less-skilled agencies, "mass" purchasing power, and so on. It also has a better chance to recognize technological and workforce trends and to take early advantage of them.

Arguments against a governmentwide policy locus, especially for large jurisdictions with several large and sophisticated data centers, are convincing as well. To begin with, a government is not a single structure and most of these policies are designed for organizations, not federations. In large and sophisticated agencies, economies of scale have already been achieved, coordination and cohesive policies that meet agency needs are already in place, little slack capacity exists to be coordinated and shared, and a workable mix of flexibility and control has probably already been established. Furthermore, there seems to be an almost natural law that posits that policy "coordinating" structures inevitably take on a control orientation, creating another layer of regulation and paperwork to make the lives of information managers within the agencies more complicated. Hence, a centralized policy structure may do little good for the agencies themselves, and by inappropriately circumscribing the autonomy of information managers in the agencies, probably has the potential for doing much harm.

The truth about the desirability of governmentwide structures to set broad information policies probably rests somewhere between these two extremes. For small jurisdictions that rely primarily on an outside data center to serve the needs of many separate agencies or departments, a centralized structure to set policy for the jurisdiction seems to be correct and needed. For larger jurisdictions with substantial data processing operations in separate agencies and a wide variety of public programs to support, a strong centralized structure for setting policy is perhaps counterproductive.

Between the two extremes of do nothing and do everything there are many alternatives. They commonly involve specialized organizations, task forces, coordinating committees, or forums of varying degrees of complexity. For example, within the federal government, the Office of Technology Assessment provides a technical research and "think tank" capacity helping to shape legislated policies toward new and emerging technologies. Voluntary associations of information professionals, perhaps with membership from key users across the government, can provide peer consultation and a vehicle for sharing information, as well as serve as an informal center for policy discussions. The low level of authority in this form of centralized policy can be strengthened by the addition of a permanent staff or policy oversight functions. Finally, some governments have established permanent forums of data processing professionals, program managers, and policy makers to encourage continuing dialogue on the full range of information policy issues. These are more stable than ad hoc task forces and usually offer a broader view of governmentwide policy. However, they generally do not have control powers or operating responsibilities. Rather, these are left to the agencies designed to handle them. Broadly based, yet flexible governmentwide policies can result from this kind of permanent mechanism for exchanging ideas and experience.

CONCLUSION

In this chapter, we surveyed the interplay between public organizations and information technology. We considered the technology itself as well as the economic, organizational, and political dimensions of information and information technology management. We reviewed some current issues and examined a wide range of possible policy responses through which work groups, entire organizations, and entire governments might create strategic information policy. Throughout the discussion, we noted that many of the forces that shape our information future are indeed beyond our control. However, by combining an acute awareness of the issues with a commitment to find a balance between stability and flexibility, effective policy alternatives can be found.

The key to managing government information resources rests with work unit, agency, and governmentwide policies that respond to the wide range of issues raised in this chapter. There is no cookbook to tell us just how to formulate them. In a rapidly changing world of technological innovation, teams of technical experts, information users, and decision makers must combine their experiences to chart government's information future. The policies that take us there must consider technology, its costs and benefits, its effect on organizations, and the political considerations that define the unique nature of the public sector. These organizational, legal, and institutional factors form the basis for the next three chapters.

EXERCISES

1. Under the section "Managing the Costs of Information," we discussed a State University department that made a $15,000 investment in some new microcomputers. That department was the Biology Department. As a member of the Psychology Department, you have been impressed with what a relatively small investment has been able to do for the biologists. You are interested in having your chair make a similar investment, but she is hesitant. The $15,000 would have to come out of funds that she has tentatively scheduled for the long-overdue renovation of the animal-housing facilities in the experimental psychology unit. Furthermore, she has heard that the experience in the Biology Department may not be as advantageous as it appeared at first. She is concerned about the $3,000-per-year maintenance fees and about a continuing need to commit future funds to file conversions and equipment maintenance. Her immediate reaction is that individual faculty members who want such equipment should purchase it from their own grant funds. She believes, for now at least, that this project is not such a good use of departmental funds.

   Since you are so much in favor of the department's making the investment, you have been asked to draw up a document that lays out as clearly as possible what will be the full lifespan costs of installing this network of equipment. The "hard" cost figures, at least for the first year, are easy to come by. Five microcomputers will cost $2,000 each (the university has a special low-cost purchase arrangement directly with the vendor). The network hardware and peripherals (including printers) will cost roughly $5,000. Costs to maintain the system will run around $3,000 per year, including maintenance on the machines, printing cartridges and ribbons, paper, supplies, and so on. You have been asked to identify both the projected costs and the benefits of the investment for the full life of the machines to be purchased. You believe your chair will show your document to the university's budget officer. Hence, while you really want to see the project "fly," you realize that your cost and benefit estimates must be solid and pass the scrutiny of both your chair and the budget officer. (Hint: For a quick brushup, review the discussion of cost-benefit analysis contained in Stokey and Zeckhauser's *Primer for Policy Analysis* as cited in the readings at the end of this chapter.)

2. You have just turned in the cost-benefit document your chair requested. However, even before you get a response, she has another request. Apparently impressed by your earlier arguments, she attended a seminar on information technologies of the future. There she learned that many researchers today have microcomputing machines on their desks that rival the processing speed and peripheral storage capacity of what were considered mainframe machines in the late 1960s. The seminar leader told her these improvements will continue for the next decade or more. She also learned that one of the major vendors is about to release a new model—rumored to be a major advance in technology—later this year. These new machines would be totally compatible with the older series but would also allow for easier communication between machines and would have dramatically enhanced graphics and audio capabilities, introducing a new generation of user-friendly interfaces. Given her relative inexperience with computing, your chair is impressed by such easy-to-use machines. Software for these new machines is not yet released but will be soon. The new machines will cost $3,500 each, but the networking hardware (when it is finally released) is projected to cost only $1,000 for your system of five machines.

   Your chair was obviously impressed by your previous memo, but now she wants to wait for this new machine to be released. She realizes now that it would be better to buy a machine with "the future built in" rather than to buy the older machines that the Biology Department had purchased. She is asking once more for your advice.

   Draft a second memo to your chair laying out the positive and negative reasons for buying now versus waiting for the newly released machine.

3. Something bad just happened. Your chair was on the verge of buying a network for the Psychology Department when she sat down to discuss this plan for one last time with the chair of Biology. There she learned that decisions about what machines to buy were only the tip of the iceberg. Apparently the faculty and staff in Biology have been going through a rough time since buying their new machines. They have gotten into squabbles over priorities. Some faculty want changes made to their manuscripts while others want new documents entered into the system. Which should happen first? One member of the support staff has never really adjusted to the new machines and still does most of her work on a typewriter. This causes problems when other staff have to retype a manuscript that she began. Some faculty are angry because they have already purchased microcomputers of their own and the new departmental computers are not compatible with the ones they have in their offices. Others complain because their files were lost when one of the machines had a disk failure. This was the only copy of their work and they have been set back by almost a month in their research. Finally, one of the machines was damaged during an electrical storm last summer, requiring extensive repairs and loss of faculty members' files.

   Apparently the Psychology Department will need some new procedures and policies if these machines are to function smoothly. Once again, your department chair has asked you to think through what procedural and policy changes will be needed. You hope that this is her last request to you.

Draft a memo to your chair answering the questions that she has put to you. (*Hint:* you may wish to refer to Figure 2.6.) You realize that it would be unwise to overwhelm her with details, so you decide to keep your recommendations down to the core of really important issues.

4. You are the staff assistant to Ellen Brighton, account executive for New World Telecommunication Systems. Ellen is about to meet with the chief of staff of the Senate Finance Committee in the State of Goodwill. New World will be bidding on the installation of a statewide telecommunications network to link together all the state and local offices administering the state's Family Assistance Program. The Finance Committee will have something to say about the decision. While Brighton feels confident about the technical aspects of the proposal, she suspects that politics may come into play in this project (this is the first public sector project that New World has bid on). Brighton will be leaving this afternoon and has requested that you draft a quick memo for her review telling her what types of political situations she should be looking out for in her meeting with the Senate Committee.

You only have time to get the broad facts of the situation in Goodwill. Using your political acumen you will have to "fill in" with reasonable surmises. The facts as you understand them are as follows:

In Goodwill, Family Support payments have been shared—50 percent of the costs being picked up by the counties and 50 percent by the state. Administration of the Family Assistance Program is handled by county governments with data processing for the system usually, but not always, centralized in each county's data processing center. All counties follow the same program regulations, but administrative procedures vary from one county to the next. All counties provide a monthly data tape to the state with full information on all recipients.

Informally, you are aware that the state has not been pleased with administrative procedures in some counties. In return for picking up more of the costs, the state is requiring that all counties meet more rigid state standards. Hence, all eligibility processes will have to be run through a standardized statewide information system. This system will be operated out of four state-administered regional offices. These offices will probably share facilities and site with four of the better county data processing centers. The telecommunications network on which New World is bidding will connect the county and local offices to these four regional offices as well as connect the four regional offices to the central office in the state capital.

Over the past several years, relationships between the state and local governments have been a bit strained. Some state administrators have little respect for local administrative expertise. In turn, local officials complain that the state is always producing mandates and then failing to follow through on them and fund them adequately. In fact, the proposal now before the state legislature to assume more Family Assistance Program costs was part of a gubernatorial election year promise to have the state fund its mandates more fully.

Draft a memo to Brighton detailing the major political issues she should be looking out for.

5. Today is your lucky day. Even as a relatively young entry-level manager in the city's Tax Department, you have been frustrated by the skill level of the city's workforce, both professional and clerical. You have just received a note from the newly appointed director of personnel. He is interested in setting up a citywide system of training and professional development to move the city's entire workforce into the twenty-first century. The centerpiece of his initiative is state-of-the-art training in information technology. Your supervisor has recommended you to the director as a person who would have some good ideas. You are one of ten people to receive a note from the director of personnel asking for advice on how to improve and maintain the technical skill level of the city's workforce.

In your Master's program you received good training in management information systems, decision support systems, and the basics of computing technology. That was only four years ago. However, you are already beginning to feel that your own skills are falling behind the state-of-the-art. Your review of the journals shows you that exciting new things are happening in telecommunications and distributed processing, yet you haven't been able to assess fully the implications of these new technologies. You are pessimistic about getting a chance to "brush up" on your skills at your job, even though you are a skilled policy analyst and work regularly with the department's mainframe and micro systems. In addition, you feel that many of your fellow employees have avoided taking full advantage of computing technologies in their jobs. Word processing and even elementary spreadsheet operations are seeping only slowly into your office. Operations on the city's mainframe still seem very segregated from most micro users.

You have been asked to sketch a comprehensive set of suggestions for improving and then maintaining the information technology skills of the city workforce. In addition, the new director wants to make sure that those who obtain new skills are properly rewarded at the time of promotion and pay increases. However, you need to make sure your suggestions are tempered with an awareness that not all things are possible within a collective bargaining and Civil Service-oriented system. Your recommendations must take these realities into account. Still, you are encouraged because the new director is working with the approval of the newly elected mayor. She has served on the boards of directors of several of the high-tech firms that have been fueling the local economy (prior to her election) and is favorably disposed to proposals relating to information technology within government.

You are sitting down to draft your letter of recommendations with cautious optimism about the future.

PROJECTS AND CASE EXERCISES

1. Read carefully the case study "An Information Network for the Employment Service." You are a staff assistant to Helen Frye, and as you can clearly see, she is faced with a difficult set of circumstances. Basically, she must decide to support Employment Service's request for a telecommunications network, or come out in favor of State Central Service's request for a coordinated network, or find her way to some solid middle ground between these two proposals. She perceives that the future viability of the Office of Technology Management may well rest on how she handles this, her first critical decision. Frye clearly discerns that this decision situation commingles considerations of technology itself, cost, organizational factors, and politics. To sort out these four aspects of the situation more clearly, she has asked you to analyze the situation from each of these four points of view. She wants you to make a case from each perspective and then, arguing from each of them, make a recommendation to her. In your concluding section she has requested that you discuss and attempt to resolve any competing recommendations that may arise among the four points of view. Of course, you may find you do not have enough information to make final recommendations. If that happens, Frye wants you to detail what additional information she needs to get and why that information will help her to make her decision.

2. Read carefully the case study "Managing the Introduction of a Voice-oriented Clinical Data System in a Psychiatric Facility."

    a. The price tag of the VOODS technology for the mental health system is $435 million. However, this price includes only purchase of the equipment. List the additional categories of cost that might be associated with the VOODS system over the next five years.

    b. Some analysts have argued that the real impediments to acquiring and installing the VOODS technology are organizational, not technical or financial. Taking that line of argument, discuss the organizational barriers that will make the installation of the VOODS technology most difficult.

    Acquiring the VOODS technology may change how doctors relate to patients, how groups of professionals relate to each other, and how individual patients and the public at large gain access to mental health records. All of these issues will demand a rethinking of existing policies. Make a list of the types of policies that work units, DMHS, and the state as a whole may have to change if the VOODS system is purchased and installed.

SUGGESTED READINGS

CAUDLE, SHARON L. *Federal Information Resources Management: Bridging Vision and Action.* Academy Studies, National Academy of Public Administration, 1987.
DANZIGER, JAMES, et al. *Computers and Politics: High Technology in American Local Government.* New York: Columbia University Press, 1982.

DAVIES, THOMAS R., and WILLIAM M. HALE. Implementing a Policy and Planning Process for Managing State Use of Information Technology Resources. *Public Administration Review* 46(SI): 516–21, November 1986.

EIN-DOR, PHILLIP, and ELI SEGEV. Organizational Context and the Success of Management Information Systems. *Management Science* 24(10): 1065–77, June 1978.

GORR, WILPEN L. Use of Special Event Data in Government Information Systems. *Public Administration Review* 46(SI): 532–39, November 1986.

HEAPHEY, JAMES, and ROBERT CROWLEY. Standardizing Welfare Management: The State versus the Counties. *New York Case Studies in Public Management—ER008* Albany, NY: Rockefeller Institute of Government, 1984.

KEEN, PETER G .W., and LYNDA A. WOODMAN. What to Do with All Those Micros. *Harvard Business Review* (62)5: 142–250, September–October 1984.

R&D Group Plugs Info Master Plans for Local Gov't. *Government Computer News* (March 28, 1986): 14–19.

ROCKART, JOHN F., and CHRISTINE V. BULLEN, eds. *The Rise of Managerial Computing: The Best of the Center for Information Systems Research, Sloan School of Management, MIT.* Homewood, IL: Dow-Jones-Irwin, 1986.

STOKEY, EDITH, and RICHARD ZECKHAUSER. *A Primer for Policy Analysis.* New York: W. W. Norton, 1978.

WYMAN, JOHN. Technology Myopia—The Need to Think Strategically about Technology. *Sloan Management Review* 26(4): 59–64, Summer 1985.

ZUBOFF, SHOSHANA. New Worlds of Computer-mediated Work. *Harvard Business Review* 60(5): 142–52, September–October 1982.

CHAPTER 3

TECHNOLOGY, ORGANIZATIONS, AND PEOPLE

Calvin Tyler put down the file with a sigh of weary frustration. Inside, Susan Miller, newly appointed assistant commissioner for Forensic Mental Health Services, had laid out her plan. She wanted a microcomputer-based information system to support mental health services in prisons across the state. In the eighteen months, Tyler must have reviewed a dozen of these proposals. They all seemed the same. As director of the department's Systems Development Group, Tyler had to comment on all of them, no matter how small. He had asked for this review authority just two years ago out of his concern over the mounting number of "information islands" springing up across the department. Maybe he had made a mistake.

Take Miller's proposal as a case in point. Although her previous job had given her some data processing background, she was clearly not a professional. She was entirely concerned with the parochial program needs of her own small area of specialization. She lacked an overview of the information needs of the agency as a whole. Her plan didn't even recognize or react to his group's long-fought efforts to develop a comprehensive system of integrated financial, client, and staffing data that would pull together disparate units across the agency. Should her proposal be allowed to go forward, Tyler knew he would have one more small shard of a system to deal with.

Despite his frustration, Tyler's first instinct was to be helpful. He started to jot down a list of the systemwide considerations Miller had overlooked—hardware compatibility across the regions, issues of standardized data definitions, system staffing and maintenance with skilled data processing professionals. . . The list seemed endless. A strong sense of déjà vu suddenly brought this line of reasoning to an abrupt halt. Tyler knew that the department's first deputy would want the systems staff involved in designing and implementing any suggestions Tyler made. Already most of his group's time was devoted to fighting fires and cleaning up small problems like the one now on his desk. His own efforts at major system development were being left undone while these smaller projects sapped his staff's time.

No, a better strategy would be to take a low profile. He would make few suggestions in writing and approach Miller off the record, offering to help in any way he could.[1]

Cal Tyler is living through the latest of many rounds in a continuing turf war between data users and data producers. New technologies have brought computing out of central data centers into all corners of the workplace, and users and data processing professionals are struggling to redefine their respective roles.

Sue Miller tells the other side of the story. Her attempts to serve the information needs of her program are being frustrated by a slow-moving data processing unit oriented toward mainframe operations with great concern for centralization and control. But Miller lives in a decentralized environment, with staff spread out in prisons across the state. She is used to scrambling for resources—space in corrections facilities, grants from the federal government, and even computing equipment purchased from those grants. She understands Tyler has his job to do, but that job does not help meet her unit's needs. She cannot afford to wait forever for some perfectly integrated system—she has operations to manage right now.

Miller and Tyler hold different views of what their organizations are and what defines effective performance for the agency. Tyler is oriented toward centralization and the enforcement of a stable set of standards. Miller is oriented toward flexibility, program innovation, and resource acquisition. They are living through a difficult transition, as are most government organizations. They are dealing with issues attending the creation and management of information islands, the structural relationships between data processing and line managers, and the design of new jobs that create information amphibians—half line manager, half information manager. These are the up-to-the-minute organizational problems created by state-of-the-art information technologies.

The tension between Tyler and Miller exemplifies the issues we examine in this chapter—the organizational dimensions of government information management. We will begin by looking at four types of organizations, noting how assumptions we make about an organization and about what defines effective performance predetermine how we think about informa-

---

[1]For more information about this situation, see the case study "A Forensic Mental Health Database to Implement a Suicide Prevention Program."

tion systems and policy. Next we take up three fundamental sets of organizational issues that government information managers face. Structural issues range from defining information-related leadership roles in small work units to creating new offices to manage the information policy process across entire agencies. A second set of organizational issues and associated policy responses focuses on the role of the individual worker vis-à-vis the larger organization. This section treats issues and policies relating to training and professional development, job design, and ergonomics. A third cluster deals with procedures and shifting roles. In this final category, we will discuss such topics as when to create and when to avoid information islands, data definition as an organizational process, and the role of organizational life cycles in shaping information policies.

But before we delve into these issues, we need to further develop a framework for thinking about them. Since the "bottom line" of most new information technologies is better-functioning organizations (whether measured in saved dollars, increased productivity, greater efficiency, or smoother operations), this chapter will focus on the relationship between government information management and organizational effectiveness.

GOVERNMENT INFORMATION MANAGEMENT
AND ORGANIZATIONAL EFFECTIVENESS

There is a reciprocal link between information management and organizational effectiveness. First, information technologies are expected to lead to more effective organizations—this is the very reason for adopting new technology. Second, effective organizations are expected to lead to better design, implementation, and operation of information systems. The result is a cycle of excellence: effective organizations create improved information systems, which in turn enhance organizational effectiveness. The discussion below explores both sides of this relationship.

But what is an effective organization? Is it one that can attain certain ends such as greater productivity, more resources, a cohesive workforce with high morale, or stable and predictable performance? Or are effective organizations those that sustain a desirable set of internal processes such as an ability to plan, set goals, and evaluate performance, or an ability to remain flexible and responsive to the external environment? Which of these performance measures are most highly valued?

These questions have puzzled organizational theorists for years. In 1970, Campbell and his associates surveyed a sample of experts to determine what criteria were most commonly used to define organizational effectiveness. Thirty criteria emerged from the study. In an attempt to make sense out of this maze of overlapping and apparently competing measures, in 1980

Quinn and Rohrbaugh assembled a panel of experts in organizational theory to examine Campbell's original thirty criteria. Their goals were to identify overlap and redundancy as well as to construct a coherent framework for making sense of the apparent contradictions among the criteria. In the first stage of the study, the experts agreed virtually unanimously that thirteen of the original thirty criteria were either redundant, combined versions of other separate criteria, or measures that operationalized other criteria. The remaining seventeen, when subjected to a multidimensional scaling exercise, seemed to cluster neatly around three independent dimensions of organizational performance—an internal versus external orientation, an orientation toward means (internal procedures) versus ends (organizational outputs), and an orientation toward control versus flexibility. The study of organizational effectiveness, then, is dominated by these three competing dimensions of effective performance. Note that each of the three dimensions represents a paradoxical tension of opposites. Effective organizations may be either flexible or controlled. Equally effective organizations may focus on internal processes or on externally oriented measures of productivity. These dimensions mirror many of the concerns we have already explored in the management of information technologies.

When considered together, these dimensions create four pure models of organizational effectiveness, as illustrated in Figure 3.1. The four types are the rational goal model, the internal process model, the human relations model, and the open systems model. Each type stresses different aspects of the internal versus external and flexibility versus control dimensions. In addition, each of the four models values differing ends and uses different means to achieve them.

Of course, real organizations are complex mixtures of all four ideal types. The four pure types serve as yardsticks against which to measure the competing dimensions of organizational effectiveness within a given real organization. However, Quinn and Cameron's competing values framework makes no normative statements concerning which of the four ideal types are more important or which ought to serve as a model for truly effective organizations in the public or private sector. The competing values framework is silent (as it should be) on the question of which of the four types is best. Simply put, the framework implies that the profiles of effective organizations combine aspects of all four. The exact mix appropriate to a given organization will depend on its history, mission, and environment.

The Rational Goal Model

The rational goal model is oriented toward control and toward the external operating environment. This type values the ends of productivity and efficiency and stresses the means of planning, goal setting, and systematic evaluation of feedback on organizational performance. This ideal type

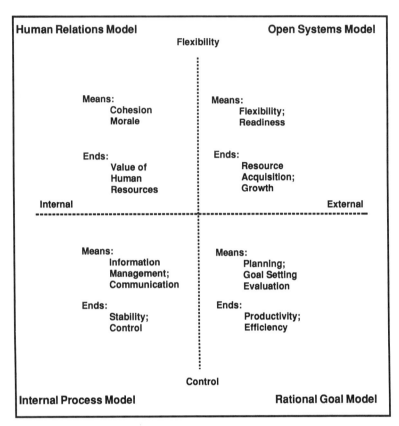

Figure 3.1   Four Models of Organizational Effectiveness (Adapted from Quinn and Cameron)

implicitly assumes a stable operating environment and a clearly defined mission. It is often associated with industrial or military systems—a platoon or squadron with a well-defined mission or a production line that operates as one component in the well-ordered environment of a manufacturing plant.

In this model the impact of information technologies on organizational effectiveness is clear and unambiguous. Information technologies are designed to increase white-collar productivity—much the same as capital equipment in the industrial sector improved blue-collar productivity over the past century. The automation of repetitive jobs like order entry and billing created greater output per clerical position in the first generation of automation. As information technologies now move toward management information systems, decision support systems, expert systems, and end-user software, productivity will increase in the professional and managerial workforce as well. Increases in white-collar productivity, so goes the theory, will allow organizations—both public and private—to produce more output with the same number of personnel. During periods of attrition or no growth, organizations oriented toward information processing will be able to do the same amount of work with fewer people. Computer-based information systems will assist the organizational processes of performance evaluation and goal setting. Information—accurately collected, channeled, and analyzed using new forms of technology—is the key to sustaining tightly controlled internal processes.

Most experts say the design, creation, implementation, and operation of effective information systems begins with a clear definition of the goals of the organization vis-à-vis a known environment, an evaluation of present operations, and clear and explicit planning around how the new system should function. This textbook approach to system design assumes information systems will be operating in organizations characterized by the rational goal model. The normative foundations of much of the existing literature on how to design, install, and operate information systems clearly rests on the ideal rational goal type. Somehow, if managers could only plan further ahead, be clearer about the organization's goals, and evaluate more carefully and clearly present patterns of performance, then information technologies would function optimally. When systems fail, designs are flawed, implementation stumbles, or operations founder, the usual diagnosis is inadequate managerial attention to planning, goal setting, and evaluation. This diagnosis often sets up a vicious cycle. Poor system performance is blamed on not enough or not good enough planning, evaluation, and control. The prescribed cure is more planning, more detailed explication of goals, and, inevitably, more control. If the organization is not actually an ideal rational goal model, this course of treatment is unlikely to improve system performance. The result is ever greater attempts to set goals, evaluate, and control with no consequent improvement in performance.

In this case, we have made the wrong implicit assumptions about the nature of the organization. Many organizations are not, cannot, and should not be oriented toward the rational goal model of control and externally oriented production. Our implicit assumptions about what the organization should be blind us to what it actually is. Perhaps the common assumption that public sector organizations ought to be oriented toward externally measurable units of production, subject to tight controls, and governed by crisply defined objectives creates as many problems as it solves. An examination of the other three ideal organization types may shed further light on this observation.

The Internal Process Model

As shown in Figure 3.1, the internal process model is a modest extension of the rational goal type. This ideal type is also based on control rather than flexibility. However, it focuses on internal operations, not the external environment. This type values stability and control and uses well-controlled communication and information management processes to attain them. Practical examples of organizations that approximate this ideal type include units within a department of audit and control responsible for the biweekly issuance of paychecks or units within a department of social services responsible for issuing client payments. While the total measured volume of production within these organizations is important, stable and predictable performance is the key measure of effectiveness. Being on time, consistent, and in control is of primary value.

Once again, the role of information technologies within this ideal type of organization is apparent. They become the basis for managing information flows and internal communications. The information manager oversees the familiar functions of analyzing information sources within the organization, designing input and output forms and specifications, developing routing procedures, and in general tracking the flow of routine information throughout the organization. Within this model, information management issues include the role of regional or distributed processing sites in the input and control of information; reacting to and recovering from information disasters such as the loss of a mainframe CPU; maintaining the integrity and confidentiality of data files; standardizing data definitions, hardware and software standards; and so on.

As with the rational goal model, another implicit assumption is that most organizations either do or should conform to the ideal type internal process model. However, many government offices that are devoted to the analysis, processing, and synthesis of information do not at all conform to the assumptions underlying either. For example, committees within the legislature, staff in the governor's office, or an instructional or research unit at the state university all process and organize information as a primary and almost exclusive mission. All rely heavily on information technologies to assist them, but none appear to conform to the requirements of a stable operating environment, clearly defined objectives, and consistently measurable output as indicators of organizational effectiveness. These organizations are vital, effective information processing units, but they conform to none of the assumptions implicit in either the rational goal or the internal process ideal types. If information technology managers become fixated on a too limited view of what criteria imply an effective organization, incorrect but unchanged assumptions clash with the realities of organizational performance and a counterproductive cycle of inappropriate control-oriented strategies emerges.

The Human Relations Model

Again as illustrated in Figure 3.1, the ideal human resources organization takes on an internal focus but has an orientation toward flexibility and adaptability. As such, this type values the development of human resources as its preferred measure of success. To achieve this goal, these organizations seek cohesion among workers and a strong sense of employee morale. While real organizations with an almost pure human resources orientation are rare, most organizations do have some sub-unit such as a personnel department that functions in this way. A governmentwide office of employee relations might serve as an example of an entire organization devoted to the end of human resource development. In addition, almost every real organization, no matter how sharply oriented toward the rational goal model or the internal process model, recognizes to at least some degree the critical importance of the ideals of the human relations model.

What, however, is the role of information technology in fostering and promoting effectiveness in these organizations? And, what does the human relations model tell us about how to more effectively manage information technologies within public sector organizations? In contrast to the rational goal and internal process types, information technologies should not be expected to have dramatic impacts on overall organizational effectiveness in this model. The introduction of information technologies may expand job definitions for some clerical and professional positions. Hence, in a minor way, the introduction of new technologies may have some positive impacts on effectiveness within the human relations model.

More importantly, however, the introduction of new technologies in organizations can be expected to create more problems than it solves. When viewed solely in human resource terms, new technologies can raise a number of ergonomic issues related to poorly designed work stations and equipment as well as prolonged, isolated work periods. These create less-vigorous and less-healthy working conditions for some and limit workforce cohesion. In addition, the introduction of new technologies can shift some workers to new functions or even push them out of the organization entirely through transfer or layoffs. From a purely human relations point of view, information technologies can have negative impacts on overall effectiveness. Even if the new technologies do not lead to displacement, rumors of displacement can create an atmosphere of mistrust and fear among employees who feel they might be hurt. These new technologies can lead to stratification of the workforce into data processing professionals, computer users and advocates, and others who do not become involved with the new technology. This can in turn lead to suspicion, strained working relations, and conflicting work goals. In reality, most organizations that introduce new technologies into the workplace experience some combination of these predicted problems. Introduced to achieve greater productivity and efficiency (as viewed from of the rational goal perspective) or greater stability of operations (as viewed from the internal process model), these innovations can often have unintended consequences, rendering the organization less effective along the human relations dimensions of employee cohesion and morale. Viewing organizational effectiveness in terms of these competing models shows clearly the multiple consequences of technological change within an organization.

Fortunately, when we look at the reverse, the impact of an effective organization on information technologies, a number of strategies and tactics for mitigating these negative effects emerge. For example, the human relations model stresses the importance of employee training and development. Mechanisms such as joint data processing and user committees that meet frequently to discuss policy directions and possible differences in points of view can be very useful. Possible insularity of the data processing center from the concerns of line managers and information users can be minimized by organizational inventions such as information resource centers where data processing professionals provide support to individual users who create their own systems and databases, often with end-user-oriented software. Attention is given as well to job descriptions and the overall design of work for both units and individuals to ensure that formal descriptions of duties and responsibilities match current realities. Finally, policy-making roles around information technologies can be clearly delineated at all levels within the organization. Work units can designate people responsible for selecting hardware and software or helping to design new procedures. The organization as a whole can clearly define the locus for policies related to information technologies (such as a chief information officer), and entire units of government can put mechanisms in place to coordinate information use across individual agencies.

In general, when managing public information systems, the human relations ideal type serves more or less as an antidote to the output and control orientations that characterize the rational goal and the internal process models. The human relations model of organizational effectiveness reminds managers to recognize that the intrinsic value of human relations, employee cohesion, and morale are important components of overall effectiveness. Explicit organizational strategies and tactics exist for helping the organization achieve effective human relations during the installation and operation of new information-based systems.

The Open Systems Model

From the point of view of the open systems ideal type, an effective organization is characterized by flexibility and an external orientation. Such organizations strive for resource acquisition and growth and they value flexibility, responsiveness, and readiness. Public organizations that acquire and operate on funds external to the legislative appropriations process typically fall into this category. For example, a state lottery must rely on its own wits and entrepreneurial initiative to achieve a larger share of its "market" and to secure the agency's operating base. Similarly, research laboratories that are within the state university or the department of health must often rely on external funding and must therefore remain flexible and responsive to the external environment. Finally, many public authorities that finance construction projects maintain a portfolio of investments and must deal competitively in the investment markets, as well as maintain a flexible and open orientation toward their external environments.

Analysts of the ideal type of open systems organization stress that information technologies are strategic resources to enhance the organization's competitive position. For example, banks use automated information systems to create twenty-four-hour deposit and withdrawal services, to secure electronic funds transfer, and to enhance service levels to their individual and corporate customers. The level of available banking services, often defined and shaped by the level of information technology employed by the bank, defines important aspects of the bank's competitive position. Similarly, several major airlines have used information systems as competitive instruments to secure a greater share of their market. By installing airline reservation systems in travel agents' offices, or by providing bonus programs oriented to individual customers (such as the popular "frequent flyer" programs), airlines use sophisticated information systems either to lure additional business or to capture valuable marketing information about individuals.

Although such highly publicized examples of the use of information technologies to achieve competitive ends are less likely to be found in the public sector, there are examples of public sector open systems organizations that can and do use information technologies to grow and acquire resources. Perhaps the classic example is the tax amnesty program. In order to increase individual and corporate payments of tax liabilities, states used computer match techniques to crack down on delinquents. Many used paid television commercials featuring announcers standing in a computer room. The clear implication was that newly installed information technologies had sharply increased the state's ability to track income flows and identify undeclared income. These advertisements, coupled with real advances in the state's ability to match diverse data files, yielded a substantial rise in tax collections as individuals and companies hastened to declare additional income and pay the required tax during the amnesty period. Similar but less-dramatic examples can be found in legislative committee structures. Legislative committees are gaining access to fiscal and program information and are using these data to make inferences about the performance of the executive branch of government. For example, in many states, both the executive and legislative branches maintain computer-based models for estimating revenue. These independent information sources are important instruments in political disputes that emerge between the legislature and the governor's office at budget time. Information technologies are perceived as a valuable competitive resource, and both sides in a partisan political system see the value of investing in them.

While information technologies make substantial contributions to the effectiveness of the open systems model, the model in turn creates a very different operating environment than do the rational goal and the internal process models. The open systems model stresses flexibility and responsiveness over stability, efficiency, and control. In this model, information systems will tend to be localized, easily created, easily modified, and subject to change on short notice. Attempts to control and standardize decrease flexibility and responsiveness, it is argued, and therefore reduce overall organizational effectiveness. Within this type, local units will strive to build and maintain locally defined databases. "Islands of information" will emerge where organizational ent, epreneurs use information resources to maximize their positions. Information systems will often be redundant as local units use similar pieces of information to achieve goals that have a local, "bottoms up" character. The importance of standard data definitions, formats, procedures, and controls will in all likelihood not be recognized. Information systems are instead viewed as competitive instruments to achieve strategic objectives. Large-scale, comprehensive systems are viewed as out of date before they are constructed. Flexibility and responsiveness are the bywords of the day.

While the ideal open systems model may appear to be a bit of a caricature—few ideal types actually exist—many agencies and organizations must respond to rapidly changing situations and will define the performance of their information systems very differently from agencies that operate in a more stable, rational goal or internal process-like environment. For example, environmental conservation agencies are quite likely to be challenged to respond to new legal mandates on fairly short notice. Specialized files of environmental hazards or site registries may be a more appropriate type of response from information managers than statewide or regionwide comprehensive databases. Many agencies must be responsive to rapidly changing external factors, and their information systems must be tailored to change and adapt with the environment. Requirements for the design, implementation, and operation of information systems within this ideal type will often run counter to similar requirements within the rational goal or internal process organization. The way issues are framed and policy positions articulated will vary considerably, however, depending on how a given real organization blends traits of the four ideal types.

The sections below will briefly sketch some of the more specific organizational issues that arise in the management of new technologies within the public sector. For each issue, a range of associated policy responses will also be considered. This discussion is organized into three sections—organizational structure, the individual worker, and procedures and roles.

ORGANIZATIONAL STRUCTURE:
ISSUES AND POLICY RESPONSES

The term *organizational structure* as used here refers to how formal responsibilities are assigned for the management of information systems. In other words, this section looks at how the boxes on the organization chart are drawn and connected to one another.

Leadership Roles within the Local Work Unit

As information technologies spread to all corners of the formal organization, so too must formal leadership roles and other structures be established to help manage it. A "grass roots" structure of leadership must emerge to manage expanding information systems within virtually all operating units. Providing leadership for this process is a problem somewhat distinct from the usual factors associated with organizational leadership. This is because most information technologies appeared so recently—long after many line managers were promoted to positions of responsibility. In many units the formally designated leader may feel uncomfortable with, or even hostile toward, new information-oriented technologies. As we discussed in Chapter 2, the implementation of new information technologies makes use of three distinct roles— technology experts, technology leaders, and technology followers. Problems may arise when formal unit heads are, or perceive themselves to be, technology followers. However, the situation is really more complicated because (as shown in Figure 3.2) two additional technology-related roles are needed to ensure the smooth design, implementation, and operation of information systems in a given work unit—the technological gatekeeper and the strategist.

Strategic choice is perhaps the key role. Someone acting in the strategist role must define the broad parameters within which the work unit will function, including decisions about what equipment and software will be acquired, who will have access, and how priorities will be set. The technological gatekeeper is always pushing the organization to try out a new operating system, or get the latest graphics gadget, or use a new laser device. While often also the unit's expert, the gatekeeper may not necessarily have all of the expert's skills. His or her key trait is an enormous interest in and fascination with new technology. The gatekeeper prevents the work unit from becoming satisfied with one way of looking at its technology and therefore keeps it closer to the mythical "cutting edge."

There is a problem associated with all five of these roles—strategist, expert, technology leader, gatekeeper, and follower. They may become attached to people whose formal positions conflict with them. For example, the person best qualified to serve the strategic choice or expert function may be a relatively junior professional, fresh from school. While technically best

ROLE	FUNCTIONS
Strategist	Sets major policy directions for such issues as system objectives, program, priorities, technology investments, and staff responsibilities.
Expert	Provides major source of technical knowledge. Is the first person to have hands-on experience, assists in setting up systems, and trains first wave of technology leaders.
Technology Leader	Personnel with greatest affinity toward technology. They are trained first and become the vanguard for large-scale introduction of the new technology.
Technology Follower	Personnel with least attraction toward new technology. Should be introduced to it slowly and carefully. Not everyone needs or wants to deal with new information technologies.
Technological Gatekeeper	Often the expert, this role is concerned with keeping the organization informed of new developments in the entire information technology field.

Figure 3.2   Five Important Information Technology Management Roles

qualified, this individual lacks the formal position and status to take on these roles effectively. Similarly, a natural candidate for technological leadership often turns out to be a very skilled person who happens to occupy a clerical title. Many organizations resist having this person (often a young female) serve as technology leader for more senior clerical or professional staff (the latter category often dominated by older males). As work unit managers strive to make the best use of their personnel and to ensure that all necessary roles are filled, a common result is that some staff (often junior ones) take on assignments that constitute technically "out of title" work. While valued within the work unit, these people can often be penalized at promotion time when they are tested for traditionally defined "in title" skills.

Work unit managers have a difficult job. They must provide for all the needed roles, not overtly violate the implicit norms of the workplace (somehow creating new norms in the process), and must try to ensure that individuals providing necessary skills and knowledge are rewarded, not penalized, by the larger personnel system.

Structural Relationship of the Data Processing Center to Line Management

Traditionally, data processing has been considered a separate technical speciality much like a medical, architectural, or engineering design unit. At present, most public sector organizations have distinct organizational units to house this separate function. The data processing office has specially reserved job titles in the Civil Service system, is often housed physically apart from line management operations (typically in a space adjacent to the machine room), and frequently maintains a distinctive organizational subculture. However, as information processing spreads through the organization, some key questions appear about the relationship between the data processing center and the line operating units and between the director of data processing and the more program-oriented line managers.

In some cases, the director of the data processing unit is given responsibility for all information technology issues. After all, he or she is the expert in the area. In other cases, the director is just one among equals as all units of the organization attempt to resolve information-related problems. These extreme solutions are seldom successful. A more appropriate middle ground must be found, taking into account the specific circumstances within each agency. The relationships between the data processing director and other line managers depend substantially on organizational history. Different staff groups may have assumed responsibility for telecommunications, for supporting microcomputer users, for physical maintenance of the micro inventory, for supporting large-scale mainframe users. The formal reporting lines of the data processing unit on the overall organizational chart will also define specific working relationships.

A "chief information officer" (CIO) is appearing with increasing frequency as an answer to these structural questions. Often reporting directly to the organization's chief executive (university president, agency commissioner, etc.), this officer has line responsibilities for the full range of information technologies such as mainframe operations, voice and data communications, networking, and machine maintenance as well as overall policy responsibility for a wide range of cross-cutting functions such as office automation, database design, and data security and confidentiality. If this position is filled by promotion, the incumbent may come from either the data processing unit or the user community. In any case, the CIO is most often an information technology "amphibian," equally comfortable with DP professionals and the concerns of users.

Locus of Policy Making

The question of relationships between data processing units and other units is a specific manifestation of a broader issue. Where is the center for organizationwide or governmentwide policies with respect to information technologies? Clearly, some issues must fall to technical experts, but just as clearly users and program managers will have strongly vested interests in the resolution of many. Numerous structural arrangements have been tried as ways to create a center for information policy in organizations. The usefulness of each structure and its exact organizational form are open questions. But organization-level policies, while complicated, seem reasonable and necessary. Whether a whole jurisdiction can usefully have a formal governmentwide information policy is a matter of considerable debate. Should such direction come from the executive branch or the legislature? Can it be formulated in a way that supports rather than interferes with program operations? Must it inevitably result in central control or is there room for decentralized decision making? It seems that organizational invention and experimentation will continue until each jurisdiction finds a satisfactory solution. These issues were discussed in more detail in Chapter 2.

THE INDIVIDUAL WORKER:
ISSUES AND POLICY RESPONSES

As stressed by the human resources model of organizational effectiveness, policy must respond to a number of pressing issues important to the morale and cohesion of the public workforce. Several of these issues are discussed below.

Training and Professional Development

As discussed in the preceding chapter, training and professional development actually means *re*training and continuing professional education. "State-of-the-art" skills will need to be updated every three to five years if the workforce is to continue to work with the most recent technology. Fortunately, skill-oriented training can often be accomplished on the job, with technology leaders perhaps involved in formal programs and then taking the lead in developing the skills of the rest of the workforce. More fundamental, concept-oriented education will need to be undertaken, especially for the professional workforce deeply involved with computing, about every six to ten years. This kind of education would follow the introduction of a new generation of machines, for example. This more fundamental education will allow the agency as a whole to make the best use of new technologies as they come on the market.

The training and professional development requirements associated with information technologies will be even more urgent over the next several years as a large backlog of users and line managers, professionals, and clerical staff with little prior preparation enter the professional development pipeline. In this process, special attention will need to be paid to the field of government information management as more workers become involved with the special set of skills, problems, and requirements associated with technological change in public organizations. Given the absolute rate of change in the technology, it is impossible to determine in advance what will be needed in either the content or even the structure of future professional training and development. Undoubtedly, though, it will represent a key investment in the human capital of the organization. And given that hardware takes up five cents of each dollar invested in information technology, software ten cents, and orgware the remaining eighty-five cents, this investment may pay the highest returns.

Job Design

Between now and the turn of the century, the key information management issue relating to job design will be bridging the gap between formal and informal descriptions of work. This will be a problem for data processing titles as well as for the growing number of nontechnical titles that involve a degree of information technology concepts and skills. By *formal* descriptions of work we mean formal job descriptions, entry requirements, promotion standards, and the detailed design of promotion instruments such as Civil Service examinations. By *informal* descriptions of work we mean actual work expectations reflected in office routines as well as qualitative judgments expressed in work evaluations and performance programs. Here are two examples illustrating the problems that arise when informal and formal descriptions of work conflict.

A unit secretary is working with voice recording and transcription equipment and a microcomputer configured as a word processor. However, he or she is working in a title series that still tests for traditional typing and stenographic skills. Promotion within the formal system is not directly linked to measures of excellent performance on the job. In a second example, a junior conservation analyst is both skilled and interested in micro-processor applications and has taken responsibility for running her unit's microcomputer-based information systems. However, her professional advancement is predicated on her knowledge of wildlife management, not on her knowledge and skill with computers. One possible solution in these cases is to create new specialized titles tailored to meet just these circumstances. Of course, over time this strategy results in the proliferation of titles to include hybridized skills. Unless the Civil Service system can stay up to date with all the new combinations of skills that arise, these titles will quickly lose their value.

Personnel managers already face a number of challenges. First, formal descriptions of work must encourage and provide incentives rather than disincentives for technological innovation. Second, data processing and other new technological skills can be viewed either as skills embedded in new and separate titles or as general competencies, much the same as reading and writing, assumed at a basic level for all workers. Third, if technology-specific skills become integrated into special titles, then almost certainly formal job descriptions will lag well behind the reality of how work is actually being accomplished on the job. This leads to the fourth point of how to balance skills specific to specialized hardware and software systems against concepts that transcend individual technologies and hence have a longer useful life.

Ergonomics

A discussion of the impacts of new technologies on individuals would be incomplete without some mention of the safety and comfort of the workplace. Examples of the stresses and, in some cases, threats to well-being brought about by new technology appear in almost every work site—exposure to the sustained clatter of a printer, sitting for prolonged periods at chairs and desks not designed to accommodate new pieces of equipment, eye strain induced by working at a glaring video screen for hours at a time, or stress and its adverse effects caused by social isolation as workers toil in too much solitude at a self-contained work station. Solutions to most ergonomic problems have already been identified—silencers for printers, specially designed office furniture, lighting and screen design to cut down on eye strain, new work scheduling and priority rules, attention to variety in the design of work over a day or a week. All of these solutions require managerial attention, and some money. One common strategy for surfacing and dealing with ergonomic issues is to regularly convene small groups of workers to discuss frankly with management the problems and their possible solutions. Explicitly modeled after the Japanese-style "quality circles," such groups provide a forum for detecting and dealing with ergonomic, scheduling, and other types of problems before they become large enough to affect employee morale and productivity.

PROCEDURES AND ROLES:
ISSUES AND POLICY RESPONSES

The sections above focused on organizational structure and the individual worker. Another set of issues centers on work procedures and processes and how groups of users and technicians interact.

Technology Professionals and Technology Users

In the not too distant past, it made sense to distinguish clearly between "DP users" and "DP technicians." One always knew the difference between the two. The technicians lived near the machine room, had desks piled high with printouts, had flow charts on their walls, and existed in a somehow strangely different culture. Users, on the other hand, could always be recognized because they felt uncomfortable in the machine room, knew nothing about programming (and hence didn't really understand data processing), and were always asking unfocused and impossible questions.

While stereotypes of this sort still persist and may have some reality at the operational level, at the managerial level such sharp distinctions are clearly obsolete. At the highest levels of organizational management, a new breed of executive is emerging who is a mixture of the two pure types—user and technician. This blended identity is the wave of the future and, over time, the tide will move further down the organization through mid-level management to the operating level. While separate technical and user subcultures will continue to exist within most organizations for some time, from the point of view of the information manager, rigid and impermeable barriers between these two professional groups are counterproductive. Strategies are needed to break down these distinctions and create a more unified organizational culture comfortable with a broad spectrum of new technological tools.

For example, several major computer vendors now require their own MIS and data processing specialists to learn about corporate operations outside of data processing (i.e., to "know the business"). Before they begin working on a corporate information processing application, they spend time in the field working with production or sales personnel to gain a firm understanding of the business they are supposed to be supporting. At higher levels in these organizations, chiefs of corporate information processing units are as likely to have been promoted from one of the line-operating units such as finance or marketing as from data processing.

People in all occupations are now entering public sector organizations with substantial information processing skills. They are often experienced users of microprocessors and their competence usually meets, and often exceeds, that of the so-called computer professionals whose careers have primarily been invested in mainframe applications. Once again, the old stereotyped distinctions between technicians and users are crumbling. Increasingly, the information resource center is emerging as an organizational invention to promote closer collaboration between technicians and users. It offers a common turf where experience and skill can be pooled in solving specific information problems. In the center, the user retains ultimate responsibility for providing a technical solution to the problem at hand, often with the application of sophisticated end-user software tools. But users also receive advice and consultation from technical professionals who can help them solve specific problems—for example, how to download or upload data sets from their local database to the agency's mainframe.

The handwriting is already on the wall. At the level of upper management, the distinction between technical professionals and users is already obsolete. Mid-level managers (especially those who aspire to higher levels) and even professionals at the operational level are witnessing the demise of traditional distinctions between technicians and users. The challenge to information managers is to devise strategies, inventions, and tactics such as job rotation and information resource centers to facilitate and expedite the creation of this new generation of professionals.

Information Islands

With the advent of powerful and inexpensive microprocessors and flexible end-user software packages for database, spreadsheet, and decision support applications, virtually every kind of organization has experienced the proliferation of information islands. By this we mean a free-standing database, model, or analytic capability that is housed on its own CPU, has procedures separate from the organization's main databases, and serves a well-defined, usually very local purpose. Variations on this basic theme include possibilities for downloading data from the organization's centralized data systems to the island, uploading information from the island to main information systems (rarely seen), or islands that are located in regional facilities, other agencies, or other units of government. Information islands are often assumed to be a problem because they create multiple, often conflicting sources of information within the same organization and are difficult to standardize or control. The inevitable problems of information islands include "polluting" data sets within the organization's main information files due to nonstandard data-entry and control practices, multiple data definitions that make the generation of agencywide figures for key variables impossible to achieve, acquisition of nonstandard hardware and software systems that leads to costly duplication, creation of fragmented and incomplete views of overall agency operations, and so on. However, as discussed above, most of these criticisms stem from the rational goal or internal process models of effective organizations. When viewed from the human resources or, more importantly, from the open system model, information islands can be an important way to ensure organizational flexibility and adaptability by giving local users control of their own information environments. Furthermore, users can often develop and maintain their own applications, freeing them from scheduling bottlenecks and priority conflicts within the central data processing unit. At the same time, the data processors save the time and effort that systems analysts and programmers would have spent on developing those applications.

Information islands represent two quite different conceptions of what constitutes an effective organization. A generally safe management strategy is to allow the creation of information islands but to manage and control their development so the organization can reap the benefits without paying heavy costs. There are several strategies for managing and controlling their evolution. The first class of management tools consists of technological fixes. Advances in telecommunications and distributed processing promise creative integration of information islands into the overall information processing system of the organization. The emergence of more stable and workable protocols for local area networks (LANs), as well as the emergence of more widely accepted standards for wide area communication such as ISDN, promises the technological answers necessary to link the hardware supporting a wide variety of separately maintained databases across the organization. However, the simple existence of ensured CPU-to-CPU communication is still a long way from ensuring effective integration of information. A number of other organizational innovations must also be employed to ensure that the formats in which information is being collected are compatible, that software is standardized or at least shares common interfaces, and so on. These strategies include the creation of organizationwide (or governmentwide) data dictionaries to specify the exact format and definition of key data elements commonly used across the organization; the creation of information resource centers to help solve problems associated with the uploading and downloading of information from islands to main systems; the creation of explicit policies delineating what hardware and software will be supported; and the definition of hardware and software standards, to prevent unnecessary variation. In fact, the majority of the policy levers listed in Figure 2.6 apply quite directly to the management of information islands.

Data Definition as Organizational Process

Most professionals with experience in public sector systems have encountered the situation where a record of interest to the organization (such as a client record in a social service agency) is controlled by two or more unstandardized data elements. An example would be two primary client identifiers, one a sequentially generated agency identification code and the other a Social Security number. Perhaps each of two databases contains both fields, but in each case the primary identifier in one database is not verified for completeness or accuracy in the other. Another example is varying definitions of common terms. "Name," "Household," "Address," "Occupation" are all terms used in many files, often with different definitions. This, of course, is the classic data dictionary problem.

Often articulated as a technical problem involving how to rationalize disparate categories and classification schemes, the data definition problem is more often a fundamental issue of organizational dynamics. At best, different units have invested considerable time, effort, and energy in the detailed structure of their present information systems. Therefore, simple inertia will cause them to resist attempts to change the definitions and fine-tuned descriptions of their basic data elements. Since the local system has been designed for and serves the needs of the unit, "small" changes to accommodate some global notion of compatibility will create much work and will yield few, if any, benefits to those who must do it. For these simple reasons, local units are seldom enthusiastic about efforts to standardize data definitions. And this is the best case. In the worst case, organizational sub-units have a vested interest in not sharing information or complying with a systemwide set of standard data definitions. Consider, for example, a mental health system where the dominant organizational form is the local treatment facility (a similar example might be a state university system or a corrections system where strong internal management of a campus or a prison is the norm). In this situation, considerable local autonomy exists around most management decisions. Often local managers are constrained only within certain broad parameters such as the total budget, patient load, or level of authorized staff positions. Local managers (correctly) perceive that refined data dictionaries can lead to closer supervision of local operations with eventual curtailment of local operating autonomy. It is, therefore, not diffi-cult to understand why local managers drag their feet or even sabotage efforts to create rationalized and standardized data definitions.

Less than five years ago, effective integration of important data items posed formidable technical as well as organizational problems. In the case just cited above, it is quite likely the several local mental health facilities each operate different hardware systems using different software. Hammering out a standardized agencywide information system would involve convert-ing multiple facilities to similar or identical hardware, operating systems, and software—not a small undertaking. Today, there are technical strategies for integrating data across disparate hardware and software systems. For example, databases can be integrated through a system of mapping pro-grams that track files from local or regional databases into a centralized relational database for organizationwide analysis. UNIX, a recent develop-ment in operating systems, promises to open the gateways among the hard-ware and operating systems of nearly every manufacturer. It may eventually be the basis for an international standard.

While technical solutions to the data dictionary and information island problems are becoming available, the difficult and most persistent problems will continue to be organizational—creating the right set of incentives for all units and levels of government to work together cooperatively. Solutions to these problems require determination by the organization's top leadership, usually an infusion of considerable resources (at least on a one-time basis), and effective persistent management. Apparently innocuous attempts to standardize data definitions can arouse surprisingly strong organizational reactions and should not be undertaken lightly.

Organizational Life Cycles

To end this section on organizational procedures and roles, a word is in order about organizational life cycles. Theorists have suggested that organizations typically go through phases in their development from youth through maturity to decline. As organizations move through these cycles of growth and development, their information strategies and tactics will evolve as well. Two examples may help to make these points.

Quinn and Cameron have hypothesized that organizations typically move through four distinct stages in their normal path of development—an entrepreneurial stage characterized by innovation, creativity, and the marshaling of resources sufficient to survive; a collectivity stage characterized by informal communication structures, a sense of family and cooperativeness among members, high commitment of employees, and highly visible, personal leadership; a formalization stage stressing stability, creation of standard operating procedures and rules, and more conservative, control-oriented activities; and finally the elaboration of structure stage where the organization returns to a monitoring of its external environment to renew itself or expand its domain of operations. In each stage, the factors that define overall effectiveness change. In the first and second stages of development, the open systems model of organizational effectiveness is stressed, while in the latter two stages an emphasis on the internal process and rational goal ideal types emerges as most important.

In light of their theoretical discussion, Quinn and Cameron analyzed a developmental disabilities facility within a state-operated mental health system. The facility had undergone a stressful period involving adverse publicity, ultimately resulting in the resignation of the director and a major shake-up in operations. According to Quinn and Cameron's diagnosis, the problem with the facility stemmed from its inability to enact a smooth transition between the collectivity and formalization phases of organizational development. That is, working under the charismatic leadership of the director, the organization had developed a highly cohesive staff, informal communication structures, and a flexible human resources-oriented organization. As the size and complexity of the facility grew (a measure of its success), a need for more formal communication structures and standard operating procedures emerged. But because it could not effect the needed transition to a more formal stage of development, it went through a serious crisis. In terms of information technologies, the formalization stage would have involved the development of more formal client tracking, financial accounting, and personnel systems. These information systems, not really necessary during the organization's collectivity stage, became the key (missing) ingredients leading to the organizational crisis at the transition to the formalization stage in its life cycle. The lesson is simple; its application is not. Appropriate technologies change as an organization grows and matures through predictable cycles.

Consider a second organization, one heavily oriented toward regional operations but with its data processing functions centralized in the main office. A Department of Transportation or Office of Parks and Recreation might operate like this. A decision has been made to introduce computing capabilities in the regional offices. While the ultimate system appropriate for the regional offices might be a large minicomputer linked to the agency's mainframe, it might be inappropriate to introduce this as the first step in regional computing. Systems of this size would in all likelihood involve putting together an operations staff to deal with the new machine and developing system management procedures as well as many of the accoutrements associated with a system of that scale. Since the regions are novices about information systems, a wiser strategy would be more incremental: introduce microprocessors into the local offices for one or two years while plans are under way for the design and installation of the minicomputer system. In this way, local technology leaders, experts, and a cadre of applications would be encouraged to develop naturally within the regional offices. In this example, the organization itself has not undergone any major shift in its life cycle of development. However, the use of information technology within the organization has gone through dramatic growth—its own life cycle of development. The appropriate level of hardware and software will vary considerably over the course of that cycle. Again the level of technology within an organization should match where the organization is in the life cycle of both organizational processes and technological competence.

SUMMARY

This chapter has sketched the organizational implications of information management in the public sector. Using the concept of organizational effectiveness, the dual nature of the interactions between emerging information technologies and organizational performance has been considered. On the one hand, information technologies have the ability to increase organizational effectiveness as measured along many diverse scales, and, in turn, the way we think about the effectiveness of an organization shapes how new technologies are managed. Four models of organizational effectiveness—rational goal, internal process, human resources, and open systems—were discussed in relation to information management strategies. Both the rational goal and internal process models stress the need for control and stability of information systems in promoting organizational effectiveness. The human resources and open systems models stress the need for a more open, flexible, and adaptable approach. Finally we examined a number of more specific issues and associated policy responses clustered around the concepts of organizational structure, the performance of the individual within the organization, and organizational procedures and roles.

EXERCISES

1. In actuality, no pure examples of the rational goal, internal process, human resources, and open systems organizational models exist. Real organizations are some combination of these four models. Consider the following organizations, all of which could primarily be viewed as information processing operations:

    —Office of Management and Budget

    —The Library of Congress

    —Department of Civil Service

    —A regional office of the Internal Revenue Service

    —The House Armed Services Committee

    —The National Security Council

    —The Council of Economic Advisors

    a. For each of these organizations, allocate 100 points between the four pure type models in proportion to what percentage of the "pure" model you believe each of these organizations to be. That is, if you believe that an organization is a balanced blend of all four types, allocate 25 points to each of the models. Your point allocation should add to just 100.

    b. Describe the important features of each of the organizations that led you to give it the score that you did.

    c. Based on your point allocation and the discussion of the ideal type models in the chapter, predict what kinds of information processing systems should function best in each of these real organizations.

2. Refer to Exercise 5 in Chapter 2. In that exercise, the director of Personnel had requested your advice for a citywide plan for professional development and training, with special emphasis on the development and retention of information processing skills. Based in part on your advice, the director has now developed and is in the process of implementing a citywide training and professional development program. The director has now gotten back to you with a request for some additional advice.

    a. The director is concerned about how to handle technical data processing skills and concepts in the promotion process. Specifically, he is interested in your advice as to how best to design promotion examinations for data processing professionals, management analysts, and clerical titles. He is considering several options. First, data processing skills could be treated like other basic literacy skills such as reading and writing, being tested for at a level of minimum competence for all positions. Second, specific data processing skills related to specific occupational titles could be designed into the examination process. Finally, new "generic" information resource titles could be defined with their own technical specializations independent of specialized program areas. Which of these options should the director pursue? What are the advantages and disadvantages of each option?

b. The director is also concerned about the safety and the health of the city's workforce, especially as they relate to the use of information processing equipment. This issue is also of great concern to the city's public employees union. Should the city adopt special ergonomic regulations? Or should it issue broad guidelines to be interpreted by agency managers? Or should the city not issue any sort of statement or policy and instead rely on the good judgment of its department heads to recognize and deal with problems as they occur? In a word, what policies, if any, should the city adopt with respect to ergonomic issues for the white-collar workforce using information processing equipment?

3. The Department of Parks and Environmental Management maintains a number of disparate databases all of which essentially contain geographic site information of one sort or another. These "information islands" have grown up within separate units of the department over time and for differing purposes. For example, there are separate databases for the Air Quality Monitoring System (Division of Air Quality), the Historic Sites Registry (Division of Historic Preservation), the Water Quality Monitoring System (Division of Water Quality), the Park Facilities Registry (Division of Public Recreation), and the Solid Waste Dump Site Registry (Division of Solid Waste Management). Recently the new commissioner was embarrassed when under questioning at a regional press conference on water quality, he was unaware of his department's own activities in the same region with respect to air quality and solid waste management. Upon his return to the capital, the commissioner wanted a fast improvement in his information base. The director of Information Services dusted off an existing proposal for a unified and comprehensive geographically defined database for the department. This database would code and locate all of the department's sites and facilities on a geographically defined grid. Standards for such a grid were defined by the National Geographic Survey, and recent advances in satellite cartography would, in principle, allow such a database to be linked to detailed satellite-generated information files concerning all regions in the state. For example, ground cover could be categorized and coded (e.g., grasslands, deciduous cover, and so on) down to a resolution of one square meter using existing technology. In principle, this database could do much more than just solve the problem with individual data islands. Ultimately, it could link the department's databases to regional or statewide, or even multistate, land-use planning systems. A host of additional applications have also been recommended in the proposal.

a. The commissioner is initially disposed to consider the proposal. However, he is concerned that it may be too costly and have too many unnecessary "bells and whistles." He is not a data processing professional and seeks your advice before taking up this issue for further discussion. Especially since this proposal has come forward once in the past (before he was commissioner) and was not implemented, he is cautious. He wants your advice on how best to structure an advisory committee to consider the proposal. Give the commissioner your best advice.

b. A very quick background check tells you that the last time this proposal was considered, the issue of the basic definition of records was raised. At present, each of the separate databases has a different definition of what constitutes a "site" and different ways of locating sites geographically (some use region, some use county, some use city or town, some use zip code, and none use a geographic code). While managers cannot agree on what coding to use, they all seem to agree that an abstract geographic code defined by the National Geographic Survey will do them little good. How should the commissioner handle this issue in his charge to the advisory committee?

4. Refer to Exercises 1 through 3 in Chapter 2. It is now six months after you wrote an initial flurry of memos to the chair of the Psychology Department proposing that the department purchase some computing equipment. Nothing of any substance has happened in those six months. The chair has surveyed the faculty and received essentially two competing recommendations concerning how to proceed. The two "camps" boil down to two different machines and network technologies, with the "camps" apparently being defined by what machine a few faculty members already own. Roughly half the faculty don't really care one way or the other (you suspect this group includes the chair). The chair has purchased two prototype machines—one from each "camp"—and is waiting to see how things shake down within the department. A colleague of yours has just received a grant and has $8,000 that she would be willing to invest in equipment that is compatible with the department's equipment. Unfortunately, no one has yet made a decision concerning what the department should do.

In an informal meeting over lunch with some of your junior colleagues, all of you frankly discuss the two proposals that have apparently frozen the department in indecision. You agree that each proposal has advocates and that each proposal would probably be adequate if fully implemented. However, it also seems clear that going in one direction will offend (slightly) one group and going with the other proposal will offend (slightly) the other camp. The key question is who is willing to "take the ball and run with it."

In that meeting, you realize that it would be easy for you to advocate your proposal and win broad-based support for it within the department (remembering that half the department is really indifferent). You also realize that the other "camp" wouldn't really be offended very much if you did this. All of your colleagues seem to agree that having someone take the lead in what they consider an adequate (but from their point of view suboptimal) solution is better than the present state of no action. The problem is that you believe that you would soon become the "expert" and the "leader" within the department. You suspect that following through on a proposal to install a departmental computing system could be a real time drain. There seems to be little doubt that everyone would appreciate your efforts—the job clearly needs to be done and no one is doing it. But you are keenly aware than in two and a half years you will come up for your tenure review. Time spent working on departmental computing is time not spent publishing your work. Everyone advises you that this is a "publish or perish" place. You suspect that in two years' time you would be a hero within the department for your efforts to rationalize the data processing question, but you wouldn't get tenure (nice guys finish last). On the other hand, it seems a shame not to get something going within the department. You decide to sit down and write a note to yourself analyzing how you might get these new computers installed within the department without jeopardizing your own chances at tenure.

Write the memo analyzing the situation and giving yourself some advice.

PROJECTS AND CASE EXERCISES

1. Read the case study "The Information History of the Office of the State Treasurer."

    The new state treasurer, Reed Jones, is rapidly coming to believe that possible problems with information technology within the Office of the State Treasurer may well be organizational rather than technical in nature. Since Jones is new to OST, he has asked that you draft a brief memo for him outlining how the locus of policy making has shifted within OST since 1960. Draft the needed background briefing.

    Reading your historical overview has convinced Jones more than ever that a reorganization is called for. Do you believe that a reorganization is wise at this point in time? If so, how should Jones proceed? Draft a further memo laying out for Jones his current organizational options. Make a recommendation to Jones and support it in your memo.

2. Read the case study "Reorganization of the Information Functions at the State University-Wilmington." Respond to the assignment at the end of the case study.

3. Refer to the case study "A Forensic Mental Health Database to Implement a Suicide Prevention Program." The appendices to that case study contain the data dictionaries for the department of Correctional Services Information System as well as for the department of Mental Health Services Forensic Mental Health Information System.

    a. Carefully study those two data dictionaries. Remembering that the actual databases will contain up to fifty thousand records and could probably not be scanned visually (at least not at a first cut), analyze the technical problems that will occur when one attempts to "match" the two databases. Draft a memo to Susan Miller and Calvin Tyler detailing an approach to efficiently accomplish the match.

b. What are some of the organizational reasons for the technical incompatibilities in the two databases that you have just analyzed in the above exercise? In a continuation of your memo to Miller and Tyler, analyze the organizational causes of the database incompatibility problems and propose solutions for keeping the databases for the two departments synchronized.

SUGGESTED READINGS

Campbell, J. P. On the Nature of Organizational Effectiveness, in P. S. Goodman and J. M. Pennings, eds. *New Perspectives on Organizational Effectiveness.* San Francisco: Jossey-Bass, 1977.

Kanter, Rosabeth Moss. *The Change Masters.* New York: Simon & Schuster, 1983.

Management's Newest Star: Meet the Chief Information Officer. *Business Week* (October 13, 1986): 160–64, 170, 172.

Nolan, Richard L. Managing the Crises in Data Processing. *Harvard Business Review,* 57(2): 81–93, March–April 1979.

Porter, Michael E., and Victor E. Millar. How Information Gives You Competitive Advantage. *Harvard Business Review* 63(4): 149, July–August 1985.

Quinn, Robert E. Impacts of a Computerized Information System on the Integration and Coordination of Human Services. *Public Administration Review,* 36(2).

Quinn, Robert E., and Kim Cameron. Organizational Life Cycles and Shifting Criteria of Effectiveness: Some Preliminary Evidence. *Management Science* 29(1) 33–51, January 1983.

Quinn, Robert E., and John Rohrbaugh. A Spatial Model of Effectiveness Criteria: Toward a Competing Values Approach to Organizational Analysis. *Management Science* 29(3): 363–77, March 1983.

Zuboff, Shoshana. *In the Age of the Smart Machine.* New York: Basic Books, 1988.

CHAPTER 4

INFORMATION AS A PUBLIC RESOURCE

It was the most sobering moment of the campaign. In the space of five hours, gubernatorial candidate James Akers had visited a family shelter and a posh suburban high school. Little children with hopeful faces living in crushing poverty. Rich kids with every opportunity who didn't know the others existed. They lived worlds apart but ironically shared a common—and uncertain—future. They had to be prepared for it. That day Akers decided. If sent to the statehouse, the status of the state's children would be at the top of the political agenda.

He began to consult with experts, to seek the counsel of parents, employers, and educators. There were so many problems and so many ways to attack them. He felt certain he could draw a broad coalition of support. It would be expensive, of course. But the state was already spending hundreds of millions of dollars to educate and care for its children. New money would not be the answer, he thought. First we have to know more. How are we spending it? What works and what doesn't? How can we keep a finger on the pulse of this vulnerable generation?[1]

---

[1] For more details on this vignette, refer to the case study "A Policy Maker's Database: The Status of Children."

Akers has hit upon the critical resource combination for conducting a major public policy initiative—consensus, money, and information.

In the preceding chapters, the word "public" has been used to mean the location of information systems in government agencies. These systems share much in common with those in private and nonprofit organizations. Many of the technical and organizational issues that apply in public agencies can also be found in businesses. But other factors also define "publicness"—factors that are unique to government. Public organizations differ from private ones in key characteristics of both context and purpose. They serve values such as political consensus, participation, due process, and constitutionalism. Personnel decisions are typically dominated by a Civil Service system, and annual budgets are determined by legislative action and political compromise rather than by the market. Public sector information use is circumscribed by the Constitution and statute and is further shaped by the policies of elected and appointed officials. This is strikingly different from the collection and use of data by private individuals or corporations seeking private ends. Moreover, information collected and maintained by government is not exclusively an organizational resource as it is in a corporation. It is also a public resource. Much of it is used in programs that benefit or serve the public at large. Like other resources, it needs to be protected from deterioration, loss, and abuse; preserved for the future; kept available for use by the people; and employed by government itself in pursuit of that elusive ideal, the public interest.

In this chapter and the next we examine how information technology is transforming the business of government—in part changing the way we think about the rights of citizenship and the role of the modern state. To begin, we examine briefly the impact of information technologies on the nature of government: the interaction between technological innovation and the political process, the added tension technology inserts between expert administrators and generalist elected officials, the government's dual roles as owner and trustee of information resources, and the responsibility of government organizations to actively inform the public. Later we discuss six specific information management activities: planning for agency information needs; the procurement process; maintaining information quality; records management; archives and preservation; information resource sharing; and security. The next chapter explores the legal aspects of public information resources and their effect on basic relationships between the state and private citizens.

Both chapters are best understood in light of a cycle of effects (Figure 4.1). Our democratic institutions, laws, and political culture define the context within which information systems operate. In turn, the procedures, structure, and operation of information systems influence and modify that environment. We begin with a question: How does the advent of modern information technologies alter the nature of our government institutions?

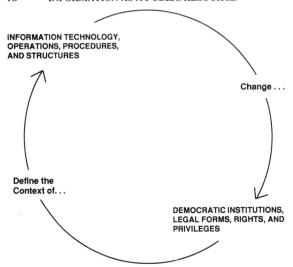

INFORMATION TECHNOLOGY,
OPERATIONS, PROCEDURES,
AND STRUCTURES

Change . . .

Define the
Context of. . .

DEMOCRATIC INSTITUTIONS,
LEGAL FORMS, RIGHTS, AND
PRIVILEGES

Figure 4.1   Mutual Interactions Between Information Technologies and Factors That Define the Public Sector

THE IMPACT OF INFORMATION TECHNOLOGY
ON GOVERNMENT

While democratic institutions, legal frameworks, individual rights, and political and judicial processes define the context and influence the development
of information systems in the public sector, the reciprocal impact of information technology on these same institutions and processes is equally important. That is, the design, capabilities, and operation of technologically
advanced information tools change the nature of government operations
and management and can affect the basic relationship between citizen and
state.

Look at a program like Medicare. An expensive program with widespread effect demands that the agency responsible for it be fully accountable
to the public. To achieve public accountability, information must be collected, stored, and verified against other sources (some of which are
databases maintained elsewhere by the government). This generalized accountability principle requires an agency to delve more deeply and persis-
tently into the affairs of private citizens and employ information sources
other than the beneficiaries themselves. This is an unquestionable intrusion
into their lives—but for an unquestionably benevolent purpose.

Once the technological tools are employed in this way, new opportunities present themselves. It becomes obvious to conservatives that they can be
used to cross-check among various programs to prevent fraud and abuse
and, as a result, cut the size and cost of government. Liberals then embrace

them as ways to shore up the credibility of (and thus public support for) programs they care about. Over time, technology used in this way approximates a centralized national database—something some embrace as a powerful tool of good government and others reject as a threat to traditional democratic values.

Our assertion that information technologies shape how governments function should not be surprising. Throughout history, technologies have shaped the structures and institutions of human society. In the most primitive societies, the invention of agricultural technologies transformed nomadic tribes into stable settled cultures. The invention of printing technologies hastened the rise of a literate middle class, setting the stage for the Renaissance and the Enlightenment. The railroad decidedly directed the development of the American western frontier, and the automobile is widely credited with shaping the pattern of American urban and suburban development after World War II. It seems a natural progression, then, that information technologies should redefine the economic, social, and political institutions of the late twentieth century.

Modern information technologies shape the structure and functioning of government in four ways. First, new technologies can change the detailed processes of government operations. Second, they subtly shift the relationships between elected leaders and technical experts within government. Third, government takes on new characteristics as a source of public knowledge. Fourth and finally, technological advances transform government's responsibilities as a trustee of public information, placing new demands on agency operations. Each of these topics is briefly sketched below.

Technology, Operations, and Policy

Government operations can be conducted more quickly, from more places, and with wider effect than would ever be possible without computers. This changes both administrative capabilities and public expectations about how government programs can and should be run.

Consider the IRS. Modern computer systems make it technically possible for the nation's tax department to keep track of most people's income and assets, calculate their tax liability based on historical records and assumptions about their living arrangements and spending habits, and simply send them a bill every April 15. The prospect of never again seeing another Form 1040 is certainly appealing, but this proposal violates the social and political norm that ours is a voluntary tax system. This idea has not been implemented, although automated execution of judgments against those who appear to have shirked their full share of the tax burden has been. Technology allows both. The interaction between what is technically possible and what is politically viable offers a constantly changing set of programmatic initiatives and policy choices.

In fact, our operational know-how often far exceeds the reach of even our broadest policy guidelines. We do not choose goals, set policies, and then implement them in a straightforward progression. Instead, in virtually all areas of our political life, but especially in fields heavily impacted by technological innovations, policy tends to follow practice, often by a long distance. The sequence typically begins when technology opens an opportunity like the ability to automatically calculate tax liability. Once these technological opportunities have been taken, program operations are changed in unexpected ways, and unintended results, whether good or bad, are beyond the reach of existing policy guidelines. It often takes a good deal of time, but revised policies eventually emerge. Since government deliberations are slow and technological innovation is not, policy makers are in a perpetual game of catch-up ball. Public sector program operations are the place where these out-of-step forces collide.

Roles of Elected Leaders and Technical Experts

Electronic information tools have a subtle but decided influence on the balance of political and administrative rationality in the management of public affairs. On the one hand, large scale information systems that guide and control government programs place more responsibility in the hands of technical experts. Modern public management is increasingly characterized by the rise of an administrative technocracy using tools that are not easily accessible to or controlled by elected officials. On the other hand, the ability to integrate information from a variety of sources can often lead to better-informed decision making by elected policy makers themselves. That is, the power of large-scale integrated data systems can give both legislative and executive leaders access to much information concerning the detailed operations of government itself. In principle, it is possible for legislators to move beyond their traditional oversight and policy-setting roles to become involved with the "micro-management" of program operations. The result is a blurring of the classic distinctions between policy development (traditionally a legislative function) and program implementation (the traditional domain of the executive branch, especially the career Civil Service).

Government as a Source of Knowledge

Public organizations collect information about a myriad of subjects, sometimes for their own needs and often to meet the information needs of others. The U.S. Census Bureau and the U.S. Department of Labor's Bureau of Labor Statistics are organizations whose stock and trade is data. Their standard statistical series and special reports are well-known and highly respected sources of information about the population and economy of the United States.

Most other public organizations also have a responsibility for public information but devote few resources to it. A debate is on about the extent to which taxpayers' money should be used to fulfill the information needs of various segments of our society. Some contend that information is a right of citizenship; others believe that only those who seek information should pay the cost of preparing it. Still others see government's responsibility fulfilled by the collection, storage, and preservation of data, while the private sector should be relied on to analyze, package, and disseminate it. The questions of how much information will be available from government, in what form, and at what cost will remain open for a long time to come. Before they are decided, government will collect and store ever larger amounts of information and these issues will grow in size and complexity.

Owner or Trustee?

In addition to the collection and creation of public data, government also has important roles as an information owner and trustee. More information is collected and held by government than by any other segment of our society. These vast data holdings "belong" to public agencies in the sense that they collect and manage them under their constitutional and statutory powers to provide service or levy sanctions. But government also has fiduciary responsibilities for information. The dictionary defines *fiduciary* as one who holds something in trust for another, one who stands in a special relation of trust, confidence, or responsibility in his obligations to others. In this sense, government is not the owner of information but its trustee. Its obligations include the physical security of information used to operate public programs and the ability to recover from damage or loss. It must also maintain a record of the past, preserving valued information regardless of the processes that created it or media that hold it in storage. Information about the process of governance is also a public trust. Public processes are recorded, for instance, in the Federal Register and the Congressional Record. They document the inner machinery of government operations—a matter of concern more than two centuries old.

As discussed in more detail below, new information technologies critically alter government's responsibilities, policies, and roles with respect to the ownership and trusteeship of public data. For example, government agencies must decide how and when to archive electronic data, who should have access to what information, at what cost, and in how timely a fashion. These four broad topics are part of the administrative environment of government—areas where the advent of modern information technologies is reshaping government operations and institutions. They help form the context in which six more specific issues are explored next—planning for agency information needs, the procurement process, maintaining data quality, preserving and archiving records, sharing information resources, and seeing to the security of government information holdings.

PLANNING AGENCY INFORMATION NEEDS

Information systems are large, complex, and expensive, involving significant investments in human and physical capital over extended periods of time. Careful advance planning helps ensure an optimal return on these investments. This section reviews some of the many issues associated with planning for an agency's information needs. It illustrates the importance of seeking multiple perspectives on information use and of analyzing alternatives through the four conceptual lenses described earlier—technology, economics, organization, and politics.

As a matter of theory, good information planning involves forecasting the present and future information needs of an agency and designing information systems whose characteristics meet those needs. As a matter of practice, information planning often reduces to buying hardware boxes and seeing (over time) what they can do. This gap between the theory and practice of planning is not without explanation. It is hard to forecast information needs in a rapidly changing technical environment. It is often easier to envision the capabilities of some specific system or component than to make sense of an abstract statement of needs. Experience teaches us that most complex information systems actually evolve or emerge incrementally over time without the guidance of an overall plan. But experience also tells of the operational woes and strategic failures of patchwork system solutions. Clearly, planning has value. The techniques and concepts discussed below are designed to help bridge the gap between theory and practice in planning for agency information needs. In it we distinguish between two types of information planning—tactical or operational planning and strategic planning. Operational planning occurs when an agency begins with a fairly clearly defined mission or goal involving its information systems. The questions to be answered by operational planning are how best to achieve the goals given our current state of operations. A typical example would be an agency that maintains a mainframe system, several LANs, and multiple microcomputing clusters in support of a diverse mission. The lease on the mainframe is coming up for renewal, and agency managers are using this opportunity to rethink their information systems capabilities. Agency managers wish to upgrade, integrate, and make marginal enhancements to the existing systems but do not anticipate any fundamental rethinking of overall agency mission. That is, they wish to plan for the future building upon their present base.

Strategic planning, on the other hand, often involves a redefinition of agency mission or goals and implies a reexamination of how the agency relates to its clients and constituencies and other organizations outside its own boundaries. For example, a new agency may be formed to coordinate programs and information resources in the broad area of criminal justice. This agency has a mandate to draw upon information resources in the courts, police agencies, corrections, and parole. The purpose of a strategic planning exercise for this agency would be to define its mission and goals as well as the role of information resources in helping it meet them. Presumably, more detailed operational planning will follow this more broad-gauged strategic analysis.

Strategic Planning

Strategic information systems planning differs from operational or tactical planning in that it involves rethinking an agency's basic goals or mission in light of new or changing demands, revised mandates, or the emergence of new services or programs to be provided. Strategic planning can and often does take place without an explicit information management component. But modern information technologies and their associated management potentials are increasingly seen as important instruments for helping agency managers respond to shifts in the environment, seize new opportunities for service, and meet their strategic program goals.

For example, the mayor of a large city is concerned about the multiple problems of poverty, drugs, homelessness, malnourishment, and illiteracy among young children aged ten or under. If this generation of youth is not brought into the mainstream, they will soon become tomorrow's teenage parents, drug dealers, and unemployables locking the city into a vicious cycle that threatens the economic and social vitality of the entire region. The mayor's strategic mission is to enhance and integrate what he sees as a fractured service system. Each service organization in the city touches upon these tough problems, but none of them comprehend their interdependence. That is, services being provided by the schools, welfare agencies, substance abuse agencies, the department of health, and in some cases police, courts, and corrections agencies must be integrated at the point where a case manager interacts with a single family containing children at risk. The information management component of this strategic mission is to integrate the demographic and service information available to case managers at the street level, to build a research database for understanding more fully the problems of inner-city youths, and perhaps ultimately to provide a database on children at risk for more effective screening and service delivery.

Figure 4.2 provides a framework for thinking about strategic information management in the public sector. It is adopted from a similar one developed by Porter in 1980 where he defined the key components of strategic planning for private sector firms to be the interactions of buyers, sellers, new firms entering a market, and the possibility of substitute products and services within a market. All of these external forces combine to produce the key concept of rivalry or competition among firms struggling for market share or customer attention.

However, as shown in Figure 4.2, the key focus of attention in public

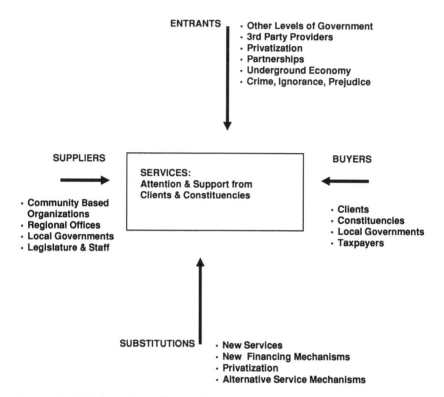

Figure 4.2   Public Sector Strategic Analysis

sector strategy is not competition or rivalry among similar units. Rather, the key strategic focus of the public sector is on providing services to clients and on receiving attention and support from the agency's various clients and constituencies. In the public sector, the analog to Porter's customers or buyers consists of our clients, those members of the public that our agencies are designed to serve. Rather than having sellers or suppliers, public sector strategic analysts think in terms of providers—the community-based organizations, other levels of government, or regional and local offices that are the means whereby we create and deliver services.

Whereas in the private sector new entrants commonly refer to competitor firms, the public sector strategic analysis of new entrants is broad enough to include notions of other levels of government (local, state, or federal government), third-party providers, or other units that may enter to assist with the delivery of much needed services. Again, in a free market framework, substitutions refer to new products or services that might be developed or introduced by a competing firm. In the realm of public sector strategy, substitutions refer to new financing mechanisms, modes of service delivery (such as privatization), or even new services that might be developed or nurtured by public agencies.

When engaging in strategic planning, public sector managers need to scan the full array of external forces sketched in Figure 4.2 and search for policy innovations that will allow an agency to capture new energy or resources in its environment, to reach out toward new goals or missions, or find new ways of relating to clients and constituencies. Often information management techniques can become key instruments in assisting an agency to realign its strategic posture vis-à-vis its external environment.

Several quick examples can serve to highlight how information management can serve a central role in helping an agency redefine its operations and goals and reach for new levels of service. In responding to the crisis in public safety discussed earlier, many jurisdictions have already created unified databases to track individuals at all levels across the criminal justice system. By hammering out a single record definition and by sharing information, the police, the courts, corrections agencies, and parole officers can create and can better maintain more accurate records on all criminal offenders. Such information systems help to create a systemwide perspective on criminal justice problems and issues, allowing coordination in the application of resources to policing, court processing, expansion of prison space, or parole capacity. In addition, better record-keeping can speed processing and ensure more uniform treatment of the people in the system.

As a second example, a research database on children at risk in the city discussed above can be created by matching and assembling records from the departments of education, social services, and health; the courts; and the agencies responsible for delinquent or youthful offenders. While considerations of privacy may prevent the creation of a comprehensive case management database with personal identifiers retained intact, the use of sophisticated encryption devices allows the involved agenies to create a complete research-oriented database for tracking the trends that tell us important information about the city's children at risk.

At a more operational level, the commissioner of Parks and Public Recreation wanted as one of her strategic goals to increase access to publicly owned recreational facilities. Viewing information technology as a strategic resource, the department made reservations for public camping areas routinely available through a commercial Ticketron agency. The strategic goal of increasing public access was greatly enhanced by looking for an opportunity to apply well-known and well-developed information technologies.

Finally, most tax departments are increasingly looking toward modern information systems to help them attain strategic ends. Increased apprehension of tax evaders and more rapid processing of income tax returns are examples of the service-oriented goals that can be attained by the skillful application of information technologies to the attainment of a strategic mission.

Using information systems as a tool for achieving strategic goals is becoming a commonly accepted principle of good management in the public sector. Good strategic information planning coupled with thoughtful and forward-thinking operational planning is evidence of good management at all levels of government.

Operational Planning

What we are referring to as operational planning is closely related to concepts such as the systems development cycle, tactical information planning, or an information planning cycle. As shown in Figure 4.3. operational planning can be roughly divided into four phases—Design, Specification, Acquisition and Installation, and Operations and Maintenance. Each of these four phases involves a linked set of issues that build upon each other through the four phases. For example, in the design phase, questions of what decisions are to be made by whom leads in the specification stage to the definition of a data dictionary, which in turn becomes incorporated into a Request for Proposal (RFP) in the acquisition and installation phase. Finally, during the operations and maintenance phase, changed circumstances predictably lead to new definitions of information needs, data dictionaries, and so on.

In addition, a number of policy concerns, all of which are more fully discussed elsewhere in this volume, run through all stages of the operational planning cycle. Security, documentation, standards, privacy, access, information sharing, and eventual record disposition must be planned for in the earliest phases and continue to be important considerations as the system moves through the acquisition, installation, and operations.

Most well-established procedures and guidelines for operational planning for information systems are based on mainframe technologies. Budget units or general service units require that agencies create mid- to long-range plans that guide expenditures for large systems. Often these plans will require a sign-off from a centralized information planning oversight unit or agency. Details of these plans will vary from one governmental unit to another.

Most standard texts on information systems contain fairly detailed and prescriptive models for how to carry out operational planning. Our intent here is not to give detailed information on the planning requirements of any specific government nor to review the many fine models for operational planning that do exist. Rather, we will sketch the general content of these planning procedures, sorted into the four rough phases of design, specification, acquisition and installation, and operation and maintenance.

Design.   Good planning begins with a sound design phase. Often involving a user survey, the design phase asks the basic question, Who are the clients for the system? What decisions must be made, by whom, based on

Design/User Survey Phase

Who is the client?
Who is the decision maker?
What functions are affected?
What is the useful life of the information to be produced?
What is the frequency of transactions?
What level of accuracy is needed?

Specification Phase

Develop data definitions.
Develop data structure.
How will information be collected?
What software functionality is required?
What hardware functionality is required?
What reports are needed?
How is staffing affected?
What training is needed?
How are physical space needs to be met?

Acquisition and Implementation Phase

Estimate life-cycle costs.
Decide whether to "make or buy."
Develop request(s) for proposal.
Manage procurement process.
Select hardware.
Select software.
Plan for conversion.
Conduct training.

Ongoing Operations Phase

Adjust to changes in operational demands.
Respond to policy shifts.
Stay abreast of hardware and software advances.
Stay in step with changing agency mission and programs.
Evaluate performance.
Revise and retrain.

Figure 4.3   Typical Considerations in Operational Planning for Informaticn Systems

what criteria to accomplish the program this system is to support? What functions are to be performed by the information in the system? What is the useful lifespan of the information being collected and what is the necessary frequency and accuracy of that information?

The important point that unifies virtually every model of operational planning is a consensus that good planning does not begin with considerations of hardware or software or even of the needed data items or structures.

Rather, good planning begins with an attempt to articulate the decision-making needs of the managers who will use the data. Questions of how to collect and structure data as well as what hardware, software, and staffing are required are necessarily and logically subsequent to the more important questions of who will be using the information for what purposes.

From the very beginning of the planning process, information system planners must remain aware of the policy issues sketched in Figure 4.3. For example, the proper time to think about designing procedures for ultimately disposing of outdated records and archiving those records with permanent value is before any records or documents are created. Too often these questions of document life cycle are left as an afterthought, creating impossible-to-manage files of raw data many years into the future. The early design phases must also pay attention to issues such as ultimate public access to information, standards for managing the information system, and adequate documentation.

Specification.   Only after the important prior questions of the audience and purposes of an information system have been clearly answered should the planning process move toward a more detailed specification of the information system itself. At this phase, the important questions are, What data needs to be captured and how should the data be defined and structured? What types of reporting capacity will be needed? What types of hardware and software functionality will be required (stopping short of trying at this phase to define what specific hardware boxes need to be purchased)? What will be the physical space and staffing and training requirements necessary to support the information system under design? In most government settings, this specification phase becomes rather formal, often culminating in a written plan for review at some control point within the government (a budget unit or information planning unit). Usually these fully specified plans become the basis for Requests for Proposals subsequently drafted by the agency.

Of course, the policy concerns first surfaced in the design phase continue to be developed and elaborated during the specification phase. For example, questions of hardware, software, and data standards become more fully fleshed out and issues of documentation standards must be completely specified.

Acquisition and Installation.   During the acquisition and installation phases, other agencies such as budget offices and general services organizations usually become intimately involved in the planning process. Most governments maintain formal procurement and bidding procedures that must be observed in the acquisition of information systems. Open competition among various vendors is the commonly accepted basis for deciding what hardware and software will be selected to support the information system under design. Because of the relatively technical nature of purchasing and installing large-scale information systems, most governments have special procurement standards and procedures. For example, in purchasing expanded memory for a mainframe system, a low bid may be received by a vendor other than the one now supplying the agency's hardware. However, this bid may include only hardware costs and may ignore staff time necessary to modify numerous applications in order to use this nonstandard memory device. To account for these nonhardware costs, most procurement regulations allow for bidding to involve "full life-cycle costs." Hence agencies are allowed to factor in conversion, training, and other nonequipment costs that they may incur in acquiring a piece of hardware.

The need for staff training and the dilemma of using external consultants versus in-house staff for installing major systems are two issues that all information plans must address during the acquisition and installation phase. Most implementation plans call for additional staff to be allocated to an operation during the installation phase and call for significant amounts of staff training. Often parallel systems are run side by side for some time when a new system is being installed to replace an older one. The details of all these installation issues must be clearly thought through in the operational plan.

Operation and Maintenance. A virtual rule of information system planning is that large-scale information systems will be obsolete before they are fully installed. The pace of technological change is so rapid, policy environments change so quickly, and system development cycles are so long that something important must change between the first design phases and the final installation phases. Hence all operational plans should make some allowance for ongoing implementation or the continual reevaluation of the implementation plan in light of recent developments. The more we plan, the more we realize the difficulty of planning in the realm of information systems.

Finally, as systems mature and develop, new policy issues that may not have been anticipated in the design phase will inevitably surface. For example, another agency may learn that yours has created a valuable new data set and may wish to have access to it or to match its own records against it. Information managers must continually be alert to these emerging information policy issues.

PROCUREMENT

Most units of government procure equipment and services according to competitive bidding procedures that are well defined in both statute and regulation. Often the bidding and contracting process is overseen by a specialized central control agency rather than by the operating agency that is requesting or making the purchase. Most government procurement regulations tend to be risk averse, seeking solid value for government investments. They rely principally on the criterion of minimum cost (the lowest bid) for evaluating proposals that meet the stated specifications for the product or service sought. Government procurement is often a relatively slow process, often tied to multiyear planning cycles with lengthy procedures for preparation of Requests for Proposals (RFPs) and extensive publication and notice procedures to ensure maximum vendor awareness and opportunity to respond.

In this kind of process, a number of apparent contradictions can arise. For example, a unit of government may bid a standard contract to purchase a certain popular type of microcomputer. By purchasing such a machine in large volume, the government may plan to achieve considerable cost savings. However, if it takes several months to bid the contract and if the contract lasts for up to one or two years, it is very likely that by the end of the contract period, a better technological option will have been introduced into the market and that the bid item will be selling on the open market for *less* than the contracted price competitively set by the government. The pace of technological change is so rapid that it simply confounds the normal contracting process.

System upgrades and conversions are often difficult to handle within existing procurement guidelines. Recalling that hardware accounts for five cents of the information dollar, software ten cents, and orgware eighty-five cents, it then becomes immediately apparent that actual procurement costs are merely the tip of the total cost iceberg. However, procurement procedures for major equipment purchases do not often factor in personnel costs associated with running or converting that equipment in future years. If full "life cycle" costs are factored in, then the current vendor has a decided competitive edge in the bidding process. To replace or upgrade while maintaining the same vendor is usually much less costly because most vendors maintain compatibility within their own lines of equipment. Hence, an agency must decide early in the acquisition process about whether and how to deal with these considerable but usually hidden orgware costs. Ironically, this apparently technical decision often determines whether the existing vendor receives the ultimate contract. So what happened to a competitive bidding process as mandated by statute?

The technical issues involved in procurement can become quite complicated and can often have significant implications for the line operations within the agency. For example, a decision by a library to acquire an automated catalog or circulation system or a decision by a social service agency to automate client claims can considerably alter both the volume and the type of work being performed by most employees of the agency. Because of the special nature of information-intensive procurement decisions, many governments have created special organizations, often within central budget units, to help analyze technology-intensive procurement decisions. Many government jurisdictions have established separate technology offices to review the full range of cost, organizational, and service impacts of proposed major procurements. These offices also serve as governmentwide sources of information technology policy and help coordinate procurements, data standards, telecommunications, and other issues that cut across multiple agencies.

MAINTAINING DATA QUALITY

Since so many public records contain personal information or control financial transactions, the importance of maintaining quality control over databases should be apparent. Incorrect entries (whether due to error, sloppy procedure, or fraud) could lead to incorrect payments to eligible beneficiaries or erroneous payments to ineligible ones. They could prevent people from receiving other rights or benefits like driver's licenses, passports, admission to colleges, or eligibility to vote or hold office. Government information is a building block of the physical infrastructure. Roads, bridges, airports, and nuclear power plants all depend in one way or another on government information. Public data is also used to support broad policy decisions and specific programmatic ones. Businesses use it to help plan new ventures. Consumers rely on it to make informed purchases and exercise their rights. All of these are reasons to actively pursue data quality and usability.

Procedural controls are important tools for maintaining data quality. Measures designed to ensure physical and electronic security automatically help to ensure data quality. Controls over data entry and inquiry (passwords and other restrictions on persons who input data, dual verification by two or more employees of important entries, and electronic security measures designed into data-entry protocols) all help to achieve data integrity. In addition, routine and random audits of computer operations and records are an additional check on data security, as well as a deterrent to those who might otherwise consider tampering with government data systems.

Networks present special problems of data integrity. Since many users in different locations share data, protocols that specify when and from where information will be updated, how conflicts will be resolved, and how local information needs will be meshed with central requirements all need special attention. Differential levels of access to central databases are another tool that restricts the ability of users to see and manipulate information in accordance with their level of expertise or specific job.

The ever-declining cost of data storage can be a problem as well as a blessing. Since comparing and evaluating old information against new is expensive, there is a tendency to simply keep it all. This contributes to "information overload," the chronic problem of finding the right information in an ever-growing storehouse of useless data.

Not all quality control measures relate to technology. State and federal laws give individuals access to records kept about them and specify procedures whereby errors can be identified and corrected. These are another mechanism for ensuring accuracy, although as we shall see in the next chapter, these protections are not always easy to understand or implement.

Finally, most government information still begins with a person filling out a form. Clear instructions, explicit definitions, and a source of human assistance all contribute to getting accurate data in the first place.

RECORDS MANAGEMENT, ARCHIVES, AND PRESERVATION

The problem of archiving and preserving public information resources is, in principle, simple to state. Given its immense volume and current and historic value, which information should be kept for how long and which discarded? How should permanent data be stored and cataloged to ensure future access to what one state calls "a usable past?"

Figure 4.4 illustrates the life cycle of a typical document or record. The management of active records is most often limited to the processes of information creation, imaging (whether in paper copy, electronic form, or other media), and immediate and near-term use. The hidden costs of data and file management are illustrated in Figure 4.4 to the right of the domain

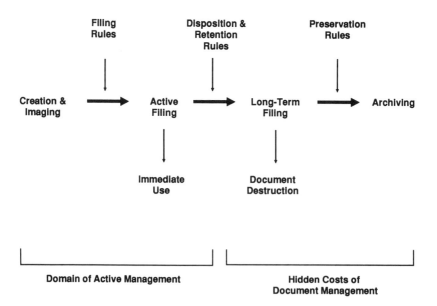

Figure 4.4   Life Cycle of a Typical Document

of active management. Here the information is first placed into an active filing system where it is available for rapid, frequent access. Active files might include, for example, currently valid driver's licenses or currently active clients in a rehabilitation program. The downgrading of active files requires either the destruction of the record or a transition to a long-term resting place. For example, case histories of former social services clients or blueprints and maps of historic places might go in these longer-term files. The selection of specific records or data items to form the permanent archives of an agency is the final step in the life cycle of a record or a document. Selected for their intrinsic, legal, or historic value, archived records need special, expensive handling if their preservation is to be ensured.

Information in machine-readable form offers several advantages in the archiving and preservation processes. First, it is typically stored in very compact form, significantly lessening the burden of physical storage. Second, using the technology with which it was created, machine-readable data can be more systematically sorted and evaluated for archival value. However, the existence of information in electronic form also poses some special problems. Primary among them is vulnerability to environmental factors and possible loss of data due to undetected or unprevented changes in the physical characteristics of the storage media. For example, tapes or disks can deteriorate in their magnetic properties over time, especially if exposed to unusual heat, humidity, or magnetic fields. Even minor disruptions can make an entire file virtually unreadable. While paper records are subject to similar problems (loss due to fire or flood, or physical deterioration due to light or humidity), the possibilities of massive information loss from seemingly minor disturbances in the storage environment have not existed in the past.

A closely related problem is the rapid obsolescence of the equipment and media used to store and read information in electronic form. Tape drives, disk drives, and the size and format of tapes and disks change every few years. Equipment and formats considered standards as recently as fifteen years ago are no longer in use. It seems likely that fifteen (or one hundred) years from now, the brand-new technologies like compact disks and optical storage devices necessary to read and interpret today's electronically stored information will no longer be used. Even twenty years from now the equipment needed to read today's government records may well be antiques. But twenty-first century libraries and archives need to have as good access to information preserved in electronic form as today's have to the nineteenth century's written records. Deliberate steps will have to be taken now to ensure continued access to electronically archived material in the future. This will most likely involve plans to build archival considerations into current records management activities, to periodically evaluate stored material, and to rerecord it in new media formats for continuing accessibility.

An even more fundamental issue needs attention. Many records of lasting value have already been lost simply because they existed on electronic media. The problem here is not a technical one. It reflects an attitude among modern office workers that information in electronic form is somehow less "real" than information stored on paper. Since people cannot read it directly, they tend to forget that electronic information represents relationships, transactions, authority, and history—matters of intrinsic value that should be evaluated before being discarded. For this reason, archivists recommend that the evaluation process begin when systems are in the design stage in order to raise awareness as well as lay the groundwork for eventual appraisal of the data.

Fortunately, mainframe managers are in a good position to deal with preservation issues. It is common practice to frequently back up and save current files. This simple procedure is an essential step in a complete plan to preserve a record of the past. As is the case for physical security and disaster recovery, the training and standard operating procedures used by mainframe managers give them a strong base from which to participate in preservation activities. More severe managerial problems arise around the rapidly growing microcomputer systems. As more and more computing is deployed to these small distributed systems and away from central data centers, the problems associated with providing for uniform assessment, storage, and preservation of an agency's operational records multiply. Unless top-management support and organizationwide awareness of these issues are explicit, the variations in local operating procedures will virtually ensure that records generated and maintained on these disparate systems will be archived in an, at best, uneven way—if at all.

SHARING INFORMATION RESOURCES

The topic of information resource sharing is a critical one for public agencies and illustrates an entire range of information resource opportunities and problems. Information resource sharing is a complex concept covering a wide range of activities. At the simplest level, two organizational units may share the CPU of a large mainframe machine. At a more complicated level, two agencies may match records on individual people for some oversight or control purpose (such as matching unemployment records with income tax records to check for persons illegally receiving unemployment insurance). Many other sharing alternatives exist. Agencies may use uniform data dictionaries for common functions (such as accounting or personnel systems). Agencies or units of government may share a telecommunications network or may jointly purchase an expensive software license. Agencies may share the technical expertise of their employees. All of these information-sharing functions can save hardware, software, and personnel dollars. They can also improve the quality of government operations. But in practice, sharing proves to be difficult business. A good initial idea often takes a surprising amount of effort to implement. Such efforts at resource sharing are the topic of this section.

Hardware and software are important ingredients in information resource sharing. Taken together, they form the technological bedrock upon which many other questions of sharing must rest. Hardware issues cluster into two groups: the computers themselves and the telecommunication linkages that tie them together. Software covers both the programs that control equipment and those that handle users' applications.

Sharing Technologies—Equipment

First, different organizations can share a common CPU, usually a mainframe. In the not too distant past when the cost of mainframe computing was extremely high and no inexpensive alternatives were available, shared hardware was the rule. Often a central service agency purchased or leased and operated a mainframe machine to serve other units of the government. Especially when large applications were involved, the direct sharing of hardware was the first and most obvious way to approach information resource sharing. However, the rising scale of most agency operations and the decreasing costs of mainframe and other computing devices are making direct sharing of a mainframe device less and less common.

Common purchasing procedures and the promulgation of equipment standards are a second way to promote information resource sharing. These are usually instituted in an attempt to exercise mass-purchasing power or to secure substantial discounts. Initiated as a way to control costs and the headaches of maintaining multiple acquisition and maintenance contracts, these standards have a second important effect. They tend to standardize the hardware in an organization, making it possible to upload, download, and otherwise share information from one unit to the next. While this is by no means a universal condition, it emphasizes the unrealized potential for making better use of existing information by making more deliberate decisions about equipment.

Sharing Technologies—Telecommunications

The more interesting technological issues, however, center not on computers but on telecommunications. Rapid advances in this field promise the emergence of formal industry standards. At present, however, telecommunications arrangements are most often vendor-specific or application-specific or not very flexible. That is, individual vendors have worked out fairly flexible local and wide area networking arrangements for their own families of equipment, but the general problem of ensuring rapid and easy communications between any two arbitrarily defined machines with two different operating systems has not yet been settled by industrywide standards.

Low-level standards such as the transfer of simple ASCII formatted files have been in existence for some time. But when complicated data structures must be transferred from one operating system to another, cumbersome transformations of the data as well as the associated control characters must often be performed. The market is likely to work out the problem of higher-level telecommunication linkages in the near future. At present, however, most vendors have greater incentives to ensure easy communications within their own product lines than across those of their competitors.

The resolution of these telecommunications issues partly involves questions of building design and physical plant (for example, where wiring closets are located and what types of wires are pulled where in the retrofitting of older buildings). Other considerations are related to communications technology per se (what types of communications protocols and machines control networks, what are the preferred physical media for various applications—fiber optic cables vs. simple twisted pairs vs. coaxial cable, etc.), and questions of new advances in the hardware to control transmission and switching.

In addition, basic ideas about telecommunications standards are still evolving. Several under discussion by international standards bodies (the Integrated Standard Data Network—ISDN and the Open System Interconnect—OSI) would form the basis of a flexible communications architecture—independent of hardware—so necessary to effectively move, manage, and share information.

Sharing Technologies—Software

At one level, the software component of information resource sharing cannot easily be separated from the hardware component. For example, software embedded in CPU operating systems and software that controls networks must eventually conform to the same developing industry standards discussed above. Hence at this rather fundamental level, they are nearly coincident.

A second level of analysis centers on the ways agencies use or share common software products. For example, separate software licensing agreements signed by two agencies in the same jurisdiction double the cost of product purchase. As an alternative, the jurisdiction itself could become the licensee, usually reducing software costs. Options like these are especially important when considering the purchase of expensive software tools such as those used to design and construct mainframe databases, and they are even more common when hundreds or even thousands of units use the same word processing, spreadsheet, or statistical packages. But a danger also lurks here. A jurisdictionwide or even agencywide software license can easily become an unreasonably rigid standard, forcing everyone to use a one-size-fits-all product unsuited to special needs.

Finally, simple mechanisms such as a directory of major software products already in use can be valuable. When augmented with the names of current users willing to serve as peer advisers, directories support informal consultations among organizations, allowing users who are "up to speed" with a specific product or application to assist newer users.

Information Sharing within an Organization

Most hardware and software issues, requiring technological skill and often a considerable dollar investment, are more amenable to solution than many of the associated organizational problems. In large measure the question of information resource sharing within and between levels of government is more an organizational than a technological issue. We may eventually have standardized hardware, operating systems, and telecommunications protocols supporting databases and software written in a common language. But the fundamental questions of data ownership, definitions, control, access, security, integrity, and confidentiality all remain. These are issues technology cannot solve. They exist even when information is used by a self-contained unit. When information is to be shared with others, these problems become magnified in both difficulty and importance. Our managerial and political skills are the only tools we have to deal with them.

Sharing anything within an agency is essentially an organizational problem. Information islands, the office of the chief information officer, the changing role of the director of data processing, the invention of the information resource center, the definition of data elements, and the use (and misuse) of user advisory groups form the core of the information-sharing issues, problems, and policy solutions within a given government organization. All of these topics were discussed in Chapter 3.

Information Sharing between Units and Jurisdictions of Government

Additional complications arise when information resources are to be shared between agencies or jurisdictions. Struggles for organizational turf are even more fierce than those within agencies. Take the case of an information system designed to track employment services provided by the Labor Department to welfare recipients otherwise under the jurisdiction of the social services agency. There are no clear answers about who should be responsible for, staff, and take the credit or blame for the performance of such a system. These questions transcend usual organizational dynamics because the various units do not share a common executive structure.

Often ethical, legal, and even constitutional issues arise when data is shared across agencies or jurisdictions. Consider a tax department using Medicaid payment records maintained by the social services agency to cross-check the accuracy of selected physicians' tax returns. Or the reverse, a welfare department using tax data to cross-check eligibility for assistance payments. These cases and others like them characteristically involve competing goals: maintaining public access to public information, protecting the privacy of individual citizens, improving the accountability and creditability of public organizations, and achieving the policy objectives of the government.

Shared information resources can alter traditional balances of power in intergovernmental relations. For example, a statewide information system that supports county-operated welfare programs puts the state in a better position to control and monitor the payment policies and practices of local units of government. It increases the state's power over the administration of public welfare and diminishes local discretion even though no laws or regulations have changed. On the other hand, such a system could set the stage for a successful local initiative to transfer more of the costs of welfare programs to the state. The loss of local policy control could be turned into a local fiscal advantage if laws regarding financing could be changed to reflect the de facto shift in power.

Information resource sharing between units and jurisdictions is complicated. No one can say whether it is a uniformly good thing that should be consistently promoted or whether it should be subject to scrutiny at every step. Whether or not information resource sharing will work depends on what is being shared, how much each party benefits and at what cost, the nature of the applications, and the organizational culture of the units involved. In general, large-scale efforts can work if "the business" of government calls for or could benefit greatly from sharing. It makes good sense, for example, when several units are dealing in a single policy area such as criminal justice or child welfare, or in a common functional area such as personnel or financial management.

When different organizations share information resources, technical questions are interwoven with political ones—debates over common procedures and data definitions become proxies for the larger questions of power and program control. When the involved parties belong to the same agency or jurisdiction, strong executive leadership is a key to successful resolution. When sharing is interjurisdictional, however, no common executive influence can be brought to bear. In these cases, both parties must see benefits flowing from the considerable resources they will invest in solving their mutual information problems.

The Role of Information Itself

Technological, organizational, and political issues are not the only constraints on information sharing. There are also issues that arise from the content and meaning of the data itself. The nature of the information to be released or exchanged influences the technical choices that underlie data sharing. For instance, when confidential data is released to another agency, security problems are compounded. Copying and transferring information means databases must be easily formatted, duplicated, and transported.

These characteristics also make them more vulnerable to unauthorized disclosure, alteration, or loss.

Other difficulties spring from the information histories of the organizations involved. It is unlikely that they have separately come to the same conclusions about identifiers, data element definitions, update schedules, and the like. Sharing information between them means changing things that may be working quite well for them individually. There are the associated problems of training, retraining, and documentation, which all arise even if there is complete agreement on the need for the changes. And once basic questions of definition have been solved, the closely related questions of how to change and update files so that the common definitions do not drift apart arise almost immediately.

Finally, there is the ultimate question of what has actually been created when databases are linked. For example, in a drive for improved nutrition, the Food Stamp file and the School Lunch Program file could be matched. It is likely that families participating in one program are also eligible for the other. Families not found in both files could be the targets of outreach campaigns to notify them of benefits that could help them eat better. If successful, this match could be costly and might violate the privacy of the families involved. But it also helps to focus resources on those most in need and offers a tangible benefit.

In another hypothetical example, imagine that a toxic substance exposure file is matched to a motor vehicle registration file to obtain the current names and addresses of people who are now known to have been exposed to a dangerous toxin. Administrators need to decide whether that data should be released to the individuals, who should bear responsibility if the data released is in error, and how its disclosure affects the liability of the cooperating agencies.

Take another case involving a match of motor vehicle files with client files from the agency that administers alcohol treatment programs. In this case we are creating a file that identifies people whose driving abilities might be dangerously impaired by substance abuse. Civil libertarians would certainly have a problem with this procedure. Other groups might support it. In either case it would be ethically and politically controversial. But note that technically and procedurally, all three examples are nearly identical. Where are the lines drawn? We will leave this issue for the moment but will return to it for a much fuller exploration in Chapter 5.

PROTECTING PUBLIC INFORMATION RESOURCES

Think for a moment about the government information systems you personally depend on. What would happen if one suddenly became inoperable? You might not get your paycheck or tax refund. You could not register your car or renew your driver's license. Your passport might expire just when you need it. Your mother's Social Security check might not show up when the rent is due. The fundamental problem in each situation is that you have no alternative. For this reason alone, government data systems must be reliable and secure. Both agencies and individuals are dependent on the reliability of government data systems. This means physical security and the ability to recover from disasters—important issues. Advance planning, working with simulated disasters, and other precautionary measures help secure the continuous operation of government information centers.

The range of possible failures (and their impact) varies widely. At the lower end of the scale are interruptions of the power supply, defects in a storage device, or programming problems. At increasing levels of severity are malfunctioning peripheral hardware components, loss of telecommunications links, loss of a mainframe CPU, or ultimately, the loss of an entire data processing facility.

Securing Mainframe Systems

All the foregoing are essentially random problems with equipment that can be minimized by good advance planning. More difficult to plan for and avoid are human errors or intentional tampering. Ranging from innocent errors such as inadvertent erasure or alteration of a data element, human threats to data security can include "hackers" tampering with data or inserting "viruses" more or less as a source of amusement, theft of data (either physically or electronically) by an employee or an outsider, deliberate sabotage of databases or, in extreme cases, of information processing equipment and facilities.

Mainframe users and managers, especially those with responsibility for critical operations, have long recognized the possibility (indeed probability) of disasters large and small. In response they follow procedures designed to guard against failures in public information systems. As a matter of good operating procedures, mainframe databases are routinely written to tapes or other backup media as frequently as daily to minimize the effort required to recover from a temporary loss of capability. Peripheral equipment on mainframe systems is often designed with built-in redundancies. That is, disk drives operate in parallel or several communication controllers feed the same input stream. If any single peripheral fails, the parallel equipment handles continuing operations, resulting in diminished, but not lost, capacity. The design of telecommunication systems linking separate offices can allow for multiple routes among the nodes in the network. A design like this allows for the continued operation of the entire network (although perhaps with bottlenecks or reduced capacity) in the face of a hardware failure or natural disaster that physically interrupts some, but not all, communication links. In some critical facilities, redundant CPUs handle the daily operational load. Often one machine is routinely designated for critical operations (such as local access to an on-line client registry) while the second CPU is used for training, new program development, and other less critical functions. A substantial failure of the main operational machine can be swiftly compensated for by the second, redundant CPU serving as an immediate backup. A related concept involves locating twin facilities at a physical distance from one another. Several agencies may run identical or nearly identical mainframe configurations thereby allowing one unit to serve as a temporary backup for another in case of a critical failure. Of course, this solution could only work on a limited basis and for a very short time, as the backup site must also process its own workload in addition to the "down" site's overload.

Ultimately, full-site backups may be put in place for some highly critical functions. Given the extreme reliance of government operations on some data processing functions, the cost of maintaining a separate fully operational reserve site might be justified. "Hot" backup sites, although extremely expensive, allow for the almost immediate resumption of processing and support functions. They are fully powered and equipped twins of operational sites. In the event of a disaster, interrupted operations can be resumed almost immediately. Of course, this means a huge financial investment that lies idle or handles only very low priority jobs in order to remain instantly available to serve its real purpose. "Cold" sites allow for the orderly, although not instant, transfer of operations from the damaged site to the backup. Often called "shell sites," these facilities have all the environmental requirements of a computer center (raised floors, fire protection systems, air conditioning and humidity controls). They also are wired for the electrical demands of a computer center in full operation and have telecommunications ports ready for network operations to be installed on short notice. Cold sites are much less costly and can be used for a wide variety of other purposes (albeit ones that are easily moved or suspended) when they are not needed. They have the further advantage of flexibility—many different organizations could contribute to the cost and maintenance of a shell site that can be custom furnished with whatever manufacturer's equipment is needed to recover from a specific disaster. The disadvantages are also important to understand: Over time, the "temporary" functions allowed to operate in the shell will become more permanent and more difficult to relocate or disband. Equally important, equipment vendors must be able to deliver and install equipment on very short notice. Both will be causes of delay that need to be anticipated.

For most mainframe systems, the key barrier to disaster recovery is inadequate planning. The procedures and technologies available for ensuring the security of information systems by far outstrip our managerial will to make use of them. The critical, and often missing, ingredient is the attention of the top management and budgeteers within an organization. It is understandably often difficult to keep major disaster planning on the agenda of an administration concerned with the more immediate pressures of active agency operations. In this light, disasters are only hypothetical questions—until they occur. Of course, focusing attention on the issue is only half the battle. The cost questions associated with securing continuing operations are tough ones. The more complete the security, the higher the price tag of the precautionary measures. The question becomes how to evaluate the benefits of having contingent security against the continuing costs of insurance against various types of accidents or interruptions in service that may never occur. That is, how much security is enough?

Regardless of the amount invested in physical security, recovery will depend on organizational factors. Perhaps the most important and most difficult is priority setting. Managers need to decide which applications must be recovered first. Of course, each program area will have its own list of critical applications, but someone must decide which of the first-priority items will actually be first. Moreover, if program operations have been supported by automation for any length of time, manual procedures and associated paper processes may have been forgotten or may no longer do the job. Alternatives need to be thoroughly investigated and periodically reviewed as part of any good disaster recovery plan.

Securing Micro-based Systems

However difficult these questions may be in a mainframe environment, they are even more problematic in micro-based systems. Unlike mainframes, these machines are typically installed by many users and are under little or no centralized oversight with respect to system operations. In general, data files are seldom even backed up and saved on a routine basis, much less archived in secure locations. As microcomputers proliferate, they often become viewed more or less like toasters or radios. No one provides backups for these things—they are inexpensive and easily replaced. In fact, where one micro is installed, there are usually many, so the question of equipment backup is actually much less serious than in the case of mainframe machines. However, the physical security of the machines themselves is less difficult to ensure than that of the data they contain. While mainframe managers routinely back up and store their data files and applications software, micro users seldom do. The severity of recovery problems then for these two kinds of systems is reversed. Figure 4.5 compares the risks and ease of recovery for mainframe and micro system components. For mainframe-based systems, the data and specialized software are relatively easier to recover because they are routinely copied and stored. The biggest problem is finding a hardware configuration to house and run them. Micro-based systems have the opposite problem. The hardware can easily and inexpensively be replaced, but casually maintained databases and undocumented custom software may have to be rebuilt from scratch.

COMPONENT	MAINFRAME ENVIRONMENT	MICROCOMPUTER ENVIRONMENT
Hardware (Loss)	Difficult and expensive	Easy and inexpensive per unit
Hardware (Damage)	Varies. May be easier and more economical to replace certain components	Varies. May be easier and more economical to replace entire configuration
Software Packages	Easy to recover	Easy to recover
Custom Software	Easy to recover	Difficult or impossible to recover
Databases	Easy to recover	Difficult or impossible to recover

Figure 4.5   Comparison of Typical Mainframe-based and Microcomputer-based Recovery Efforts

Malicious Threats to Security

Science fiction writers have imagined that hostile forces could obtain for nefarious purposes information about all of a nation's citizens. A recent admission by the Canadian government that it had, in fact, lost a copy of its complete taxpayer file with all of its citizens fully identified shows convincingly that serious breaches in the quality and security of government data systems are more than a figment of the imagination. Almost all the preceding discussion has been premised on the assumption that threats to physical security are from natural events, equipment failure, or an innocent mistake. Deliberate threats to information systems are more difficult to plan for and deal with because one must work against intentional, intelligent actions, not mere random events. This is the area where problems are most difficult to detect. Often they do not involve misuse or abuse of equipment, but rather fraudulent manipulation of a properly functioning system—such that benefits can be illegally authorized, services stolen, or selected information changed or destroyed. These problems are not obvious while they are occurring—everything still works as expected. For this reason, preventive measures are better than corrective ones. Thoroughly trained supervisors, carefully thought out procedures, and an organizational culture that gives security highly visible support are three of the best ones.

Many of the strategies for dealing with malicious threats, however, are similar to those for dealing with naturally occurring events. For mainframe systems, precautions against intentional abuse can be enhanced by securing the physical location of the equipment and by limiting access through such devices as security guards, badges, and entry check points. Electronic security may be enhanced with simple identification and password requirements (often sufficient to deter violations of data by nontechnical staff or to prevent inadvertent data violations by trained personnel). More complex encryption techniques increase the level of sophistication needed to breach the security of protected information systems. Some of the techniques being designed for military systems are highly sophisticated and very difficult, but not impossible, to breach.

Beyond measures aimed at physical and electronic security, procedural safeguards such as double verification of key entries by two or more employees, limiting input points for certain types of transactions to physically isolated work stations, requiring both preaudits and postaudits of selected data entries, and system designs and data architectures that conform to easily audited standards can provide for additional degrees of confidence. Specially organized security units can help detect, and in some cases prosecute, incidences of abuse and fraud. For example, upon the apprehension of especially skilled hackers who gained access to its long-distance lines, the telephone company actually hired them to work in a special security unit designed to detect and secure against further abuse by others. While the example is amusing, the problem of providing security measures against the breach of private and sensitive data is a most serious matter and one that is engaging the attention of more government managers than ever before.

While all of these problems are challenging in centralized environments, they are additionally complicated when micro and mini systems are linked through networks to a mainframe. By their very nature, these systems are designed to be open to use by many people. As the community of users and the number of access points to the system multiply, however, so do threats to the integrity of the data and the possibilities for inadvertent error or intentional abuse or sabotage.

SUMMARY

Government information systems, because they function in the public domain, are constrained by limitations and expectations that do not exist in the private sector. Our fundamental notions about the proper relations between the state and the public result in often conflicting requirements for due process as well as efficiency, for openness as well as confidentiality, and for keeping an eye on the future and simultaneously preserving a record of the past. Yet, while the tenets of our government influence the choice of technological tools, the tools themselves bring about change in the very nature of modern government. On an operational level, nearly every public program and millions of individuals depend on their smooth, uninterrupted, reliable functioning. They also contribute to a new confusion among the roles of political leaders, professional managers, and technical experts. Intergovern-mental systems change the relationships between branches and levels of government, often in unexpected ways. All of these general trends raise a number of more specific issues that require the attention of public adminis-trators. We need to pay attention to the issues of physical security and disaster recovery, archiving and preserving public records, and maintaining the quality of public information resources. Even if all of these could be handled with aplomb, there still remain important questions about promot-ing or restricting information sharing and actively or reluctantly disseminat-ing information directly to those who need or want it. Government procurement processes try to serve multiple goals as well: competitiveness, cost control, predictability, and long-term value. These considerations give government information management its special character and unique re-sponsibilities.

EXERCISES

1. The Mid-State Cooperative Educational Services Region (Mid-State CESR) provides special and vocational education services to eight low-density suburban and rural school districts. Mid-State is governed by a Board of Overseers consisting of one member from each of the eight boards of education of the participating districts plus one of the local superintendents. The overseers recently voted that Mid-State consider providing management assistance to the administrators of the eight member school districts. As an analyst working on the staff of Mid-State, you have long suspected that the districts could share common informa-tion and computing systems. The administration of all eight districts is nearly identical in terms of size, scope, and complexity, and they all use the same forms to report to the state education department. You suspect their attendance, inventory, payroll, purchasing, accounting, budgeting, and scheduling systems are all very similar. Your boss, the executive director of Mid-State, asks you to draft a memo for his review (and possi-bly for the Board of Overseers) showing what could be done in the way of shared information services for the eight districts.

   a. Draft a memo to the executive director sketching how common information systems might be developed. Describe what systems might be developed and list what could be their economic and other benefits.

   b. The Board of Overseers bought your argument and instructed the executive director to move forward. In your opinion, the attendance system would be a good first target for automation. It is a labor-intensive process involving extensive reporting every month to the state education department. Considerable time of classroom teachers, school secretar-ies, and central administration personnel is taken up in keeping atten-dance records. Furthermore, with the exception of just one district, these chores are all done by hand in the individual schools. Three additional districts have ad hoc systems at the central office level for generating the monthly report (merely spreadsheets for adding up sums reported by individual schools). You develop a piece of attendance software that can be run on a machine that virtually every school has in its inventory for instructional purposes. Preliminary reviews by a committee from the Board of Overseers (as well as a working committee of a principal, a school secretary, and a central office clerk) hail it as a great timesaver. However, none of the eight districts are willing to implement the system. It seems that teachers, school secretaries, and central office clerks are comfortable with how they are now doing things. They don't want to experiment with a new system. Moreover, this reporting has been going on for such a long time that few people within the system appreciate the whole reporting cycle (they just do their own piece each day), and hence they fail to appreciate the regionwide benefits that can be obtained from your new system. Your first attempt at a shared administrative system seems to be faltering on organizational, not technical, grounds. Your boss is hesitant about continuing the project. Draft a memo to your boss analyzing why you feel the project is not working and what should be done about it. *You* feel that the project should move forward—now convince *him* that it should.

2. New Technologies, Inc., is a software development firm that has just released an impressive new piece of software especially designed for public sector budgeting. The package combines spreadsheet, database management, and simulation capabilities, with an impressive report-generating feature. The package is ideally suited to making last-minute changes in the overall budget during eleventh-hour legislative negotiations.

   Five units within Orange County government are considering acquiring this package—the Budget Committee in the County Legislature, the Budget Division, the Office of the County Manager, the County Social Services Department (staffed by county employees whose funding and operational budget comes from the state), and the County School Board (which is financially independent from county government).

   The package is expensive. The initial purchase price is $20,000 for the license and $200 for each micro-site that will be installed. The annual maintenance fee is $3,500. Not all five units want the package equally as much. The Budget Division first discovered the package and definitely wants to acquire it. They will need up to ten installations. The Legislative Budget Committee is very interested but won't want as many installations. The county manager, social services, and school board are being "brought along" on this deal. They are price-sensitive users. If it becomes too expensive, they will back out. How many copies each unit wants depends on the final price.

   As an analyst in the Budget Division, draft a memo to the county manager proposing how the software costs should be shared.

3. The governor was just reelected on a platform that stressed statewide economic development—promising to attract high-tech, international

trade and new manufacturing into the state. Fortunately, the Department of Commerce has been developing for some time a comprehensive economic development database. This database contains tax base and tax rate information from the Assessment Department, labor market information from the Department of Labor, income data from the Department of Taxation, and individual-firm specific data from the Department of Commerce's own files. In addition, all of the state's census data is available in machine-readable form. To date, this combined database has been used for planning and policy development purposes within the Commerce Department.

Private developers would like to have access to this information, and recently representatives of the state's Business Council (a group that represents business interests to the government) approached the governor asking that this information resource be made available to the public. The governor, convinced, has directed the commissioner of Commerce to make this database publicly available. The commissioner has asked you for a preliminary plan for opening this database to the public. The file is massive and unwieldy. Updates from various departments come at odd times, and the master database is never uniformly up to date. Missing data items in the unaudited portions of the file could wildly skew analytic results. The department currently has three persons who handle the "care and feeding" of this database. Hence, whenever the department uses this data, these experts carefully scrutinize how it is being used, employing their collective years of expertise to ensure that data are valid and are being properly interpreted. You fear that if the data were simply opened to the public, contradictory and erroneous conclusions would be based on "government data sources." On the other hand, you don't know what a "standard data set" might look like. It is hard to predict exactly what uses the public might make of the information. On the other hand, responding on a request-by-request basis would require an immense amount of effort. You estimate that up to four or five new staff positions might have to be created just to handle these requests.

Draft a memo to the commissioner of Commerce detailing his options for making this data publicly available. Sketch the benefits and drawbacks of each option. Make a preliminary recommendation concerning how the commissioner should proceed.

PROJECTS AND CASE EXERCISES

1. Read the case study "Disaster Strikes the Hazard County Welfare Department." Respond to the assignment at the end of that case.
2. Refer to the case study "A Forensic Mental Health Database to Implement a Suicide Prevention Program." Some observers would argue that Susan Miller is the true heroine of this case study. Working against almost insurmountable odds, over the past four years she put in place the

rudiments of a forensic mental health database. Absent her efforts, nothing would have existed, and the public outcry and scandal would have been much worse. She has been working diligently to get a job done while statewide procedures and politics within her own department conspired against it. She succeeded, if only partially, in the face of these daunting odds.

Other observers would argue that Miller is the problem. Her maverick actions, setting up an information island without adequate consultation and coordination with other units, has caused the present mess. Had she worked out rather than skirted and avoided these problems of coordination, the present embarrassment would never have happened.

Which of these two versions of the news is true? Is Miller a heroine or a villain? With the advantage of hindsight, analyze her actions over the past four plus years. What, if anything, could she have done differently to avoid the present difficult situation?

3. Read the case study "A Policy Maker's Database: The Status of Children." Each of the proposals for an information base to support the governor's initiative has special characteristics. Williamson would index a wide variety of information to the key factor "person." DiLello favors an index to "time." Wing argues for the benefits of indexing to "place." Moreau's proposal is different. The essential ingredient is specialized knowledge. Discuss the strengths and weaknesses of these four approaches. Which, in your opinion, best supports the sweeping goals of the governor's idea?

4. Read the case study "Integrated Information for Policy Making: A System for Services to People with Disabilities." The legal mandate and the pledged cooperation of the involved agency heads do not guarantee the success of this system. These factors ensure only that the organizations will be represented at the negotiating table. This situation seems to call for a series of incentives, in other words some advantage that each organization will realize in the process of cooperation. Review the description of each agency and suggest a way that SSDI might help solve an internal problem, bolster its public image, improve its resource position, or set the stage for future developments.

SUGGESTED READINGS

Burnham, David. Ruling Pressures IRS to Modify Its Ways Significantly. *Times Union.* Albany: December 13, 1987: B-6.

Kraemer, Kenneth L., and John Leslie King. Computers and the Constitution: A Helpful, Harmful, or Harmless Relationship? *Public Administration Review,* 47(1): 93–105, January–February 1987.

McCaffrey, David P., and Ronald H. Miller. Improving Regulatory Information: New York's Transition to Environmental Fees. *Public Administration Review* 46(1): 75–83, January–February 1986.

Porter, Michael E., and Victor E. Millar. How Information Gives You Competitive Advantage. *Harvard Business Review* 63(4): 149, July–August 1985.

University of the State of New York, State Education Department, and State Archives and
    Records Administration. *A Strategic Plan for Managing and Preserving Electronic Records in
    New York State Government: Final Report of the Special Media Records Project.* August 1988.
U.S. Congress. Office of Technology Assessment. *Federal Government Information Technology: Management, Security, and Congressional Oversight.* Washington, DC: Government Printing Office, 1986.
Whistler, Thomas L. *The Impact of Computers on Organizations. New York: Praeger,* 1970.

CHAPTER 5

INFORMATION, CITIZEN, AND STATE

Melody Mallory stared at the terminal screen. There was something troubling about this case. In all the time she had worked for Travelers Insurance she had not seen one quite like it. The boy was only seven years old, but the claims record on the screen showed broken bones, concussions, burns on the feet, lacerations, even a broken hip. Mallory thought of her own daughter, only five years old, and of the terrible stories of child abuse she had read about in the papers.

Her research over lunch revealed that Lebanon County, Pa., the boy's home, had a Child Abuse Hotline. Mallory knew she had to make a call to report what she had found. How could she live with herself if she didn't? As she dialed the number, Mallory could not have suspected that this expression of concern was about to cost her job.[1]

After her call to the Hotline, Mallory found herself snarled in a labyrinth of Travelers' own policies on disclosure of policyholder information, as well as government regulations on freedom of information and personal privacy. Her dilemma was a complicated mixture of ethical choice, institutional policy, and the law. Clearly, her predicament would not have occurred but for modern information systems. Travelers' automated insurance claims system allowed a detailed personal record to be assembled easily in one

[1] For details on this vignette, refer to the case study "Where to Draw the Line: Public, Private, and Illicit Uses of Personal Information."

place. The boy had been treated by several doctors in several hospitals. Without the insurance claims system, no one outside his family would have known of the long string of accidents and injuries. That nationwide system made all that personal information available to Mallory at her computer terminal in Schenectady, New York. Similarly, the Lebanon County Child Abuse Hotline was an innovative use of telecommunications technology. It was also integrated into an automated information system. Mallory's call was entered and tracked in a system expected to observe confidentiality strictures to protect callers, children, and parents. But the system was also a tool for investigating, validating, and prosecuting or dismissing reports.

Melody Mallory's experience sets the stage for the issues we will cover in this chapter. It shows how the tenets of our political system help define, delimit, and complicate the uses of information systems. As government information managers, we are expected to sort out and balance contradictory mandates of law, ethics, and service. This fundamental characteristic of the public sector shapes the context of government information management.

In Chapter 4, we examined how information technologies are transforming the way government does business. This chapter explores the other side of that relationship—how the business of government circumscribes applications of information technology. Special attention is given to two parallel issues, public access to government information and personal privacy.

"PUBLICNESS" SHAPES THE CONTEXT OF INFORMATION MANAGEMENT IN GOVERNMENT

Managers of public information resources shoulder competing responsibilities. On the one hand, they manage one of the most important assets of democratic government—information about what government does and how it does it. On the other, they must handle sensitive personal data that deserves special protection from disclosure. They are expected to use resources efficiently, yet our form of government pursues multiple goals beyond simple efficiency. Their technical decisions are subject to override in the political arena and by the courts. They must employ their skills and tools in the service of their agencies but also in the "public interest." These constraints, not found in private sector organizations, are inherent in the business of government.

Several centuries of political thought, the U.S. Constitution, federal and state statute, and a significant body of administrative law all define the context within which public information systems must operate. The classic view of the state-citizen relationship is, at its base, quite simple. Rights, privileges, and powers originate with and are held by the people. Through the Constitution, defined powers and responsibilities are granted to the federal government and remaining powers are reserved to the people or the states. The Bill of Rights protects the privileges of citizenship and limits government intrusion into individual liberty. From this view, the citizen is the primary source of sovereignty, granting the power to govern at the ballot box.

In the classic view of our economic system, productive activity results from the free interactions of private individuals in an open market. Government frames the context within which the economy operates by providing for a uniform monetary system, a physical infrastructure, and the common defense.

Reality is more complicated. When left to its own devices, the free market produces monopolies that exploit citizens and foster fundamental inequities in the distribution of wealth. Firms are free to maximize profits while sacrificing the safety of workers, and groups of people live in poverty in a land characterized by great wealth. Government intervenes to correct these problems by regulating business, insisting on safety in the workplace, establishing social programs to support disadvantaged citizens, and authorizing transfer payments to ameliorate poverty. To accomplish these ends and remain accountable to the electorate, government needs complex organizations to collect information and monitor the economic, social, and physical well-being of individual and corporate citizens. In the process, the cherished protections of some can be viewed as so much red tape by others.

Our system is designed not so much to resolve as to balance conflict. Its stability depends on an uneasy equilibrium among competing claims, each of which we support vigorously in the abstract but find difficult to mesh in practice: the right to privacy and the right to know, the right to due process and the right to a speedy trial, the individual's claim to civil liberties and the state's interest in social order. The list goes on. The enduring tension among these competing "goods" is evident in the way we approach government's information needs as well. This balancing process, a fundamentally political activity carried out within a legal framework, is characteristic of information management in government. For example, a constitutional amendment gave the federal government the authority to tax personal income. To implement this power, government acquired massive files of information about the private finances of individual citizens. Later, as nationwide benefit programs began to be established, it became important for programs to be uniformly administered from place to place. Centralized processing systems and databases help ensure consistency in programs whether they are administered in Arizona or Vermont. They follow the same computerized rules in Minnesota and Massachusetts. In these cases, we have chosen technological tools that will help achieve agreed-upon policy ends.

Other laws and procedures respond to different interests. The Privacy

Act is designed to protect personal information in government data systems from unwarranted disclosure. However, the administrative procedures governing the Privacy Act and the Freedom of Information Act are designed not only to implement provisions of law but also to support the orderly conduct of agency affairs and to preserve the discretion of administrators. The effect is mixed. Modern information technology can serve all of these purposes, but not equally or simultaneously.

Some critics of information technologies suggest there has been a fundamental change in the relationship between the citizen and the state. They believe the concentration of vast amounts of information in huge bureaucratic institutions cannot be counterbalanced by individual rights or claims. They say the complexity of computerized data negates even the most ardent desire for information to be available for public inquiry and scrutiny. Others argue that it is not the technology that is at fault but our information policies, set by both design and default, that threaten the open nature of American government and the private citizen's relationships with it. The modern public information manager must understand and deal with these issues.

Below we review the interaction of technology and public policy in two key areas, public access to government information and protection of personal privacy.

PUBLIC ACCESS TO GOVERNMENT INFORMATION

Since the founding, Americans have placed faith in the openness of their government as a protection against tyranny. The First Amendment, guaranteeing freedom of expression, is probably the most widely known and commonly revered tenet of American government. As early as 1789, Congress enacted laws regarding the orderly recording of government activities. But as the nation became more complex, the simple approaches of the eighteenth and nineteenth centuries became less effective means of public information. Accordingly, other pronouncements strengthened the record-keeping responsibilities of public agencies and the ability of citizens to know about and have access to them. The Federal Register Act requires an official record of executive branch activities much like the Congressional Record documentation of the proceedings of the national legislature; the Administrative Procedures Act requires agencies to follow prescribed rules for executing their powers and to publish in the Federal Register information about their organization, rules, decisions, and procedures; the Freedom of Information Act (FOIA) prescribes other "fair information practices" designed to allow public access to the vast holdings of government records systems, as long as access does not threaten national security or invade personal privacy.

Freedom of Information in the Computer Age

"Freedom of information" has at least two common meanings. In everyday parlance it literally means what it says—free access to *information* held by government. Under the law, however, it means free access to the pre-existing *records* of public agencies. The FOIA specifies how citizens may gain access to public records and spells out procedures agencies must follow in responding to those requests. But FOIA has certain limitations that are complicated by modern technology: It is not a guarantee of information but a guaranteed procedure for accessing existing records. It does not require an agency to create records to respond to specific questions, nor to answer questions at all if no official record system in its possession is appropriate. More important, it does not ensure accuracy, comprehensiveness, or completeness of records released to requesters. Nor does it require an agency to change the physical format of its records to suit a requester or prohibit it from changing the format to suit itself. On the other hand, nothing in the law prohibits agencies from doing all of these things. Information technology can support any of them. In short, the law is a guide, but public policy, administrative practice, and technology play inextricably intertwined roles.

Agency administrators must recognize and resolve many practical issues that arise from this complexity. These include creating and maintaining carefully designed classification systems for records and specifying access procedures and internal controls. Training and clearly articulated agency policy are necessary to ensure that requests that go through the commissioner's office, through a bureau chief's office, and across the desk of an operator in the data processing division will receive similar treatment and responses. An agency must also explicitly decide what purposes its information access policy actually serves. It may follow the law to the letter and not one step more. It may view itself as an aid to public access and understanding. It might help requesters to better define their needs, or it might simply respond to questions as they are posed. It may allocate specific resources to public access, or handle them within the limits of existing funds.

This in an area where many of the organizational issues discussed in Chapter 3 come into play. For example, work unit, agency level, and jurisdictionwide policies need to fit together. An agency may intend to support broad access and citizen assistance, but its budget request for resources to carry out that kind of policy may be denied. Fees for information services are another sensitive issue. Some believe it is fair to charge fees high enough to cover the actual costs of access, arguing that they would allow agencies to give more public support, individual assistance, and responsive service. Others contend fees would be a deterrent. Public organizations will treat these issues in different ways. Some will lean toward greater access and public service, others toward consistently applied clear-cut rules that do not disrupt agency operations or drain away unplanned resources. Still others will put the agency's interest in protecting its discretionary powers first and other considerations later. It is easy to see, then, why FOIA, designed in principle to give the "citizen on the street" access to government operations and data resources, is often evoked in confrontational settings involving investigative reporting or litigation. While responding to FOIA requests can be, and often is, a routine matter, it can also be an adversarial process.

Routine Dissemination of Government Data

While the foregoing discussion pertains to providing access to government information on request, another class of issues centers on the accessibility of information released as a matter of course. Some of the data routinely collected by government agencies have always been designed to inform the public. This information, largely statistical in nature, describes government operations and the condition and performance of the social systems in which we live. For example, census data, employment trends, and economic indicators such as national and regional computations of the cost-of-living index are information "products" designed for public release. In addition, most government agencies collect data that, when released in summary form, are important sources of public information concerning the functioning of government, the economy, and the society at large. Reports concerning state and local finances, schools, corrections, agricultural production, and health care fit this class of data. The primary problem with the publication and release of this kind of information is its low priority among the other routine operations of an agency. The missions of the agencies collecting this data seldom emphasize (or even recognize) the resource commitment needed to sort, analyze, and prepare it for public release. The time and effort needed to locate and understand raw data, analyze it, prepare summary statistics, and publish statistical abstracts is, in fact, the key impediment to the dissemination of this kind of information.

Releasing information in machine-readable form creates additional complications. Most agencies are neither willing to provide free public access to their complete data files nor willing to tailor-make tapes or disks for each special request. Furthermore, most agency files contain data from a number of different sources, collected for different reasons and with different instruments, updated in different ways and on different schedules. This makes them, almost by definition, in a continual state of flux and makes knowing how and when to release information extracted from them much more difficult than it would seem at first glance.

Imagine that a state department of education is asked for information about the financing of elementary and secondary schools. This information would be of critical interest to teachers' unions, the association of school boards, the legislature, the governor's office, and associations of superintendents and school business officials as they try to formulate school aid proposals or attempt to see how specific districts are faring. However, this data might be collected from a fall head count of pupils, a spring full-time census, a spring and summer analysis of local income tax from the taxation department, a biennially updated estimate of property tax values from yet another agency, and so on. The answer to the deceptively simple question "How much is spent per student?" must come from a continually changing, uncoordinated database whose composition will vary, even if only slightly, from week to week and place to place. Furthermore, the fully documented, not-so-simple answer probably exceeds in sheer volume what any single user either wants or needs to know and would take far too long to prepare than most situations demand. If this data were simply released in raw form when requested, one almost guaranteed result would be confusion. There would be conflicting data definitions, analytical approaches, and conclusions all traceable to the same set of original data.

This simple example illustrates a common and growing problem with government information. Some of its dimensions are technical: the need for standard definitions, procedures, and formats and the need for "metadata" or information about information (How was it collected? When? How reliable is the source? How often is it updated?). Standard statistical series usually handle such questions well. Often releases are made several times a year presenting a snapshot "frozen" at a point in time. The main database, however, continues to be updated and an all-inclusive annual summary is later released covering the entire year. Moreover, definitions have been settled for some time and any changes are heralded by long notice periods and extensive explanation.

Different technical questions affect the vast stores of government-generated information that have already solved the data problems just described. National Depository Libraries, for example, house the official documents of the executive and legislative branches for all to use. These paper collections are enormously expensive to establish and maintain. If, as some advocate, these documents were issued on electronic media, they would be easier and cheaper to produce, store, find, and categorize. But that may remove them from the reach of people without the technological means to use them. Are paper records the only answer? Clearly not. But it is important that the "availability" of public information (which is independent of its format) not be confused with its "accessibility" (which depends on format directly).

Many of the issues related to dissemination of government information, however, are not technical ones. They are policy questions about the priority such activities receive, the resources allocated to accomplish them, and the performance standards applied to gauge their effectiveness. Today, we know that multiple sources of related information could help answer many questions about our society and our economy. Tying disparate data systems together toward that end is no small task. It also generates some tough questions: Should government simply ease access to the data it has? Should it be responsible for routine analysis and release of statistical series and summaries? Should it charge fees for information? Should it interpret its data and make its conclusions available? If so, would that effort preempt private sector initiatives or investment in better information resources for everyone?

Collecting and processing data is costly. Analyzing, interpreting, and publishing information is even more so. The degree to which a public agency, a state, or any other jurisdiction invests in these activities rests mostly on the value both leaders and constituents place on publicly available information resources as a legitimate function of government.

PERSONAL PRIVACY

Not so long ago, interactions we had with government were few and all were based on face-to-face relationships. The information that government agencies had about us came from us directly or from people or organizations who knew us personally. A century ago, official records of citizens included information about birth, death, marriage, property ownership, and little else. These were, of course, paper documents, recorded locally and seldom circulated beyond the place where they were made. The most complete records were not likely to be held by government, but by churches. Each record was made for a specific reason.

Today, each of us is far more likely to be known to the world by official records than by our personal interactions. As the complexity of our society has grown, so have the institutions we rely on to make it operate. Many of our most important relationships are now no longer with people but with organizations. And the way they know us is by our records. It is in this sense that we have become an information society. Records substitute for face-to-face contact not only for getting goods or services we want but also for obtaining those we consider necessities. Records of one organization are supplemented by or verified against those of others. Decisions about us are based on impersonal organizational data banks at least as much as they are derived from information we give freely about ourselves.

Government is no exception. Two twentieth-century trends have put enormous records systems between people and government: the explosion in government programs begun in the New Deal and expanded in the 1960s and 1970s, and the introduction over the past three decades of computer technology into government operations. Together these two trends—more numerous, sophisticated, and far-reaching programs, and the means to administer them—have changed the relationship between citizen and state. Even though most personal data are collected for benevolent ends, the process of government intervention has become highly impersonal and therefore remote and indifferent. In part due to the availability of large-scale information systems, government's response to social needs is now less individualized than the social services offered during the Great Depression of the 1930s under more decentralized, local control. Furthermore, the possibility for fraud and abuse of removed, complex government programs has led to a widespread and politically popular call for increased accountability and auditability of government records. The result is a further layer of data collection and intervention, adding more distance—psychic, geographic, and social—between the state and the people it intends to assist.

There are also ethical considerations. New information technologies raise questions of how public managers and employees ought to act that often go beyond, and even challenge, the strictly legal standards we are given. For example, should people's lives be disrupted by an official investigation simply because their records fit the profile of a hypothetical problem? Have we dispensed with due process when we allow a computer to make and implement an adverse decision?

Consider an agency charged with the management of alcohol and controlled substance abuse programs that collects highly personal and confidential data on its client population. Principles of government accountability for the funds it expends would require that this information contain unique (i.e., unduplicated) client identifiers. But the privacy of these clients must also be respected. To complicate matters, the existence of a centralized information system, often necessary to manage the agency's programs, virtually ensures that multiple copies of this database can and will exist. In the days of exclusively paper files, confidentiality often boiled down to a locked file cabinet. Today, many copies of complete files exist, and they can easily be replicated and transported. In fact, for many operations, backup and archiving multiple copies is a standard requirement of responsible program operations. Hence, all the procedures and policies for providing for the security and integrity of information systems become doubly important in this case. The precautions are no longer just a matter of good operating procedure; they are part of an intrinsic ethical obligation to protect confidential data about private citizens.

Informational Privacy

Informational privacy can be defined as the ability of individuals to control when, how, and to whom information about them is communicated to others. The Privacy Act of 1974 expands this definition into the five principles listed in Figure 5.1 that prohibit secret systems, give individuals access and other rights to their records, and summarize agency responsibilities with respect to personal data.

In the period since the 1974 Privacy Act and the Report of its Privacy Protection Study Commission, major advances have been made in informa-

---

The existence of government record systems containing personal information cannot be kept secret.

Individuals must be able to find out what data is in their records and how it is used.

Individuals must be able to correct or amend the data in their records.

Individuals must be able to prevent information collected for one purpose from being used for other purposes without their consent.

Government organizations must assure the reliability of personal information in their record systems and prevent misuse of that data.

Figure 5.1   Information Management Principles of the Privacy Act

tion technology—and government agencies have taken full advantage of them. Computing power has increased geometrically in both capacity and speed. There has been a simultaneous decline in cost. Data is no longer only stored and retrieved as it was in the early 1970s. It is gathered, manipulated, exchanged, and analyzed in electronic form. Extended storage capacities make it easier and cheaper to collect, store, and expand masses of data than to cull old, outdated information to make room for newer, more accurate records. Telecommunications networks connect computers without regard to time, place, or distance. Microcomputers have introduced hundreds of thousands of new machines, and millions of new users to the constellation of government information resources. What was once a collection of individual records systems organized in traditional ways has become something quite different. It is not simply a change in degree, but one in kind. Individual liberties are threatened not by the computer's speed or processing power but by the ability to integrate and connect many small systems (each of which was built for a specific, justifiable purpose) and to use them for new ends. The result of technological advances is a whole list of new "routine uses" for government information. They can be classified into three broad categories—computer matching, front-end verification, and computer profiling.

Computer Matching

Matching projects involve passing computer files of one organization against those of another using a unique individual identifier, usually the Social Security number, as the match criteria. Raw matches, or "hits," must then be further reviewed to verify that the match is indeed between records of the same individual and that any discrepancies between them cannot be explained. Computer matching was begun in the federal government in 1977 by the Department of Health, Education and Welfare in the Aid to Families with Dependent Children (AFDC) program. This soon led to other matching projects between AFDC and Social Security files, between Veterans Administration and Supplemental Security Income records, and a number of others. Most involved welfare or other benefit recipients or federal employees. The number of matching projects grew rapidly. In a 1986 study, the Office of Technology Assessment identified 110 federal government matching programs in use between 1980 and 1985. The number of matches conducted had nearly tripled during the period, involving in all seven *billion* personal records.

End-Front Verification

Federal verification activities are conducted today through the FBI's National Crime Information Center; the Social Security Administration's Beneficiary, SSI, and SSN Data Exchanges; and others. States use similar techniques in programs they administer. Verification differs from matches in several respects. Individual inquiries are used rather than mass comparisons. They are usually conducted before, rather than after, eligibility has been established or a benefit awarded. They are generally conducted on-line rather than in batches as matches are. Because of these characteristics, some believe front-end verification is leading directly to the creation of a de facto national database.

The issues here are important and very controversial. Congress has rejected the idea of a single national data file as too great a threat to civil liberties, and too heavy a reliance on a single kind of information resource. Yet the idea is used effectively in Western Europe and appeals to many in this country. It might significantly lessen the burden of information exchange between individual and government. It offers a better opportunity for private citizens to actually know what information the government has about them and take action to correct errors. It is more amenable to coordinated regulation and control than the thousands of data systems it might replace. Still, some fundamental ideas about our government seem violated by such a system. Many will participate in this debate before it is decided.

Computer Profiling

The third technique made possible by new technologies is computer profiling. In these, databases are searched not for specific individuals, but for information profiles matching certain patterns of characteristics. The Drug Enforcement Administration uses profiles to screen airline passengers for possible drug runners, the IRS uses them to identify potential tax compliance cases, and the Social Security Administration applies "error-prone" profiles to identify cases likely to have eligibility or payment errors. Issues here relate to the constitutional guarantees of due process. People are targeted for special investigation, not because a specific event or individual action warrants it, but because a computerized record fits a set of hypothetical conditions suggesting criminal conduct or civil violation.

Today, government matching, profiling, and verification programs touch nearly all Americans in some way. For example, every state tax depart-ment exchanges taxpayer information with the Internal Revenue Service. The IRS has expanded its matching activities even beyond the government and reportedly uses the mailing lists of private mail-order houses to verify the financial situation of taxpayers. Motor vehicle departments around the nation routinely offer their vehicle and driver registration files to interested parties, sometimes even for profit. These techniques are usually intended to improve government services or accountability or to crack down on misuse of government programs by private citizens or service providers. Their advocates point out that they have been effective in detecting cases of fraud and abuse as well as serving as a deterrent to those who might consider cutting a corner or two in their dealings with the government. As the proba-bility of apprehension rises due to these improved information technolo-gies, they argue, voluntary compliance with regulations will rise due to the deterrent effect. From the same data, others hypothesize a deterioration of voluntary compliance. Once private citizens perceive that government agen-cies do not preserve strict single-use confidentiality of personal data, they may become less willing to comply with government's requests voluntarily. While no reliable research exists on this question, the possibility causes census and taxation officials in particular to be especially cautious regarding how any of their data are presented. Moreover, civil libertarians point out that these same technologies that are used to detect fraud and abuse could lead to infringement of constitutional rights. Indeed, to guard against this possibility, some Scandinavian countries require that all computer matches of personal information, whether from public or private databases, be ap-proved in advance and in writing by a special government commission before the match is performed. Recent changes in federal law regarding computer matching are also moving in this direction.

Return for a moment to the principles underlying the Privacy Act. They are based on expectations of personal knowledge of the uses to which information will be put and on informed consent to those uses. Yet the newest technologies are not used for one-by-one transactions but to apply sweeping generalizations to millions of records—activities citizens do not know about and, therefore, can neither consent to nor stop. Here is where the ethical responsibilities and practical problems of public information resource management intersect. Each public administrator who deals with personal information needs to be keenly aware of the interplay of individual rights, administrative responsibilities, and technological tools.

SUMMARY

The preceding chapter examined how the advent of modern information technologies is transforming government operations. This chapter explores the reciprocal relationship—how political ideals, constitutional guarantees, law, and administrative regulations circumscribe information technology applications in the public sector.

Issues of public access to government information and personal privacy have received considerable attention. Grounded in legal principles important to the functioning of a democratic society, these two issues pose a series of dilemmas for government information managers. They must understand the provisions of the Freedom of Information Act and be prepared to implement them with respect to public information in electronic form. In addition, they must provide for routine public access to the immense stores of government information that is prepared specifically to add to the store of knowledge. Originally designed to secure individual privacy in a much less sophisticated technical environment, personal privacy statutes and administrative regulations represent continuing challenges for government information managers. New procedures such as computer matching, front-end verification, and computer profiling offer important new opportunities to enhance the efficiency of government operations. At the same time, they raise fundamental ethical and constitutional questions concerning how far government managers may pursue efficiency before they begin to infringe on personal privacy. Both of these issues stem from the unique place government information systems occupy in a free society.

EXERCISES

1. The legislature in the State of Goodwill has just voted in an income tax for the first time. The tax is to be administered by a reporting form sent out to all taxpayers on or about January 1 and is due back by April 15. The form is to be keyed explicitly to the federal Form 1040 and its attached schedules to ease the reporting burden on taxpayers. A new division within the Department of Revenue is being created to handle administration of the new tax.

    a. You have been requested by the new division head to think through in broad terms the preservation and archiving functions of the newly created division. She is interested in issues such as physical security, confidentiality, how and when to archive data, and guidelines for the possible release of data tapes to other government agencies. Draft a memo to the new division head detailing the issues that she will have to set policy on. Where possible, make specific recommendations. She is especially interested in your ideas concerning how to destroy and archive old taxpayer files.

    b. Impressed by your previous work, the new division head once more turns to you for assistance. She is about to travel to Washington to meet with representatives of the Internal Revenue Service. She is interested in data sharing between your state and the IRS. She suspects that such data sharing could be of mutual help. However, she also suspects that some tricky issues may exist with respect to matching the personal information contained in these records. Draft a memo for her private review, sketching all the issues that she should consider during her trip to Washington.

2. Refer to Exercise 3 in Chapter 4. In that exercise, the commissioner of Commerce asked you to draft a memo detailing options for making a comprehensive economic development database, currently used only within the Commerce Department, available to the public. In your review of this project, you discovered that some of the key fields in that database contain information that is aggregated from individual taxpayers (data from the Department of Revenue) as well as data aggregated from individual firms (Department of Commerce and Department of Labor data). The problem is that under some circumstances, you believe this aggregate data may actually reveal characteristics about individual taxpayers or businesses. For example, a request about all steel plants in a single county would yield firm specific data if that county had only one steel plant.

Create an addendum to your memo that lays out the commissioner's options for dealing with this new round of confidentiality problems.

3. The Department of Environmental Conservation, division of Air Quality, regularly collects information on air emissions from industrial plants. This information is used to monitor compliance with federal and state clean air standards. Until recently, this information has been primarily for internal use within the division. However, several recent lawsuits under the Freedom of Information Act have made it clear that the division will have to develop a more systematic data dissemination policy. Environmental advocacy groups demanded access to data about a chemical plant that is upwind from a new housing development. Owners of the plant claimed that the information they filed contained vital trade secret information related to the products they manufacture. In the litigation, a number of legal points turned on issues of information. Questions were raised about the form in which the data was collected and about the division's stated policies for releasing that information. The assistant commissioner for Air Quality, a new appointee, was upset by the lack of divisionwide standards.

The assistant commissioner has asked you to draft a preliminary memo detailing what such an information access policy for the division should look like. In your memo pay attention to what considerations need to go into the policy; who should be consulted in drawing up the policy; how the policy will be implemented; and how you will know if it is working properly. Draft such a memo for the assistant commissioner.

SUGGESTED READINGS

Burnham, David. *The Rise of the Computer State.* New York: Vintage Books Division of Random House, 1984.

Cooper, Philip J. Acquisition, Use, and Dissemination of Information: A Consideration and

Critique of the Public Law Perspective. *Administrative Law Review* 33(Winter 1981): 81–107.

Cooper, Philip J. The Supreme Court, the First Amendment, and Freedom of Information. *Public Administration Review* 46(6): 622–28, November–December 1986.

Deitz, James. *Federal Government Computer Data Sharing and the Threat to Privacy.* 61 U.Det.J.Urb.L. 605 (1977).

Feinberg, Lotte E. Managing the Freedom of Information Act and Federal Information Policy. *Public Administration Review* 46(6): 615–21, November–December 1986.

Hernon, Peter, and Charles R. McClure. *Federal Information Policies in the 1980s: Conflicts and Issues.* Norwood, NJ: Ablex Publishing Corporation, 1987.

Laudon, Kenneth C. *Dossier Society.* New York: Columbia University Press, 1986.

Miller, Arthur. *Personal Privacy in the Computer Age: The Challenge of a New Technology in an Information-oriented Society.* 67 Mich.L.Rev. 1091 (1969).

Privacy Protection Study Commission. *Personal Privacy in an Information Society.* Washington, DC: Government Printing Office, 1977.

Relyea, Harold C. Access to Government Information in the Information Age. *Public Administration Review* 46(6): 635–39, November–December 1986.

Relyea, Harold, and Lotte Feinberg, eds. *Symposium: Toward a Government Information Policy—FOIA at Twenty. Public Administration Review* 46(6): 603–39, November–December 1986.

U.S. Congress. Office of Technology Assessment. *Federal Agency Information Technology: Electronic Record Systems and Individual Privacy.* Washington, DC: Government Printing Office, 1986.

U.S. Congress. Office of Technology Assessment. *Federal Government Information Technology: Electronic Surveillance and Civil Liberties.* Washington, DC: Government Printing Office, 1985.

U.S. Congress. Office of Technology Assessment. *Informing the Nation, Federal Information Dissemination in an Electronic Age.* Washington, DC: Government Printing Office, 1988.

U.S. Department of Health, Education and Welfare. *Records, Computers and the Rights of Citizens.* Washington, DC: Government Printing Office, 1973.

Westin, Alan F. *Information Technology in a Democracy.* Cambridge: Harvard University Press, 1971.

Westin, Alan F., and Michael A. Baker. *Databanks in a Free Society.* New York: Quadrangle Books, 1972.

CASE STUDY 1

MANAGING THE INTRODUCTION OF A VOICE-ORIENTED CLINICAL DATA SYSTEM IN A PSYCHIATRIC FACILITY

The case study presented here depicts a technology that does not actually exist. That hypothetical technology, however, sets the stage for important dynamics among public sector decision makers. The issues and choices they face in this case study have occurred in the past; they continue to be relevant today and will surely reappear in the future. No organization can face the prospect of adopting (or adapting to) changing technology without dealing with these issues. Moreover, as the pace of technological change accelerates, the ability to handle its operational implications will become increasingly critical. The details of the case situation are pertinent to many real jurisdictions, but the situation, agencies, and characters are fictional.

The year is 2007 and the information industry is entering what many observers believe to be its most profound transformation since the late 1940s. Fundamental developments within the past decade, coupled with several new advances in nonlinear laser optics, promise to redefine the very nature of information processing machines (formerly known as computers). It is predicted that the traditional distinction between processing capacity (often measured in units such as MIPS) and core storage capacity (traditionally measured in units such as megabytes) will soon be obsolete. Shannon's definition of information embodied for decades in bit-oriented logics has given way to a new generation of machines that bears little resemblance to anything ever produced in the past. The classic categories of "hardware" and "software" no longer apply. Since the processing and storage of information are no longer separate in any way, these traditional distinctions no longer have meaning.

Several dramatic theoretical and engineering advances have combined over the past decade to bring about this new generation of machines. The first prototypes are now several years old, and a handful of small firms in the Silicon Valley and off Route 128 in Massachusetts are rushing to the market with new products (the industry is still marveling at their meteoric rise). Foremost among these is Voice Office Systems, Inc. (VOS). Thus far, traditional giants in the field such as IBM, AT&T, Digital, Unisys, and CROWN Data Systems have failed to introduce product lines using this revolutionary new technology.

BACKGROUND OF THE NEW VOODS TECHNOLOGY

The advent of Voice-oriented Optical Data Systems (VOODS) resulted from the convergence of five basic and applied engineering advances since 1997. The fundamental discovery that made this new technology possible came from a Danish mathematician, Erling Svensen. Svensen had demonstrated that, in theory, an infinite amount of information could be stored within the so-called attractor for a specialized set of non linear differential equations. His proof had broken a several-centuries-long stalemate among mathematicians concerning nonlinear equations and had opened numerous new fields of research. Svensen himself had received the Nobel Prize in 2000 for his proof.

Charles Farnworth, a physicist at Cal Tech working on the Defense Strategies Project, had demonstrated that Svensen's "attractors" could be nearly perfectly described using less than one megabyte of information (using the classic Shannon definition of information). Hence, in theory, an essentially infinite amount of information could be stored within a structure that itself could be described with a finite (and relatively small) amount of data. Brain researchers were quick to realize that human recall from a limited structure of neural networks must conform to the "attractor" structure defined by the Svensen-Farnworth hypothesis.

All of these developments would have been so much theoretical mathematics had it not been for the development of the first truly nonlinear laser devices at the Massachusetts Institute of Technology in 1999. For the first time, a physical device was capable of producing the theoretical attractors originally posited by Svensen. Using a small bit-oriented program to define the structure of the attractor, virtually endless amounts of information could be stored in unending combinations within the deep structure of the attractors themselves. In much the same way that a single set of nerves controlling the muscles of an arm or leg can produce an almost infinite variety of movements, so too the limited, but cleverly structured, information defining the attractor allowed for the development of virtually infinite new combinations of information.

The third breakthrough emerged from the Japanese initiative in "fifth-generation AI–oriented" machines first launched in the early 1980s. While this research program had not paid off for many years, deep understanding of the so-called knowledge frame and inference-generating technologies of Artificial Intelligence had emerged from that effort. While these advances had been operationalized in traditional list processing languages such as LISP, PROLOG, or IXLOC, the theoretical propositions developed by this research were directly applicable to the new VOODS technology.

The fourth breakthrough was in the systematic work on voice encoding and decoding that had been ongoing in many research centers since the late 1970s and early 1980s. Reliable protocols for coding voice commands had become available in traditional bit-oriented machines in the late 1990s. This technology was taken wholesale into the devices used to code the structure of the attractors.

Finally, dramatic advances in laser optics, beginning with the development of optically oriented logical devices in the late 1980s, provided the final advance necessary to bring about the new generation of VOODS technology. The creation of fully optical logic devices had clearly obviated the need for semiconductors or any form of electronically oriented circuits. This, of course, was necessary for the final development of nonlinear, attractor-oriented information processing machines.

PRACTICAL APPLICATIONS OF THE NEW VOODS TECHNOLOGY
(See the accompanying schematic.)

While the theoretical and applied innovations that brought VOODS into existence form an interesting chapter in the history of science, the practical applications of the new technology are no less than astounding. Voice Office Systems, Inc. (VOS) brought about the first commercial applications of this new technology in the very early twenty-first century.

Its new system was capable of actually learning the voice, syntax, and style of an individual user. Each of these features of speech would be programmed into separate and ever-increasingly complex and unique attractors. Hence, the combination of these three attractors could literally learn to recognize and mimic the voice and speaking patterns of an individual.

Furthermore, using knowledge frames and inference-generating structures, additional modules of the system could literally learn routine office procedures. Using this powerful combination, such machines could actually carry out assignments given broadly worded instructions. For the first time,

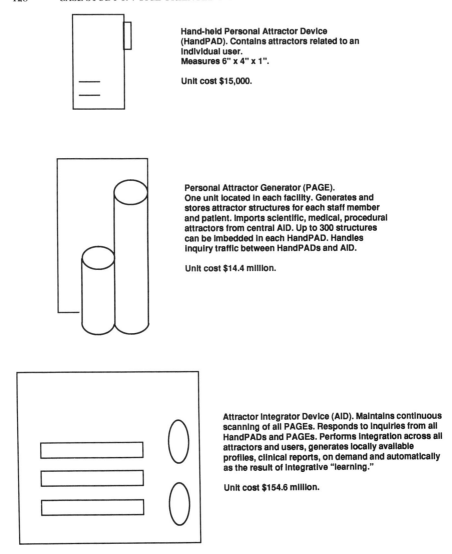

Hand-held Personal Attractor Device (HandPAD). Contains attractors related to an individual user.
Measures 6" x 4" x 1".

Unit cost $15,000.

Personal Attractor Generator (PAGE).
One unit located in each facility. Generates and stores attractor structures for each staff member and patient. Imports scientific, medical, procedural attractors from central AID. Up to 300 structures can be imbedded in each HandPAD. Handles inquiry traffic between HandPADs and AID.

Unit cost $14.4 million.

Attractor Integrator Device (AID). Maintains continuous scanning of all PAGEs. Responds to inquiries from all HandPADs and PAGEs. Performs integration across all attractors and users, generates locally available profiles, clinical reports, on demand and automatically as the result of integrative "learning."

Unit cost $154.6 million.

Figure VOODS.1   Major System Components

a machine could receive and "understand" abstractly worded verbal instructions such as "Draft a letter to Smith at Keystone Industries requesting an update on progress on the Generator contract." Attractor structures within the memory contained the necessary specific information on Mr. Smith, on Keystone Industries, and on the generator contract to create the necessary letter. In effect, the machine could play the role of a junior administrative assistant of infinite patience and untiring energy, if only limited intelligence.

VOS quickly came to realize that this new technology could be invaluable in patient care within a medical situation. Various attractor modules could learn the pattern and style of an individual physician. Others could learn the knowledge frames associated with a broad range of well-defined (and some not so well-defined) clinical situations. Finally, each patient could be assigned a single attractor, so that in some sense one could imagine that the machine had come to learn about or "know" each patient. The machine could act as an intelligent physician's assistant, helping the physician to consistently monitor patient care. Other health-care professionals could query the system or update it when they interacted with the patient. The bottom line? The expert human judgment of physicians could be extended through this system, allowing fewer physicians to attend to the needs of more patients. The nonexpert aspects of patient care could be greatly streamlined by the unique "intelligence" of the VOS system. Moreover, clinical personnel would have far greater resources to draw upon in making diagnoses, prescribing treatment, and following a personalized plan of therapy. Since the system would have better, more complete information about a patient than the old paper or highly structured electronic records, and since it could continually stay abreast of changes in medical technology and the biological sciences, each patient would receive better-informed, more consistent, more specially suited treatment. In short, health services could be revolutionized.

GENERAL PROBLEMS WITH THE VOODS TECHNOLOGY

While the new VOODS technology offers immense advantages, it is not without its practical problems. Foremost among them is the uniqueness of individual attractor structures. The simple facts are that VOODS systems programmed to be used by one manager or physician cannot be used in any effective way by another. That is, these so-called junior assistants can be responsive to only one combination of voice, cognitive structures, and operating procedures at a time.

Second, these machines are not easily compatible with any of the old electronically-oriented machines. This is especially a problem, since most of the data systems developed in the 1980s and 1990s were in the form of fully relational databases in electronic form. While these relational databases are clearly obsolete in a technological sense, they are in use everywhere and represent immense capital and staff investments. More importantly, they contain essential information concerning, for example, patient demographics, which should be transported from these old systems into the new VOODS system. At the moment, only a "low-tech" solution is practical: optical scanning by the new system of individual data records in the old system, plus the creation of additional attractors that specify how the scanned data elements relate to each other.

Third, VOS has moved toward a new unit of information, the MERG (memory encoding and recall generator), for creating the attractor structures. MERGs bear no relationship to old memory units such as bits, bytes, or words.

In addition to these technical incompatibilities, the new VOODS technology creates a host of personnel and management issues. For example, data processing professionals have been trained for some time to work in an environment of fully integrated micro and mainframe systems with fully distributed processing through local area networks (LANs) and long distance data networks (LDDNs). This orientation will lose most of its functionality in the new world of VOODS technology. Existing data processing professionals were brought up on old concepts of fully integrated, relational databases and traditional hardware and software systems. The retraining costs will be immense.

THE SITUATION WITHIN DMHS

Dr. Sally Ehrlman, a young and aggressive director of the Adirondack Psychiatric Center, has been watching the development of the new VOODS technology since it first hit the press in the early 2000s. She had closely followed the first clinically based systems pioneered at the Harvard Medical School and decided early on that they were ideally suited to the management of patient care in state psychiatric facilities. She applied for and received a demonstration grant to introduce the new technology within her own facility in 2005. This grant had been provided by the VOS corporation itself, with VOS providing equipment and expert assistance in the project.

Her experiment had been an overwhelming success. Physicians were able to maintain individualized records on all clients and to use these data profiles for patient management. There was a demonstrated increase of 35 percent in the number of patients who could be served by the physicians on staff. Yet, even with this greatly increased patient load, they applauded the results and felt that patients were not being shortchanged in any way. In fact, just the opposite—they took great satisfaction in giving better care to more people with the same level of effort. It was an actual case of that elusive goal "doing more with less." The results in community-based facilities were not as certain, but if even half the success of in-patient care could be shown, this technology promised to become the first real hope for improvement in the community mental health world since the unexpected effects of deinstitutionalization took hold around the state in the 1970s and the need for these services exploded far beyond the services available. Physicians and clinicians were flocking to use this new technology, practically leapfrogging over the facility managers and data processing personnel in their understanding and use of the new technology.

Features of the new system included

Clinically oriented information storage and retrieval

Profiles of individual patients tailored to the "clinical style" of the individual physician

Powerful heuristics to aid in diagnosis and in prescription of treatment

The ability to "learn" new clinical procedures or new information about individual clients as such knowledge becomes available, apply it to already stored facts and relationships, and identify patients who could benefit from revised treatment

A high degree of decentralization allowing the attractors to be tailored to the needs of individual physicians and other users

The overall system has worked in what can almost be described as a miraculous fashion. Capabilities that could not have been imagined five to ten years ago are clearly operational. The Department of Mental Health Services (DMHS) commissioner has recommended that this system be implemented across the state over the next five years. The estimated cost of purchasing this new equipment is $435 million. However, the estimated payback period is expected to be less than four years.

PERCEIVED PROBLEMS WITH THE VOODS SYSTEM

While clinicians within DMHS have unanimously given the VOODS system for patient information the highest ratings, not everyone is totally pleased with the new technology, certainly not the technology as being marketed by VOS.

The popular press is filled with rumors that IBM is about to release its own version of the VOODS technology. Informed speculation is that IBM will not adopt the same MERG standard as has VOS. These rumors suggest that IBM has developed and is testing a more powerful new technology for shaping attractor structures that will not be compatible with the VOS system and may work better. It is likely, however, that VOS will institute a patent fight if IBM attempts to enter this market. A major lawsuit could push the availability of competitive systems off for years.

Laying this problem aside, there remains the technical problem of incompatibility between VOODS information systems and the more traditional bit-logic electronic machines. Information processing professionals in DMHS predict that the adoption of the VOODS technology will lead to the creation of two entirely separate client-oriented information systems within each facility. Furthermore, there appears to be little hope in the near future of reconciling the VOODS data structures to the more traditional structures necessary to maintain the existing bit-logic relational databases. Some specialized transfer protocol is needed, and although much R&D work is going on, nothing has yet been tested and on the market. Having just spent the past decade gaining integration of hardware and software capabilities within DMHS, information processing professionals are understandably reluctant to allow a fracturing of information systems again.

The unions have already expressed stiff opposition to the new technology. Quite frankly, their fears stem from the belief that the new VOODS technology will strip aides and other health-care workers of the last vestiges of professional responsibility. They believe the allied health-care professions will become devoid of clinical judgment and almost routine in nature.

Civil Service is concerned about the new technology for several reasons. First, it seems clear that their newly completed conversion of several job series to reflect an electronic age will become obsolete. For example, after what everyone agrees was much too long a struggle, Civil Service titles finally reflect the reality that stenographic positions no longer exist. They were only recently reclassified entirely into the word processing and information processing series. Since these new VOODS systems are truly voice oriented (they even have proper grammar and can spell), Civil Service is beginning to realize that the very nature of clerical work is about to be completely transformed again. Furthermore, a two-decade-long debate still rages over the role of technical information skills in professional job classifications. Do they belong in specialty titles or are they so fundamental that, like literacy, they belong in the description of every skilled occupation?

Program managers in the facilities have yet another set of concerns. Using a sophisticated network of the latest generation of so-called micro-mainframes, they have finally achieved a relatively uniform information environment. Most facilities have completed the transition to a paperless office, and internal and external communications, as well as client records and financial systems, are all being handled within it. The new VOODS technology now threatens to create self-standing information systems within every clinical unit—perhaps with every clinician having his or her personalized information environment. The administration of information resources is bound to be complete bedlam.

THE CASE ASSIGNMENT

The advent and practical application of this new technology raises a number of organizational, strategic, financial, and professional issues. The traditional lines dividing technicians and users become blurred, and coalitions form around various aspects of the problem. For example, many of the facility administrators and nonmedical program managers have joined with the data processing professionals in their desire to protect the stability of their existing information systems. The medical professionals and those charged with delivering mental health services around the state (the physicians, the Adirondack facility director—also a physician, and the DMHS commissioner) see in this technology a powerful tool to advance both professional and public service goals. The control agencies are struggling to both maintain a stable environment and make wise investments in the future.

The Senate is about to hold appropriations hearings on the $435 million funding request being put forward by DMHS. Senator Edgecomb, who will be leading the hearings, expects that a wide diversity of opinion will be offered by a number of constituencies. You are an administrative assistant to Senator Edgecomb. He has asked you to prepare a briefing that anticipates the types of testimony he is likely to encounter during the hearing. (*Hint:* Scan the three "points of view" depicted below as a starting place for your memo.)

THE CONTROL AGENCY POINT OF VIEW

Put yourself in the place of the agency's budget examiner in the State Budget Office. You are reviewing a request to invest $435 million over the next five years to acquire this system. How would you react to this request? What reservations might you have? What additional information might you request? Can you suggest strategies short of approving the entire five-year acquisition plan that you might adopt?

Look at the concerns of the state's other control agencies such as State Central Services, Civil Service, and Audit and Control concerning this acquisition. Are these reservations justified or are they just attempts to block progress on a good idea? Should a public agency be on the leading edge of technology or are the risks that attend radical change inappropriate to the purposes of government? Should this new technology be acquired in a way that would make it more available to other agencies or should the risks, if taken, be limited to one agency setting?

THE INFORMATION PROFESSIONALS POINT OF VIEW

A coalition of information processing professionals and facility managers have argued that acquisition and implementation of the equipment should proceed at a slower pace after being pilot-tested more thoroughly in several other sites. They urge that the complete acquisition of the technology be delayed until such time as a coherent updated information policy can be worked out for the agency as a whole.

What issues should legitimately be addressed in this information policy? Have past efforts to define information policy for the state and for the agency been helpful in this situation? What features of the new technology make it especially difficult to define policy for the new technology? Should information policy be technology-specific or should the agency be able to develop policies that are general enough to survive several generations of new technology?

THE USER POINT OF VIEW

From the point of view of clinicians, delay in adopting VOODS simply means lost time, money, and opportunity. The technology has been proved effective in a pilot trial. Even by conservative estimates the technology will pay for itself in less than four years and thereafter provide improved client services at literally no cost.

Should the leading edge of technology be held up due to bureaucratic caution and technological myopia? From the clinician's point of view, argue why the state should be buying in early to the leading edge of this new technology. What sort of coalition could be developed to advocate for this point of view?

Further Reflections

1. In this case, three important perspectives interact in the active policy discussions surrounding acquisition of the VOODS technology—the control agency point of view, the information professionals point of view, and the user point of view. As discussed in Chapter 1, these three perspectives continually shape government information management and policy. After reading Chapter 1, discuss how the issues treated in the VOODS case are similar to or different from issues that arose when government agencies made the transition from a mainframe computing environment to a mixed mainframe and micro environment in the late 1970s and 1980s.

2. Chapter 5 discusses the companion issues of personal privacy and freedom of information rights that grant access to government collected and held data. After reading Chapter 5, discuss how the issues of personal privacy and rights of access interact with the VOODS acquisition decision.

CASE STUDY 2

A FORENSIC MENTAL HEALTH DATABASE TO IMPLEMENT A SUICIDE PREVENTION PROGRAM

This case analyzes a hypothetical, but quite possible, set of events. It illustrates how information communicated between organizations shapes perceptions, decisions, and actions. The case is not meant to refer to any similarly detailed real event. The characters are fictional.

Trouble has been brewing for the past year within the state's correctional system. A series of inmate suicides in state prisons and in county detention centers has drawn adverse publicity about the provision (or lack) of mental health services to inmates. These incidents most often occur in minimum security prisons or in detention centers while prisoners are awaiting trial. The Legislative Commission on Program Audit and Review has issued a special report on the subject charging that the absence of reliable screening and identification procedures is a root cause of failure to prevent suicides.

More recently, an audit by the State Auditor General revealed that the data systems necessary to support such services in most facilities were nonexistent. That is, where forensic mental health units did exist, clinical personnel did not have access to the information that they needed to perform their jobs well. Caught in a cycle of adverse publicity and critical audits, personnel within both Corrections and the Department of Mental Health Services (DMHS) redoubled their efforts to deal effectively with what they candidly admitted was a problem statewide.

For some time, the State Budget Office (SBO) has been concerned about the ability of DMHS fiscal analysts to systematically relate client levels, staff levels, and expenditures through the budget process. Typically, DMHS could present client, staff, and budget data at the facility level, but a finer-grained analysis of these data, including staffing levels per client by type, had been difficult to achieve. For years, SBO had been pressuring DMHS to create a data system that would allow a first-class programmatic analysis of its overall budget request. This recent spate of bad press, centering on the audited inability of the DMHS's data systems to track clients (much less relate them to dollars and staff), was the proverbial "straw that broke the camel's back." The leadership within SBO called for a full-scale review of the budgeting and data management procedures of the mental health agency.

However, the critical catalyzing event took place last month when a spectacular suicide occurred in a minimum security upstate correctional facility. The press had a field day with the event, and shortly thereafter a court order mandated an overhaul of forensic mental health services, with specific emphasis on a suicide prevention program. The court ordered a minimal screening program for all inmates in minimum security facilities with a subsequent program of follow-up. The legislature immediately began to consider a series of bills that would replace the provisions of the court order with new language in both the Penal Code and the Mental Health Law.

To implement the court order, DMHS's Forensic Units would be required to maintain a minimal data profile on all inmates identified through the screening procedure as being "at risk." This group would receive top priority for treatment services. A report to the court on progress toward a permanent screening and treatment program is scheduled in ninety days.

THE DMHS PROGRAM PERSPECTIVE

The DMHS program perspective on this problem is best told by Susan Miller, assistant commissioner for Forensic Mental Health Services. Miller has been in her post for four and a half years. Her previous experience included working as an active and knowledgeable user of information systems with the Division for Youth. Ironically, one of Miller's priorities in recent years has been exactly the kind of information systems for her treatment units that might have helped avert the suicide incident.

From Miller's point of view, those information systems have been problematic partly because the systems and the staff who need them are not physically located within DMHS facilities. By and large, the systems development efforts within her own agency have focused on information needs within mental health facilities. The needs of her units, located in correctional facilities, have been left unsupported.

With the assent of the commissioner, Miller has created self-standing information systems within her treatment units. Since the primary data on corrections inmates is maintained by the Corrections Department, Miller's objective has been to put up a complementary clinically oriented system. Her staff defined a standard data record (see Appendix A) to be kept on all clients statewide. They had then sought and received budgetary approval to purchase microcomputers and software to support the system.

From the beginning, Miller has wanted to coordinate the development of her data system with the central system within Corrections, but the Corrections staffer assigned to consult on the project missed several key meetings and, in any case, offered little assistance even when present. Working with a consultant from State Central Services (SCS), Miller's task force settled on a CPM–based machine that was on state contract. (At that point in time, SCS was still providing consultation services on the acquisition of micros and approving their purchase.) To get the project under way, Miller assigned one DMHS program analyst with special expertise in microcomputing to pilot the new system in one third of the Forensic Units.

Within a year and a half of a strong start, things began to unravel. The state dropped its contract on the CPM machine they had selected. In any case, it soon became clear that IBM was becoming the informal industry standard with its DOS operating system. Furthermore, dBase was emerging as a more powerful and widely accepted software package than the one they had piloted. Nonpilot sites began to move toward a DOS and dBase configuration. In the midst of this transition, Civil Service held a new exam and issued an appointment list for DMHS program analysts. The vast majority of the analysts who had developed and were now maintaining the forensic mental health database were not on the new list. The exam had concentrated on program design and treatment theory, but Miller's people were specialized in program operations and small-scale systems development. Civil Service suggested they be replaced by systems analysts, not program analysts. Miller, of course, had no access to lines in the systems title series and, in any case, disagreed that technical experts would fit the bill.

The SBO has now rescinded its approval for additional microcomputers pending its review of the entire information systems development effort within DMHS. Her unit and commissioner are under attack in the press, she has little internal support from the department's data processing professionals, and the bureaucratic constraints of the state system seem to be making a difficult task at best, virtually impossible.

THE DMHS DATA PROCESSING PERSPECTIVE

Once the Forensic Units had begun to get such bad publicity, Calvin Tyler, director of DMHS's Systems Development Group, had been called in to review the situation. Several years ago, the Systems Development Group made a strategic decision to concentrate on the mainline function of providing a coherent and comprehensive system of financial, client, and staff data for the agency as a whole. DMHS has been under perpetual attack by SBO and other control agencies because of its fragmented information bases. In the past, the Systems Development Group's energies had been diverted from solving this critical issue because numerous program units had been absorbing staff time with localized requests to deal with emergencies. As a result, Tyler's staff had continually been deployed to "fight fires" while the important and long-term work of developing a comprehensive data system was deferred.

Over time, Tyler's major objective had become protecting his staff from these diversions so the long-range goal of designing and installing a comprehensive system could move forward. The advent of micros had been both a blessing and a curse for Tyler. With every unit now purchasing its own microcomputers, his staff was under increasing pressure to build interfaces with numerous, uncoordinated groups of new users. On the other hand, many users were now beginning to solve their own information needs, decreasing the demand on his staff to support stand-alone systems with no design relationship to the comprehensive data systems so desperately needed by the agency as a whole.

While he at first opposed vigorously the creation of self-standing "information islands," Tyler has come to realize this trend is inevitable. Program managers who acquired micros allegedly to handle word processing almost immediately began to amass their own databases. With the relaxation of SCS controls over the purchase of micros, the entire world was breaking loose. Helpless to turn the tide, Tyler had come to take a more or less permissive attitude toward these systems, redoubling the efforts of his own group to create the comprehensive integrated database that would lend coherence to the overall information environment.

The bad publicity around the forensic data system was one of Tyler's worst dreams come true. In fact, his group had not really participated in the development of that system (or fragment of a system), and now they were being drawn into the controversy as if they should have somehow been involved all along.

THE CORRECTIONS PROGRAM PERSPECTIVE

Bill Petersen, director of Highmountain, the upstate facility where the suicide took place, best represents the Corrections' program perspective. Corrections is not primarily in the business of providing mental health services. While he welcomes the presence of these units within his facility, he makes it clear (when spoken to off the record) that these services are not "mainline" from his agency's point of view.

Petersen has worked over the years to maintain a good neighbor relationship between his staff and the forensic mental health personnel assigned to Highmountain. When questions of space or support (such as the use of limited computing resources) have come up, he has worked to address these as fairly as possible. He has always known that these DMHS personnel were a drain on his central support resources, and in a period of declining resources overall, tensions had emerged between them and his own staff. However, with the public attacks on both Corrections and Mental Health, Petersen understood that now was the time to stand together and to work toward a common solution to this problem. Cooperation was the password of the day.

THE CORRECTIONS DATA PROCESSING PERSPECTIVE

Quite frankly, when this fracas broke out, Ellen Farley, director of Data Processing Operations for Corrections, was unaware of the existence of a separate forensic mental health database in any correctional facility. Being relatively new in the job, Farley requested and received a file several years old pertaining to that system's development. The file was incomplete. Apparently DMHS had not maintained good liaison with Corrections staff in developing this proposal.

In an after-the-fact way, Farley could lament this as another example of lack of interagency cooperation. Here DMHS had moved forward with yet another micro-based system when probably a better solution would have been to integrate their needs with the statewide data system within Corrections. After all, access to the statewide system existed in every correctional facility. Why not just share access to that system rather than build a new micro-based system? But apparently those questions were now so much water over the dam. The micro-based system was in place, and its performance (or lack of performance) was creating problems for all of them. Farley viewed this as a perfect example of what happens when non–EDP types try to develop systems on their own. Hardware was not standardized (some CPM, some DOS machines with differing software packages). Furthermore, no one in the facilities seemed to know how to modify the system. It was developed by staff who had by now moved on and virtually no documentation had been left behind.

Farley was glad primary responsibility for this debacle rested with DMHS. Nevertheless, the bad publicity reflected poorly on Corrections, and she was prepared to cooperate in any way possible to rectify the situation. She would assign a staff liaison to work closely with the DMHS team looking into the problem.

THE CASE ASSIGNMENT

As new actors and program responsibilities place new demands on our information processing capabilities, problems of coordination almost always develop. As in any really complicated situation, there are several sides to this story. In this case, at least three important perspectives exist: those of the users (Miller and Petersen), those of the data processing professionals (Tyler and Farley), and those of the control agencies overseeing statewide operations. Working from their own points of view, managers strive to create "best" situations all around. However, and ironically, problems can and do arise precisely from people striving for the best as they individually see it. Diagnose this situation from the point of view of data processing managers, program managers, and control agencies. Try to suggest how agency or statewide policies, or their absence, contributed to the problem. What different policies might help solve it?

VIEW THE PROBLEM FROM A TECHNICAL DATA PROCESSING PERSPECTIVE

Examine closely Appendices A and B, which compare the data records on each inmate/client maintained by the Forensic Units and Corrections, respectively. Can you design a technical solution to this problem? That is, can you design a system that would draw elements from both files to create a new forensic mental health database? View this as a technical problem in merging databases from two separate systems involving different hardware, software, and data element definitions. How difficult is this problem from a purely technical point of view?

To what degree have history and the positions taken by the program managers and users complicated the development of a technical solution to this problem? List and discuss the user-generated impediments to a sound technical solution.

To what degree do the additional complications of dealing within state government impede a sound technical solution to this problem? List and discuss the specific actions and policies of various control agencies that inhibit the attainment of a sound technical solution.

VIEW THE PROBLEM FROM A USER PERSPECTIVE

Put yourself in Miller's shoes when she first began this project four and a half years ago. Critique the strategy that she pursued. With the advantage of hindsight, could you recommend a different course to her? What forces might have led her away from the course you are now recommending? Would you characterize any of her decisions as flawed or obviously bad ones given the situation that she faced at the time?

Miller was working within constraints imposed by the internal policies of the data processing shops in both agencies. How might these policies have contributed to a difficult situation for Miller? Could Farley's predecessor or

Tyler have acted at that early stage to avoid the present set of difficulties? If they had followed different operating policies in order to help Miller four years ago, what impact would those changes have had on their shops' abilities to meet their own systems development and support objectives?

How have the various control agencies contributed to Miller's difficulties? List and discuss the policies that caused problems in this case. List and discuss possible changes in state and agency policies that could have prevented the problems sketched in the case.

VIEW THE PROBLEM FROM A CONTROL AGENCY PERSPECTIVE

It is easy for users and data processing professionals alike to agree that restrictions placed on them by control agencies such as the State Budget Office, the Auditor General, Civil Service, and State Central Services create unnecessary complexities.

For a moment, take the point of view of each of these control agencies. Why did they act as they did in this case? How could they respond to the all-too-common accusation that they were blocking the efforts of well-intended public servants to get an important job done? List and discuss any changes in agency-specific or statewide policy that might have made this situation better but still allowed the control agencies to execute their legitimate oversight functions.

Appendix A

Department of Mental Health Services
Forensic Mental Health Information System

Data Dictionary

Data Element Name	Type	Field Size	Definition/Codes
Name	A/N	25	Legal name
SSN	N	9	Validated Social Security Number (primary identifier)
Corrections ID	A/N	10	
Sex	A/N	1	M-male F-female
Race	N	1	1-White, not Hispanic 2-Black, not Hispanic 3-Hispanic 4-Asian 5-American Indian 6-Other
Screen date	N	6	Date of initial screening in DMHS unit (MMDDYY)
Education	N	2	Highest grade: 00-none 01-08 elementary 09-12 high school 13-16 college 17 postgraduate
County of origin	N	2	Standard county codes (01-57)
Clinical class	A/N	1	N-not violent S-dangerous to self D-dangerous to others
Primary diagnosis	A/N	2	2-digit standard psychiatric diagnosis code (e.g., depression)
Height	N	2	Height in inches
Weight	N	3	Weight in pounds
Substance Abuse Indicator	N	1	1-Drug Abuse 2-Drug Addiction 3-Alcohol Abuse 4-Alcohol Addiction 5-Both Drug & Alcohol Abuse/Addiction 6-None

These files are updated weekly by clerical (data entry) staff in the Forensic Units.

There are twenty local units, each with its own database in the above format. There is no established communications network, nor any central data file other than summary statistical reports prepared quarterly. Each local database contains between 200 and 1,500 records.

Appendix B

Department of Correctional Services Information System

Data Dictionary

Data Element Name	Type	Field Size	Definition/Codes
Last Name	A/N	15	
First Name	A/N	10	
Middle Initial	A/N	1	
Alias Indicator	A/N	1	1-no aliases 2-has used aliases (see paper files)
Corrections ID	A/N	10	Primary identifier within state correctional system
Facility Code	N	2	2-digit correctional facility identifier
SSN	N	9	Social Security Number given by inmate
DOB	N	8	Date of Birth (MMDDYYYY)
Sex	A/N	1	M-male F-female
Race	A/N	1	A-Asian B-Black C-Caucasian H-Hispanic I-American Indian X-Other
Conviction Type (current sentence)	N	1	2-digit code denoting offense for last conviction (murder, armed robbery, etc.)
Felony Class (current sentence)	A/N	1	A-Class A Felony B-Class B Felony C-Class C Felony D-Class D Felony E-Class E Felony
Starting date of current sentence	N	8	MMDDYYYY
Length of current sentence	N	7	Years and months (YYYYMM)
County where convicted	N	2	Standard county codes (01-62)
Past convictions	N	2	Number of previous felony convictions
Past incarcerations	N	2	Number of previous state prison sentences

This is an on-line central system covering all twenty correctional facilities in the state. Records are updated daily on an overnight batch basis. Each facility and central administration has access to the entire file for inquiry. Changes can be made to a facility's records only by central administration and staff in the facility itself. The system contains a total of 50,000 records.

Further Reflections

1. The issues discussed in this case center on the broad question of information sharing between two government agencies. Read the discussion of information sharing in Chapter 4. How might information-sharing policies have been established in this case before the crisis emerged? In what other areas of government that you are familiar with do similar information-sharing problems exist? Could the existence of some boundary-spanning organization at the level of the entire state government have helped to avert the problems that arose in this case? If so, what would be the nature of such an organization?

2. Many information-sharing problems arise less because of technical problems than because of organizational ones. Chapter 3 discusses the organizational aspects of government information management. Using the four ideal type models introduced in Chapter 3, can you explain why it was logical for the problems sketched in the case to emerge as they did? Discuss how policies at the work unit, agency, and statewide levels contributed to the problems that evolved in the case. Remember that not all policies are explicitly laid down; some are evident only in practice. What different or additional policies might have averted the crisis these agencies now face?

CASE STUDY 3

AN INFORMATION NETWORK FOR THE EMPLOYMENT SERVICE

The advent of microcomputers and minicomputers has brought computer hardware into many of the most remote offices of state and local government. Increasingly, wide area data networks are being proposed as a mechanism to create an integrated information environment for operating agencies. When more than a single agency is involved, these decisions often bring in questions of statewide policy. This case explores some of the technical, organizational, and political issues that arise when such networks are acquired.

THE SITUATION IN BRIEF

Helen Frye, director of the newly created Office of Technology Management (OTM), has been placed in a difficult position. As virtually her first act in office, she has been asked to review a controversial proposal to acquire a wide area data network for the state's Employment Service agency (ES). The proposal was drafted primarily by Doug Bronson, ES assistant commissioner for Administrative Services. The proposal has been openly opposed by George Gordon, director of Telecommunications Services at the State Central Services Office (SCS), on the grounds that it would be wiser and more efficient to purchase a network that could be used by multiple agencies using similar equipment and operating systems and having similar geographic distribution of system nodes.

THE BASIS FOR THE EMPLOYMENT SERVICE'S REQUEST

The acquisition of a wide area data network linking field locations and the central ES office has been a long-held and elusive dream of Doug Bronson, ES assistant commissioner for Administrative Services. Over twelve years ago, Bronson was director of Data Processing Operations when ES operated as a time-sharing customer of State Central Services (SCS). Bronson had actually created a pilot system where ES offices in the capital region were connected on-line to SCS's mainframe. The experiment had failed because of the high cost of holding open telecommunications lines, a lack of demonstrated need for on-line access in the face of such high costs, and a frequent inability to gain access to SCS's mainframe (even when telecommunication lines were open) because of down time or because peak daytime usage had tied up all the ports into the time-sharing system.

Shortly thereafter, ES became one of the first agencies to establish an independent data center. Since then, ES has become such a large information user (and the cost of computing hardware has come down so fast) that it has been able to plan an orderly expansion of its hardware systems, creating an environment tailored to its needs and not subject to periods of severe undercapacity, as was the situation under previous leasing arrangements with SCS. Indeed, Bronson has risen from director of DP Operations to assistant commissioner because of his demonstrated ability to anticipate and plan for the agency's future information processing needs.

Telecommunications costs have also dropped dramatically in the past decade, and the emergence of an increasing emphasis on economic development has created a strong demand for on-line ES data. A critical link in the ES portion of the Gubernatorial Master Plan for statewide economic redevelopment calls for ES offices in the economically depressed eastern region of the state to have access to placement opportunities in the western regions where expanding financial service industries and high-tech growth firms are creating employment opportunities. Furthermore, successful implementation of this intrastate link would position the state to become involved in a soon-to-be-developed regional and national job placement network. This proposal represents an expanded view of the traditional ES mission: matching the skills of workers with available jobs. To be effective, however, virtually instant response is needed—the connection between employer and potential employee must be made while the applicant is present in the ES office.

In addition to advancing the ES mission with respect to economic redevelopment, the proposed wide area data network would help achieve a number of the agency's other strategic goals. For example, for several decades, ES has administered the Unemployment Insurance Program, Job Training programs, a Job Bank, and Youth Employment programs. It conducts safety checks and wage and hour investigations, participates in service programs for the hard-core unemployed, attempts to intervene in economically depressed areas of the state, and as mentioned above, has had an increasingly important role in economic development initiatives.

In the past decade, the department has also been called upon to participate in wage verification projects designed to ensure welfare eligibility and full payment of personal income taxes. Although it strives to carry out these many responsibilities, often with inadequate and even declining resources, the department has been criticized for wide variations in service quality across the state and for inconsistent attention to one or another of its mandates. Its critics especially like to call attention to those areas in which the state falls below the national average—a sensitive spot with the governor.

Its operating budget has traditionally come mostly from federal sources, and recent federal cutbacks have severely undermined its ability to serve so many purposes. The prospects for additional federal support in the near future are dim, as are hopes for larger state appropriations to fill the void.

With declining financial support, unabated demand for its traditional services, and a growing list of new mandates, Bronson has begun to stress ES's information resources as a crucial ingredient in its drive to continually "do more with less." Better availability and expanded use of existing information are now seen as critical if ES is to handle so many responsibilities without an increase in staff or federal or state dollars.

In the past year, a carefully conducted management survey, crafted by Bronson's staff, has shown that better program management and more efficient use of both staff and money will result from an immediate investment in a wide area data network. Important agencywide benefits are expected, including significant improvements in reporting from the ninety-five district offices to the central office; a streamlined method of disseminating uniform and up-to-the-minute instructions or information to the field; a way of furthering ES's economic development mission by making resource information (job openings, skills inventories, training slots, etc.) easily accessible among district offices; and providing desperately needed opportunities for field office staff to communicate and learn from one another without the expense and time commitment of physically traveling around the state.

The survey called for investment in a network that would connect the ninety-five ES field offices, the central office, and a dozen selected program operators around the state. This investment was endorsed by the commissioner, the chairman of the Assembly Labor Committee, and the AFL–CIO and other major labor organizations. The proposal calls for T1 microwave links between the major offices, and 9,600 bps (bits per second) leased lines connecting smaller offices.

The cost-benefit analysis shows that clear advantages can be gained in improved service with direct positive effects on the governor's economic development goals. Although the network would entail both a start-up cost and annual charges, the cost of the technology is declining while the cost of the staff positions it would obviate continues to rise. Furthermore, although the department's existing management information systems could stand improvement, the proposed network will more than triple the value of the Department of Labor's (DOL's) current information resources by eliminating the need to duplicate, wait for, or do without information that already exists somewhere in the system. No other single improvement could be more useful in responding effectively to the many external demands it serves. Moreover, a well-planned, smoothly operating network will greatly improve the internal functioning of the department, resulting in administrative savings (after full installation) of several million dollars per year.

STATE CENTRAL SERVICES' POSITION ON SHARED NETWORKS

State Central Services was among the first of the larger state agencies to acquire and operate a data center. Serving the needs of most of the smaller agencies through a time-sharing system, SCS maintained a statewide data network to support its users. Recently, SCS has purchased and installed on behalf of the state an upgraded voice network with access to all local dialing directories; Washington, D.C.; and several other major metropolitan centers.

Most recently, George Gordon, director of Telecommunications Services within SCS, has been working on a project to define and set standards for multiagency statewide information transmission networks. A few networks are already in operation for specific purposes (e.g., the state lottery, the welfare department), and several other agencies have begun to consider individualized networks to support their own programs. As a result of more than half a dozen agency budget requests for feasibility and management studies several years ago, the State Budget Office (SBO) directed SCS to conduct a statewide study and to make recommendations regarding a standardized approach to telecommunications for state agency operations. The SCS report to the governor is in draft form and will soon be released. The report will argue strenuously that any new network should be a steppingstone to statewide service, providing at a minimum shared capacity for several agencies that have similar or related needs. The report contains arguments for uniformity (where applicable), economies of scale, central service points, streamlined contract administration—all leading to increased efficiency. Moreover, a broadly conceived general purpose network would offer much greater flexibility in responding to future needs, making the state's investment a sound one well beyond the near-term demands of existing programs.

When Gordon became aware of the imminent request from ES for authority and funding for its own network, he drafted a memo to SBO requesting that the ES proposal be reviewed within a broader framework. Gordon strongly urged that the request be denied in favor of a coordinated response that could include the needs of at least three other, smaller agencies that need telecommunications support but could never hope to acquire it individually: the Department for the Aging, the Division for Juvenile Justice, and the Parole Service (all of which could make use of the unused trunk-line capacity of the proposed ES network and, additionally, could be customers of ES data for the employment needs of their own clientele). Furthermore, the Department of Family and Children's Services (DFCS) is also interested in its own network. Joining it with an ES–DOA–DJJ–PS network would offer several advantages: It is large enough to contribute substantially to covering the cost, and it could also use ES employment data to aid its clients in achieving self-sufficiency—one service area in which ES has taken considerable criticism.

Proved technology would allow these agencies to share a network. ES's mainframes are run under IBM's VM operating system and can run RSCS (Remote Spooling and Communications Subsystem). Emulation software for the hardware used by the other agencies is available for their machines and has been proved by use on BITNET, an academic computing network. (The technology of networks is moving at so rapid a pace, however, that it will soon become possible to provide a greater variety of services to users regardless of equipment manufacture.) The T1 links have ample capacity to handle the traffic of all the agencies and, in fact, are only marginally cost-justified on the basis of ES usage alone. Ninety percent of the non–ES office locations are in county office buildings, all of which also house an ES field office.

POSITIONS OF THE SEVERAL AGENCIES BEING "COORDINATED"

While the notion of a shared data network is technically feasible—indeed, it has some dramatic advantages in economy of scale and efficiency as measured in a static cost-benefit study—some hidden costs as well as organizational and political questions must be taken into account. For example, who should "own" and have control over the design, operation, and future expansion of the network? Should this be under the control of ES or SCS? Should the use of the network be voluntary or should the greater efficiencies be mandated by the state? The state agencies being drawn into this proposal in a quest for greater efficiency have positions of their own.

The Division of Juvenile Justice and the Parole Service have recently become increasingly heavy users of telecommunications services. However, because of their constant interaction with many other law enforcement agencies, and because of differences in their operations in the metropolitan versus the more rural areas, their use of telecommunications facilities has been highly uneven across various geographic regions of the state. At this time, an ad hoc arrangement of leased lines connects several key "nodes" of their systems (primarily within the metropolitan region). Other service points maintain leased dial-in capabilities and do not attempt to remain connected to any sort of a centralized system on an "on-line" basis.

However, the cost of this arrangement has become expensive enough that Juvenile Justice and Parole have independently initiated a study of the feasibility of leasing a statewide data network to give their operations into an integrated information environment. The two agencies anticipate they will need primarily on-line daytime capability, thereby competing with ES's need for peak-time transmission capabilities. Furthermore, they expect that as more and more of their regional facilities come on-line, they will have a growing demand for peak network capacity. They are concerned that the ES or SCS network be designed in a way that anticipates their future needs for peak network capacity.

The Department for the Aging does not at present have significant on-line data needs. From time to time, large files are transferred from one point in the state to another. These data transfers could be accomplished at off-peak times. In fact, Aging does not feel any particular need at this time to participate in any sort of statewide data network. From a cost point of view, they would resist any attempt to make them "own" a piece of any network, since they do not believe they have the traffic necessary to support such an investment. However, if SCS could provide reliable services at costs less than what are commercially available, they would be happy to purchase services on an "as needed" basis from a state agency rather than from a private vendor.

The Department of Family and Children's Services is opposed in principle to being placed in any arrangement with ES or SCS that will bind them to any long-range financial obligations. Their past experiences with "shared" statewide services have not been good. Typically, large statewide systems have been designed to meet the needs of the largest users with smaller and even moderately sized users such as DFCS being added on as an afterthought. They end up contributing to the support of a network designed to serve large agencies with few services tailored to their own needs. They have few needs at this point and, in any case, prefer to purchase services from private vendors who will be more likely to provide custom services.

In informal discussions, the four involved agencies seem to have quite different approaches as to how to share the costs of a unified system. Juvenile Justice and Parole have a clear preference for staking out a claim for a fixed share of peak capacity. They would be willing to pay for the fixed costs of their own feeder lines plus marginal costs associated with use of shared trunk lines. The real advantage to them in this proposal is that they can lease trunk capacity at marginal rather than average cost, as would be the situation from a private vendor. However, since they would be competing with ES for peak capacity, both Juvenile Justice and Parole need to have a definitive say in network design.

Aging, on the other hand, would prefer not to buy a portion of peak capacity. It would rather purchase capacity on some sort of usage charge, reserving the right to transmit data off peak or at peak with a charge differential. That is, they see no need to "own" a piece of a network for on-line transmission purposes. Rather, they would purchase services on an episodic basis. DFCS would like no part whatsoever in the whole project, preferring to pay the additional cost of a private vendor for the additional benefit of tailor-made services.

All the smaller agencies are concerned about who will control the data network, how responsive the network will be to their needs, and how the pricing structure for the shared capacity will be handled. As sketched above, they have different preferences about pricing. As an immediate reaction, they are all suspicious of "being coordinated" by any control agency—SCS is not exempt from this suspicion. However, they are not sure that leased services from ES would be any better.

THE EMERGING ROLE OF THE OFFICE OF TECHNOLOGY MANAGEMENT (OTM)

Sensing that some larger issues of statewide information policy were being discussed within the context of the ES data network proposal, SBO has requested that the whole proposal be reviewed by the Office of Technology Management (OTM). Hence, Helen Frye, the newly appointed director of OTM, has been given the delicate task of sorting out the various interests of SCS, ES, and the four smaller agencies. She has to make a recommendation to SBO concerning the ES request for approval to go to bid on a data network (in light of the dissenting opinion drafted by Gordon at SCS).

Frye recognizes that this assignment may be a very important one because it involves the crucial question of centralization versus decentralization in state-level decision making. The state had unsuccessfully attempted twice in the past to centralize the information technology decision-making process. In both cases, a special unit was given responsibility for reviewing the purchase of large system acquisitions, especially hardware and expensive software systems. Both attempts, one within SBO and one within SCS, were subsequently dismantled as unworkable. In addressing the request from SBO, Frye realizes that she must tread a thin line between the best interests of the state as a whole and the interests of individual agencies. Underlying this process, of course, is the long-run survival of her own newly created organization.

The fact is that OTM was born out of controversy. Several years ago, one of the Big Eight accounting firms had been under contract to redesign the state's motor vehicle registration system to provide a more modern and usable database. The project had been close to a complete disaster. Both title transfer and traffic ticket tracking subsystems had been virtually inoperable for periods of several months. Slow response times during the registration process had caused long lines at DMV offices where motorists were renewing their licenses or registering their vehicles. A public outcry had resulted in a gubernatorial commission to investigate state policy on information systems.

Fortunately, an interagency association of data processing professionals who had been meeting informally for several years had been drawn into the process. As a result, OTM was designed as a peer review office that would provide support and assistance rather than mandate statewide policy. OTM's mission is to foster subcabinet-level forums for coordinating the state's data needs around specific functional areas such as Corrections and services to children; to convene a group to work toward a standard data dictionary for key central functions such as payroll, accounting, and personnel; to provide a forum for the exchange of information and views on software, hardware, and policy matters; and to provide advice and encourage coordination on major purchases of technology.

All along, there had been fear that OTM would emerge as a centralized control agency rather than develop as a center to assist data users and producers in their attempts to perform a difficult job. Frye was well aware that backlash from key groups could create a difficult, if not fatal, situation for her fledgling office. She was conscious of all these factors as she sat down to plan her response to SBO's request.

THE ASSIGNMENT

1. What should Frye do? She must make a recommendation that is both technically competent and politically sensitive. Furthermore, she must also consider the nascent role of her own organization. How should she respond? What are the pros and cons of decentralized and centralized services? How can she measure the trade-offs between responsiveness and comprehensiveness, specificity and economies of scale, agency-level and state-level control?

2. Who is in charge here? That is, does the state have adequate policy mechanisms for dealing with issues like these? This request has involved ES, SBO, SCS, and four smaller state agencies. Can the state ever do its business if so many actors become involved in each decision? Should there be, instead, a clear locus of responsibility for making decisions that potentially involve several agencies?

Further Reflections

1. A difficult aspect of Helen Frye's decision is that it cannot be neatly contained within a single way of looking at the problem. To make her recommendations to the State Budget Office, Frye must balance considerations of the technology itself (both present state and likely future trends), cost considerations, organizational considerations (both interorganizational and intraorganizational), and ultimately political considerations as well. Chapter 2 provides a theoretical look at the overall field of government information management using just these four theoretical lenses. Reread Chapter 2.

As a staff assistant to Frye, you have been asked to analyze her decision from the four points of view of technology, cost, organizational dynamics, and political considerations. Within each analysis, you have been asked to detail the important factors that will impinge on her decision. Using that frame of analysis, make a specific recommendation concerning what she should do. In a concluding section, attempt to resolve any inconsistencies between the recommendations that emerge from the four theoretical perspectives taken one at a time. If Frye needs more information in order to make a wise decision, specify what information she needs and why it will be important.

2. Chapter 4, "Information as a Public Resource," discusses the issue of information resource sharing in some detail. In that chapter, six topics are identified as contributing to information resource-sharing problems—hardware, telecommunications, software, intraorganizational processes, interorganizational processes, and finally technical issues such as the standardization of data dictionaries.

Review this case in terms of each of these six topic areas. For each topic, sketch those particular facts of the case that make this choice difficult. Which of the six topics explains most of the interesting dimensions of this problem? Which of the six issue areas offers the greatest hope of a solution for Frye?

Draft a brief memo to Frye that analyzes her decision from the point of view of each of the six topics.

CASE STUDY 4

REORGANIZATION OF THE INFORMATION FUNCTIONS AT STATE UNIVERSITY— WILMINGTON[1]

This case presents a series of organizational and operations issues confronting the president of a major university within a state university system. The case situation has developed over a number of years, culminating in the need for an organizational realignment of the university's information functions and related personnel changes. Although the kinds of issues and actors depicted here can be found on many real campuses, the characters and State University—Wilmington itself are fictional.

The State University at Wilmington (SU–Wilmington) is one of five major university centers of the SU system. It has a research-oriented faculty with a strong presence in both the physical and social sciences. SU–Wilmington has a student enrollment of seventeen thousand including forty-five hundred graduate students. The Wilmington campus is located in the central region of the state.

For the past ten years, the information needs of the university have been met by a strong and effective director of the computing center, Dr. Laura Thompson. As with most other campuses in the United States, computing at Wilmington has been hit by a number of cross-cutting forces

[1]An earlier version of this case appeared as "Reorganization of the Information Functions at SUNY–Wilmington," *New York Case Studies in Public Management—ER023*. Albany, NY: Rockefeller Institute of Government, 1987.

including the proliferation of stand-alone computing centers, an exploding number of microcomputers, and a host of attendant management and policy problems. By every account on campus, Dr. Thompson has charted an effective course through these stormy waters. Unfortunately for Wilmington, she has just accepted a position (at double her current salary) as director of Marketing to the Academic Sector for a major computer corporation.

The president of the university has decided not to replace Thompson with another director of the computing center. Instead, that title will be upgraded to something like chief officer for Information Services. The president has decided this new position will encompass responsibilities for the computer center but will also entail broader responsibilities as chief information officer for the entire campus. The president is familiar with the concepts of information resource managers, chief information officers, and information resource centers and wants to reorganize around these concepts.

THE EXTERNAL INFORMATION ENVIRONMENT
OF SU-WILMINGTON

The information environment of SU–Wilmington is currently dominated by four important external factors. First, for at least the past decade, the State Budget Office (SBO) has been frustrated by the apparent inability of SU's central administration and the constituent campuses to provide uniform and coherent administrative information. For example, the student records systems in each of the five major university centers run in different hardware and software environments. These incompatibilities across the various campuses complicate the control function for SU Central, SBO, the State Auditor General, and others.

Recently, the chancellor of the statewide SU system has appointed a vice-chancellor for Information Services. Working with SBO and the auditor general, the vice-chancellor has been negotiating the purchase of a standard hardware and software environment for all the university centers in the SU system. According to rumor, it will be an IBM environment, with a software system tailored to the needs of SU Central. In part, the president of SU–Wilmington is interested in elevating the director of the computing center to a chief information officer because of the need to deal with this new SU-wide office.

A second trend is a decline in "soft dollars" available to support the computing center on campus. This has happened for two reasons. First, Wilmington is selling less and less time on its mainframe to local and state government agencies. These organizations are now increasingly acquiring their own computing facilities. Second, on-campus researchers with soft-money support are also acquiring their own specialized computing facilities.

Only those users who need very large memory or very high processing capacity continue to provide soft-dollar support for the computing center. With the loss of these external funds, and only limited state dollars available for this purpose, there is some question as to whether a first-rate general purpose computing center can survive on campus.

A third external factor revolves around a recent decision to purchase a new digital switch for the SU–Wilmington telephone system. Although its large Centrex system functions well, future cost considerations indicate the university should purchase its own phones. Preliminary estimates show that the full cost of the purchase could be recovered in less than four years. The purchase of a telephone system raises the very real possibility of integrating voice and data communications across the campus. At present, however, data communications are handled out of the computing center, reporting to the vice president for Research, and voice communications are handled within the Office for Telephone Systems, reporting to the vice president for Business and Finance.

Finally, like all computing centers everywhere, the center at Wilmington is being buffeted by the increasingly rapid shifts in available hardware and software. Minicomputers and microcomputers are proliferating with several specialized computing centers and six specialized microcomputing labs already in existence. These changes demand that Wilmington take a broader look at its information technology needs.

THE INTERNAL INFORMATION ENVIRONMENT OF SU-WILMINGTON

The basic organizational framework for SU–Wilmington was laid in the late 1960s when the state university system was consolidated following a period of rapid expansion. Since then, important information processing functions have appeared in many locations across campus. Every administrative office is supported by word processing of some sort, more and more of the classes are moving to computer-based instruction, and increasingly sophisticated administrative systems are under development. However, the organization of the university does not reflect these dramatic changes.

The first SU–Wilmington organization chart (Figure SU.1) shows the configuration of the important organizations on campus involved with major information processing systems. These units are spread across the five vice presidential areas—academic affairs, research, community affairs, student affairs, and business and finance. Appendix A summarizes the major information-related functions performed on campus within each organizational unit. When Appendix A is cross-indexed with the first Wilmington organization chart it becomes obvious that the information function is

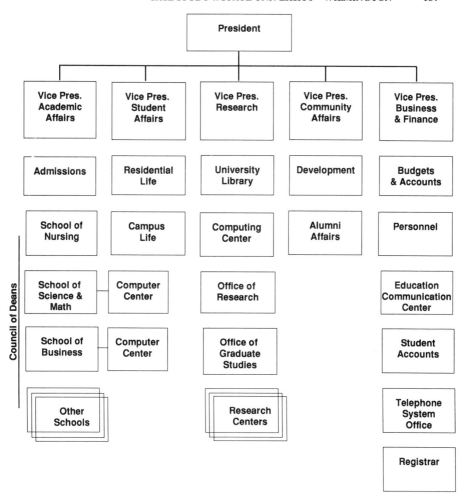

Figure SU.1   Organizational Structure and Major Functions of the State University at Wilmington

spread across the entire campus, with some important functions "falling between the cracks" of the major vice presidential areas.

However, when one looks beyond a mere listing of functions by organizational units, some clear patterns emerge. An important one is the split between academic and administrative computing. Academic computing supports the research and teaching needs of faculty and students. In fulfilling this function, the university must respond to the needs of nearly one thousand faculty and staff as well as its seventeen thousand students. Those demands are broad and diverse, with every faculty member having some specialized need that he or she believes is the most important thing on the entire campus.

On the other hand, the university itself is a large and complex administrative machine, maintaining records on thousands of students and alumni and managing the expenditure of millions of state-appropriated as well as "soft" research dollars.

Both academicians and administrators are supported by some common core functions such as the telecommunications office within the computing center and the telecommunications center within the Office for Telephone Systems.

In addition to the broad functional split between academic and administrative computing, several political factors are germane to the computing environment on campus. Four groups are especially important. The Council of Deans views computing primarily as an academic resource. This is a powerful policy-making group that views the entire university from an academic point of view. However, even this group does not have a uniform position on computing. For example, the deans of Education, Public Affairs, Social Sciences, Law, and Nursing would like to see the academic computing budget subdivided and allocated on a school-by-school basis. They believe that if they could individually control a portion of the overall computing budget, then they could combine these state funds with soft research funds to create their own computing facilities—facilities that would be more responsive to the needs of their own faculty and students. On the other hand, the deans of Business, Science and Mathematics, and Humanities oppose this move. Not only Business but Science and Math already have their own facilities and look to the central computing center to serve the needs of their big "number crunchers." These units realize that if the central resource were carved up, a large mainframe capability would probably be lost. Humanities simply realizes that it could never mount its own computer center and so supports the continuation of a universitywide resource.

The university's Policy Committee (consisting of the president, his immediate staff, and the vice presidents) constitutes the most influential political body on campus. However, even this group is split in its approach to computing. All the vice presidents realize the need for a strong centralized administrative system (being good administrators themselves). However, the vice presidents for Academic Affairs and Research form a powerful block (over 80 percent of the university's employees report through these two) that protects the interests of academic computing. Since the computing center reports through the V.P. for Research, some people on campus believe the center is too heavily oriented toward academic comput'·g. Time just never seems to be allocated to the development of much-needed administrative systems.

The Administrative Users Group, consisting of the registrar, university accountant, director of admissions, and other administrative officers, is a powerful force that defines the agenda for administrative computing on campus. While this group has no formal power (it is an informal advisory group), most people recognize that it really calls the shots with respect to administrative computing at Wilmington.

Finally, the computing center's Advisory Committee is formally charged with representing faculty and staff opinion in the development of computing and information policy on campus. It consists of three subcommittees—on instruction, research, and administrative computing—but overall has played a more or less "rubber stamp" role under Laura Thompson's leadership. Issues rarely boil up, but when they do, the presence of the three differing perspectives effectively prevents any one point of view from winning out. Given a chronic stalemate among the sub-committees, Dr. Thompson has been free to do as she thinks best. Under the surface, however, faculty members of the instruction and research subcommittees privately complain that the administrative computing subcommittee overlaps too much with the Administrative Users Group. Academic users feel that this informal cabal is tilting the overall time and performance of the computing center in favor of administrative support at the expense of academic needs.

In addition to these overall patterns in the organization and politics of information on campus, several minor themes contribute to an even richer and more complex organizational picture. For example, the library maintains its own circulation and cataloging system. The Educational Communications Center maintains a video communications capability (with satellite hookups) throughout the campus, as well as a facility that services microcomputers (hence the university provides its own service contracts on most micros). An administrative computing network is in place to support word processing and electronic mail, and the computer center maintains a network linking over three hundred "hardwired" terminals across the campus. The intricacies of how these functions have been split across existing organizational lines are only hinted at in Appendix A.

THE SITUATION WITHIN THE COMPUTING CENTER

Laura Thompson's ability to hold the computing center together has been regarded as nothing less than a triumph of personal leadership. Many people believe that the situation in the center is ready to shake apart at any moment and that she has personally been holding it together.

The organization chart of the computing center (Figure SU.2) shows that the total staff of fifty-one is divided among four units—Academic Services, Administrative Computing, Systems Development, and Operations. Each unit is headed by an assistant director. The center organization chart also details the major functions of these units. Appendix A illustrates more clearly why the staff within the computing center often find themselves in a

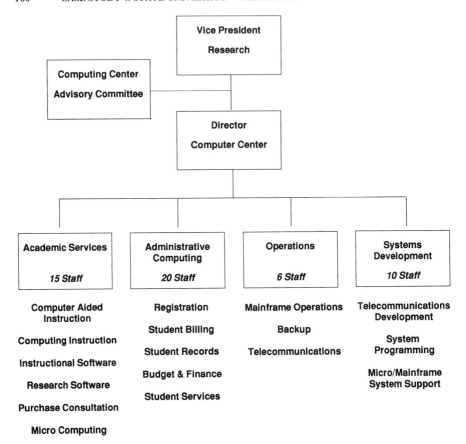

Figure SU.2   Organizational Structure and Major Functions of the State University at Wilmington Computing Center

difficult position. It shows that while many of the computing and informa-tion services on campus are delivered through the computing center, no less than seventeen units are involved in the overall hardware system. It is not surprising that staff in the computing center feel a clear need to get on top of this ill-defined campuswide computing environment.

In general, the staff of the center feel overwhelmed. While they are charged with overall responsibility for computing on the campus as a whole, the information islands and small decentralized centers are increasingly popping up everywhere. While academic and administrative users are eager to bring these labs and small centers into existence, they always seem to come back to the center's staff when they need support and assistance. Hence, the computing center is being drawn into a flurry of small projects not of its own design. Whenever a problem occurs, it seems the center is held responsible, even if the offending site had been developed without the consultation of center staff.

Both academic and administrative users believe they should control all the time of the center staff. Neither group seems to understand that staff time is limited and that all their effort cannot be allocated to one project or functional area.

Furthermore, resources are being siphoned away from the center to support other information initiatives on campus. For example, several schools and research centers have recently set up their own specialized computer centers. The net effect has been the creation of duplicate operating staffs, and diversion of needed resources from the task of providing a truly fine mainframe computing resource. If present trends continue, the university will have a series of small centers and labs with virtually no real mainframe computing power.

Relative to other centers in similar universities, the computing center's budget is shrinking and its salary scales are no longer competitive. The center is becoming a training ground for junior personnel who learn their craft in the university's rich computing environment and soon move on to better-paying jobs, often in private colleges and universities or corporations.

THE ASSIGNMENT

1. As the president's special assistant for Academic Planning, you are to prepare a draft document that redefines the former position of director of the computing center. This redefinition will necessarily include a reorganization of the information functions on campus. The report will be prepared in preliminary draft form and will be reviewed by the University Policy Council, the Council of Deans, the Administrative Computing Users Group, and the computer center's Advisory Committee.

As a minimum, your report should contain

—A title for the new position.
—A job description.
—An organization chart detailing the relationships between this new position and the units within the present computing center, including the several informal advisory and users groups.
—A discussion of any sensitive or difficult reporting and organizational arrangements that might not be apparent from the charts you have presented above. Discuss how, if at all, functional responsibilities will be shifted or reassigned. Justify and explain the major changes you are proposing.

2. For the eyes of the president only, draft a memo predicting the reaction of four groups to the proposal outlined in Assignment 1 above:

—The computing center staff

—The deans and the heads of schools
—The specific computer centers and labs
—The vice presidents

In each case, predict their reactions to the proposal and suggest to the president how he should handle their likely objections.

Further Reflections

1. One problem on the Wilmington campus is that the computing environment is a mixture of many different subenvironments. For example, administrative computing (issuing paychecks, registration for classes, and so on) must be highly routinized and efficient. On the other hand, computing to support research must be highly flexible and constantly changing. Chapter 3, "Technology, Organizations, and People," lays out four different ideal type organizations and discusses how the computing needs of each differ—the rational goal, internal process, human resources, and open systems models. Read that chapter.

> a. Review Appendix A and classify each unit at Wilmington into the organizational model that best describes its functioning. What problems did you have in making this classification?
>
> b. Some organizational theorists would argue that work units with similar functions should be grouped together during a reorganization. Use the classification that you have developed in section *a* above to examine how subunits broadly related to information management should be reorganized on campus. Cast this analysis in the form of an organization chart and accompanying memo to the president.

2. The president has taken your advice and has now appointed a new university officer with broad responsibilities for information management and policy on campus. The time has come to begin developing a campuswide information policy statement. Chapter 4, "Information as a Public Resource," suggests a number of areas where information policy, especially in units that serve the public, must be developed. Topics include maintaining data quality, archives and preservation; sharing information across units and providing for the physical security of systems.

As a newcomer to the campus, the newly appointed chief information officer is seeking your advice on what areas need to be reviewed for possible policy development. After reading Chapter 4 carefully, draft a memo to the newly appointed chief information officer detailing what campuswide issues you believe should receive his attention in his upcoming policy development exercises.

Appendix A

Major Information Resource Functions – SU Wilmington

Unit	Function
Vice President for Academic Affairs	
Deans, Schools, Departments	- Maintain Instructional Software - Maintain Research Software - Computer-aided Instruction - Maintain 6 Microlabs (150 machines) - Academic Word Processing - School-specific Computer Centers
Admissions	- Undergraduate Admissions File - Graduate Admissions File
Vice President for Research	
University Library	- Automated Catalog & Circulation System for 1.5 million volumes - Automated Inter-Library Loan System - On-line Database Search Capabilities
Director Computing Center	- (see Figure SU.2)
Office for Research	- Maintain Accounts on $28 million in Funded Research
Director of Research Center	- Maintain Research Software - Maintain Special Computing Centers (e.g., Social Science Research, Geological Research Center)
Graduate Studies	- Graduate Admissions - Graduate Student Files
Vice President for Community Affairs	
Development Office	- Maintain Accounts on University Endowment ($8.5 million) - Maintain Development Databases
Alumni Affairs	- Maintain Alumni Database

SU Wilmington Information Resource Functions, continued

Unit	Function
Vice President for Business & Finance	
Registrar	- Graduate Student Transcripts - Scheduling of Classes - Maintain Student Records - Degree Clearance
Budget and Accounting	- Maintain Expenditure Records on All State Appropriated Funds - Accounting on all grant dollars
Personnel	- Maintain Personnel Database - Annual Leave and Sick Leave - Process Appointments (Faculty, Professional, Graduate Student)
Phones	- Maintain University Phones - Provide Student Dorm Phone Service
Student Accounts	- Tuition Billing and Collection - Process Financial Aid Applications
Educational Communication Center	- Maintain Video Connection on Campus - Maintain Video Satellite Connections
Vice President for Student Affairs	
Residential Life	- Dormitory Scheduling and Billing
Campus Life	- Maintain Accounts for Student Association - Schedule Campus Activity Spaces

CASE STUDY 5

DISASTER STRIKES THE HAZARD COUNTY WELFARE DEPARTMENT

by John Peter Seagle

The loss of a computer site or the data it contains can be disastrous for any organization. In the public sector, such a loss can be a catastrophe for members of the public who depend on government services that cannot be obtained from any other source. The situation portrayed in this case could occur in any political jurisdiction involved in public welfare programs. The characters and counties depicted here, however, are fictional.

At three A.M. on February 6, Mike McGraw, director of Data Processing for Hazard County, received a call from the local fire chief. The county computer center, a light steel building attached to the historic county hall, had collapsed after an intense fire. Assured no one was hurt, McGraw rushed downtown and immediately saw the extent of the disaster—nothing was salvageable. Apparently, an underground gas line had ruptured, causing an explosion and fire. Unfortunately, a gas detector had not been installed—or even required by the fire code.

The center had served a score of county organizations. When McGraw was appointed County Data Processing director three years ago, he had insisted that his customer agencies and the county executive agree on a set of priorities for the use of its computing resources. He knew the list by heart. As he began to make phone calls, the first name on his list was Shirley Wilson, the County Social Services director.

The Hazard County Computer Center had been built nearly six years ago. The growing demand for data processing support and the installation of the county's portion of the new statewide Social Welfare System (SWS) had combined to offer a major opportunity to upgrade and reorganize the entire Data Processing Department. Although making good use of newly available state funds also meant appropriating county funds as well, the county legislature had supported the entire effort. After all, even though there were more than twenty county agencies needing the services of the center, fully half of its business came from the Social Services Department.

A dedicated communication line had connected the Hazard County computer to the main computers at the State Welfare Department (SWD), and data were transmitted between these machines at a rate of 9,600 baud, or approximately 1,000 characters per second. On a normal day, some functions could be handled on-line; others were batch updated overnight and on weekends. The county center had operated two shifts, seven days a week, while the state data center operated around the clock every day of the year. The state's system maintained all information and processed all transactions related to eligibility for social welfare programs. The county retained all data and responsibility for actually issuing benefits to eligible individuals within its borders; none of these financial transactions was recorded in the state system.

THE EFFECT ON THE COUNTY SOCIAL SERVICES DEPARTMENT

When the call from McGraw ended, Wilson's thoughts raced ahead to the situation she would face starting at nine A.M. when people who depended on county welfare programs would start arriving at the office. Many important programs depended on the computer center: issuing of Medicaid ID cards, paying Medicaid bills, tracking cases under appeal, reporting cases of child abuse, making child support payments, tracking client employment and earnings, and preparing routine reports.

Her most immediate concerns, of course, were for those needing Food Stamps and public assistance checks. All other services could be temporarily delayed or temporarily handled without computer support. People's daily lives, sometimes their very ability to eat and remain housed from one day to the next, however, depended on cash and food benefits being issued on time and in the correct amounts. The regular bimonthly issuance of benefits to six thousand ongoing recipients in both programs had occurred at the end of last week. For the next few days, only new cases and emergency situations would need immediate service—something that could be handled manually. However, getting out the next regular payments depended critically on equipment and automated data resources housed, until tonight, at the Hazard County Computer Center. Checks and Food Stamp authorizations were prepared, printed, and reconciled on McGraw's equipment. Thanks to the fire, the county had lost not only that equipment but also the information and the paper forms for preparing these documents manually. Even if the data and forms had been available, however, the caseload was too large, the time too short, and the staff's memory of the old manual procedures too dim to meet the next issuance date. There had to be an automated solution.

In fact, the idea of using the old manual system for backup had long since been abandoned. A neighboring county, Crane, had agreed with Hazard to form a mutual backup for county computing, and this arrangement had worked well last winter when Hazard had a thirty-six-hour power outage due to a heavy, wet snow. The snow fell on Thursday evening, and although the telephone traffic into the Social Services Department was enormous, few clients were able to get to the county offices for other than emergency services and those situations were handled "off-line" until the computer could be updated. By working through the following weekend, Crane County was able to handle the processing for both jurisdictions. Documents used by the two counties had the same format, so no changes in the printing control tapes were needed. Numbered continuous forms for the Hazard County checks were released from the Hazard computer room and taken to the Crane County Office Building for printing. (If only this new problem were so easy to handle.)

There were other reasons for not building a manual backup system. Most of the critical records for the county's welfare programs are kept by the State Welfare Department (SWD) in the statewide eligibility master file. Up-to-date records are kept for each client and show all actions taken, status changes, and case transaction history. Moreover, Wilson, McGraw, and the current county executive were all satisfied with the high level of security and reliability in the statewide system, which had now been in operation for more than five years. Although some of the county social services staff had resisted (even resigned, retired or transferred rather than deal with "The Computer"), most had accepted the system within a few months. Even the most stalwart of the employees had finally stopped keeping their own records or making a printout at every opportunity. Once they had become satisfied that the system worked properly, knew its arithmetic, and had a good memory, they all came to rely on it. In fact, very few, if any, of the staff could determine eligibility or calculate a benefit without it. As welfare programs had become even more complex, the computer system had become more than an aid—it was an indispensable partner.

The county had found the state central file difficult to use for statistical and internal reporting purposes, however, and so had made it a practice to periodically "take a snapshot" of both the state eligibility records and their own payment files for local use. This had also seemed a good idea in the highly unlikely event that the state system were destroyed—with some difficulty, the county's database could be reconstructed.

Perhaps, working with last month's "snapshot" (the most recent available) plus the state's database, a reasonably accurate payment file could be constructed. Wilson called the SWD commissioner to report the disaster and ask for assistance.

THE STATE WELFARE DEPARTMENT REACTION

Back at the state capital, Will DeAngelo, the director of Computer Center Operations for the State Welfare Department, met with his boss, Roberta Clemson, the deputy commissioner for Information Systems. The executive assistant to the commissioner and several agency program executives were also with them to assess the situation in Hazard County and make recommendations for state assistance. Situations of this kind, but not of this severity, had occurred often enough in the past that the technicians in the group knew how to react. Within the day, arrangements had been made (in conjunction with Hazard, Crane, and adjoining Meriden counties; the document and equipment vendors; a temporary service firm; and the SWD) to resume skeleton operations in the basement of the civic center, to issue the next benefits on time but in the amounts indicated by the state's central eligibility file (payments that would be correct for most but would probably fail an audit), and to handle resulting errors and emergencies by operating special evening and weekend hours for several weeks. In the meantime, the site would be reconstructed. Normal operations were projected to resume in 120 days.

Once the group had agreed upon a plan of action and put it into motion, DeAngelo returned to the nagging situation he and Clemson had been struggling with for more than two years. Both were very security conscious and had instituted a number of measures that successfully thwarted unauthorized access to the agency's systems and provided for immediate backup in the event of unexpected loss of power, equipment, or staff. The computer center had the latest state-of-the-art fire protection system and was continuously monitored for abnormal environmental conditions. The staff were well trained and professional. As technicians, DeAngelo and Clemson had done all they could to secure the department's information resources, both data and equipment, against irretrievable loss or unauthorized use. Yet both were uneasy in the face of the Hazard County experience.

They had tried unsuccessfully in the past to get the attention and interest of the commissioner, their "customers" inside the agency, and the State Budget Office (SBO). None had expressed much interest in planning for an information-based disaster—they had enough immediate, real problems to face and did not have the time, staff, or inclination to invent hypothetical catastrophes. Moreover, in their collective experience, the odds of a major disaster were nil—none of them had experienced one firsthand and, in truth, none was likely to. The cost of maintaining some kinds of backup capability was simply beyond reason when there were so many competing demands for state dollars.

Surprisingly, even their own technical staff showed little interest in the subject. When faced with a typical down-time situation, for example, their desire to "fix it" almost always had to be countermanded by DeAngelo with an order to switch to the backup system first. They had so much of themselves invested in the system that they simply couldn't admit that problems might not be remedied in only minutes.

Although the Hazard County loss was regrettable, it did offer a positive opportunity: It had been of a large enough magnitude that the commissioner and the program deputies had to become involved in the recovery process. Their attention had been focused on the issue. How could that attention be sustained and broadened to include acknowledgment that SWD itself might one day face such a situation?

THE PROGRAM MANAGER'S VIEW

John Ross, SWD deputy commissioner for Assistance Payments, had been in the disaster recovery meeting with DeAngelo and Clemson. New to the job, he had been startled by the extent of the loss and then impressed by the quick and decisive way Clemson had led the group through the assessment process and put the recovery plan into action.

The Assistance Payments Division was responsible for supervising the administration of public assistance and Food Stamps in all of the state's fifty-nine counties. Ross quickly realized that the Hazard County situation could have happened anywhere, including counties whose caseloads were severalfold larger. It was obvious why Clemson and DeAngelo had urged the group to consider the consequences of a state-level loss.

DeAngelo had explained the existing protections and recovery plans, noting carefully some of the questions that remained unanswered: Which operations would be curtailed or shut down if less than 100 percent capability were available? What would happen if the disaster knocked out the vendor-owned telecommunications lines rather than the agency's own site or equipment? No backup or recovery planning had ever been discussed regarding the hundreds of microcomputers in the agency, each with its own databases and applications. Emergency operations needed to be rehearsed, but that meant simulating a major loss and, however briefly, reducing ongoing support and operations to do it. There had never been a "convenient" time to do that.

As Ross contemplated these things, he began to see how important the subject was to his division as well as to every other sector of the agency. He decided to bring it up with his own staff at their regular Tuesday staff meeting. Unfortunately, before that meeting occurred he was called upon to handle an irate legislative committee and a highly critical federal audit of the state's Food Stamp Program. He also faced a major setback in the state's highest court requiring a class action settlement involving retroactive benefits to twelve thousand difficult-to-identify former recipients. As a result, he revised the staff meeting agenda, pushing off the disaster recovery discussion until next month.

THE VIEW FROM THE STATE BUDGET OFFICE

Assistant Budget director Ray Stack sat at his desk at the State Budget Office (SBO). He had just concluded a phone conversation with the head of SBO's Human Services Unit. The topic was becoming a familiar one. Two years ago it had been raised several times. Last year at least six agencies had made the same inquiries. This last call brought this year's total to nine. All were brought up informally, but none were short on merit. The details varied, but the central idea was always the same—could the agency expect any support for a major budget request to help ensure continuation of its information processing operations in the event of a disaster? In each case, the agency felt it had exhausted its internal resources and, despite the employment of every reasonably priced option, still felt unprotected. Drafts of requests for "hot" backup sites had crossed his desk, each priced in seven figures annually. Stack agreed with much of what he had heard but was reluctant to give advice or make an official recommendation. The governor wanted a major initiative in education next year, the Senate was holding out for a tax cut, every agency was requesting additional funding for ongoing as well as new programs. All of these proposals were costly. They were also real, immediate, and tangible.

How could he recommend major spending for something that would be catastrophic if it occurred but was of little or no interest until it actually happened?

THE ASSIGNMENT

DeAngelo and Clemson need to have the cooperation and participation of a number of other actors. Indeed, the agency itself would be the beneficiary of the major players "putting their heads together" over this issue in light of this recent, significant information-based disaster. Put yourself in their situation. Are they being realistic? Is it unreasonable to expect the agency or the state as a whole to invest heavily in prevention or backup capability that experience teaches will probably never be needed? Given the facts that most people and organizations perform better under stress and that each event may well be unique, would it be wiser to deal with each adverse situation as it occurs? In other words, money and goodwill are easier to come by in an emergency and perhaps, in the absence of a crisis, ought to be spent on other more-pressing current needs. On the other hand, these are information-dependent public programs on which people rely for their health, safety, and well-being and for which there are no alternatives. Is it irresponsible to conduct them without having a well-thought-out basic recovery plan? If so, should that plan include high annual "insurance premiums" such as unused or underused physical plant and equipment held in reserve in the public interest?

Explore each of these questions from three perspectives: SWD's technical professionals, its program managers and high-level executives, and the State Budget Office. What course would you recommend that SWD follow? What, if anything, should be expected from a statewide perspective?

Further Reflections

1. As discussed in the vignette opening Chapter 2, Mike McGraw's first thoughts upon hearing of the disaster in Hazard County instinctively took four perspectives on the problem—technological, economic, organizational, and political. After a long day working on the disaster recovery, McGraw returns home for some rest and reflection. In preparation for the next day, he again uses these categories to diagnose the situation.

Using the four perspectives discussed in Chapter 2, categorize the issues Mike is likely to ponder that night under each of the four perspectives.

2. The Hazard County case focuses explicitly on the issue of disaster recovery. However, as discussed more fully in Chapter 4, "Information as a Public Resource," disaster recovery is a special situation involving the more general issue of protecting and preserving public information resources. Read carefully the sections of Chapter 4 dealing with these issues.

Disaster recovery can be accomplished via several different strategies. As discussed in Chapter 4, "hot sites," "cold sites," and shared facilities are all ways that agencies can achieve backups to major mainframe installations. These facilities can be either owned by a government agency or leased from a vendor. In any event, backup sites must be subjected to close cost analyses. Alternative uses (such as for beta test sites for new systems) when the site would otherwise be idle may be a critical factor that "tips" the cost-to-benefit equation. Sharing sites is also a key cost factor.

In addition, most data protection and preservation plans must cover backup of the increasing number of micro systems, protect against malicious threats (from both outsiders and employees), plan for eventual archiving and preservation of data, and have procedures for maintaining data quality (this issue is discussed more fully under the sections on "data sharing" in Chapters 4 and 5).

As a staff assistant to Roberta Clemson, you have been asked to draft an outline for a departmentwide plan to protect and preserve the information stores of the Department of Social Welfare. After reading Chapter 4 closely and skimming the issues in Chapter 5, draft a memo that lays out for Clemson the issues that she should be taking into consideration.

CASE VIGNETTES

WHERE TO DRAW THE LINE: PUBLIC, PRIVATE, AND ILLICIT USES OF PERSONAL INFORMATION

Much of the information that government agencies create, collect, house, or use is available to the public. For example, the U.S. Department of Labor's Bureau of Labor Statistics regularly issues numerous reports about the state of the nation's economy. The U.S. Bureau of the Census is similarly engaged in collecting, analyzing, and reporting information about the American population. Public and private organizations and ordinary citizens are encouraged to make use of these information sources.

Other government data banks are built and maintained for very different reasons. They are used to administer the tax code, health and welfare programs, disability and retirement benefits, and other "private" transactions between the government and individual citizens. Much of the information they contain is related to individuals: their identities, incomes, family circumstances, and health status. For these information files, government also acts as the guardian, protecting them from unauthorized use or disclosure. Records systems, once housed only on paper and in file cabinets, are now increasingly found in computerized form or on microform media, making them much more complete, transportable, and accessible—and vulnerable to loss or abuse.

There is an open debate about where the line between public and private purposes should be drawn in the face of so much information and so many competing uses for it. Agencies, individuals, legislatures, and courts all struggle with this question. The following vignettes, taken from contemporary real-life reports, illustrate the difficult choices and the real dangers inherent in the information resources of an open society undergoing rapid technological change.

VIGNETTE 1: THE CONCERNED CITIZEN

A private citizen, in the course of her normal duties as an insurance claims clerk, suspects that the record of injuries and treatments for a particular file indicates a case of child abuse. Following the urging of public service advertisements, she reports her suspicions to the Child Abuse Hotline. When her employer learns of her action, she is fired for violating the confidentiality of company records. Using the accompanying news article, comment on the actions of the clerk, the Hotline official, and the insurance company. Were they each acting responsibly? What other actions could have been taken?

Would your opinions of this matter change if

- The clerk reports her suspicions to her supervisor, who takes them "up the line" for action. Four weeks later, the child in question sustains life-threatening injuries and the family is reported to the Hotline by hospital personnel.
- The case is one of several discovered by a staff analyst in the insurance company who noticed excessive claims for a number of children in a summary report she was preparing for another purpose. Fearing for the safety of those children, she reports the cases to the Child Abuse Hotline.
- The employee in question is a computer professional. As a citizen concerned about children, she wrote a program to search the company database for information patterns that might indicate child abuse. She then reported all suspicious cases to the Child Abuse Hotline.
- The employee is a program analyst with the Medicaid agency. In the course of conducting a utilization review against the claims file, she discovers several suspicious cases that might involve child abuse. Knowing these children might be in immediate danger, she reports her suspicions to the Child Abuse Hotline.

INSURANCE WORKER FIRED AFTER CITING CHILD-ABUSE SUSPICIONS
BY GRACE O'CONNOR, STAFF WRITER

Melody Mallory of Schenectady, the single parent of a 5-year-old daughter, is out of work today because she broke a company rule of confidentiality to report a case of what she believed to be child abuse.

Mallory was fired a month ago by Travelers Insurance Co., after almost seven years in its Colonie office, for having called a child-abuse reporting agency in Lebanon County, Pa. to alert officials to 18 different accident claims on one child.

"There were broken bones, concussions, burns on the feet, lacerations, even a broken hip," she said of the information she found on the company's computer when the boy's most recent claim came into her department at Travelers.

"Everyone is innocent until proven

guilty, but I strongly suspected abuse because the accidents were so bizarre for a 6- or 7-year-old boy,'' she said. There were no medical claims to suggest the boy suffered any illness which would cause him to be accident prone, she said adding, ''I had to make the call.''

But, in a situation that seemed to illustrate some of the concerns professionals nationwide have voiced about calling child-abuse hot lines, Mallory's call was not kept confidential. Her superiors were informed by the child-abuse agency and she was let go for violating company policy against giving out client information to anyone other than authorized people, such as physicians.

A recent study by the New York City Mayor's Task Force on Child Abuse and Neglect found that many professionals, such as teachers and doctors, who legally are required to report suspected cases of child abuse, are reluctant to do so.

Reasons for keeping quiet included the kind of retribution from superiors that Mallory encountered, according to the study which was made public this week, in Chicago during the seventh National Conference on Child Abuse and Neglect.

Four out of 10 teachers, 18 percent of hospital personnel and 8 percent of police officers surveyed admitted having failed to report at least one case of suspected child abuse to authorities despite the statute requiring them to do so.

Mallory's call was voluntary. She is not among the workers required by New York state law to report suspected child abuse and she said she was aware of company policy against releasing confidential information. But, she said, she could not ignore what she saw.

Her call went to Lebanon County caseworker Kevin Anspach. Mallory recalled that ''he (Anspach) asked my name and I gave it, but I made it clear I was calling as an individual, not an employee of Travelers. I told him I did not want it to get back to my employer that I had called.''

Joe Kirtz, spokesman for the state Welfare Department in Harrisburg, Pa., said,

''Reports of child abuse, the name of the person making it, the (name of the) alleged perpetrator, as well as the (name of the) child involved are routinely held in confidence under Pennsylvania law.''

However Anspach did call Travelers and did give Mallory's name. He told *The Times Union* he had no choice but to talk to the company to confirm information Mallory gave him.

The father of the suspected abuse victim, Anspach said, ''had come in and asked for her (Mallory) regarding the report.''

But, Anspach said, ''I don't think she should lose her job over this. She had a feeling and tried to make a contact. I feel she did the right thing.''

Although Anspach acknowledged the number of accident claims filed on the boy ''seems kind of unusual to me,'' he said an investigation found no abuse.

''It seemed awful strange to us the child was injured so much, but the father said it was not because of physical abuse,'' Anspach said.

''According to their (the child's family) doctor, there's no problem,'' Anspach said. ''And we talked to the child alone and he said no parent was abusing him.''

The family physician said the parents always brought their children in for regular checkups and medical attention, Anspach recounted. ''The doctor said it was no problem, that all these things were routine.''

A finding of no evidence in a suspected child-abuse case is not unusual according to another study discussed at this week's Chicago conference by Dr. David Young, clinical director of the Kempe National Center for the Prevention and Treatment of Child Abuse and Neglect in Denver.

His study of 576 reports of possible sexual abuse of children to the Denver Department of Social Services in 1983 showed 267 of them were unfounded, either because there was insufficient evidence or because the incidents did not happen.

Nonetheless, experts at the conference still urged increased reporting of suspected child abuse.

"We think the public is becoming more and more aware of the problem and prevention programs are having some impact," said Christine Holmes, spokeswoman for the Chicago-based National Committee for the Prevention of Child Abuse.

In Mallory's case, however, it cost her job. Anspach's call to Travelers prompted the company to let Mallory go, a company spokesman confirmed.

Alan Fletcher, corporate spokesman for Travelers Insurance in Hartford, Conn., said the rules of professional conduct for people working in the group claim department, "the area Melody is in," are given to every employee. These rules are set down in a manner designed to "ensure the individual's right to privacy," since people working in the claims department handle "sensitive personal and medical data."

"The rules must be obeyed by employees," he said. "We must take precautions to protect the insured."

Because of her good service record with the company, Mallory said she was surprised when the company fired her. But, she added, she does understand their action.

"They said I knew I was not supposed to release company information to anyone on the outside," she explained.

What she cannot understand is why her name was not kept confidential by the agency she called. She had given it because she believed it would not be used, she said.

Terry McGrath, spokesman for the New York State Department of Social Services, said callers to the child-abuse hot line in this state are encouraged to give their names to protect people from being falsely accused. There are, however, rules to guard against staff breaching confidentiality.

In both New York and Pennsylvania, whether or not a call reporting suspected child abuse is made anonymously, it is investigated.

Source: *The Times Union,* Albany, NY, November 13, 1985.

VIGNETTE 2: THE THEFT OF INFORMATION

The tax records of 16 million Canadian citizens, stored on two thousand four-by-six-inch microfiche cards, were stolen from the Tax Ministry and returned two weeks later. The motive for the theft and the use made of the records while they were missing are both unknown. The accompanying news article suggests some of the possible ramifications of fraudulent use of the stolen information. Use the following questions to help examine them:

- Unlike other commodities, the value of information is not diminished by legitimate use or sharing. In fact, it can become more valuable—if its integrity is maintained. What are the implications of this theft and its unknown threats to the integrity of the data?
- Social Security numbers have become a universal identifier for American citizens. Many activities, benefits, ownership rights, and other aspects of our lives might be called into question by the theft of so much identifying information. Should the public be notified? Should the government consider issuing new numbers as a consequence of the theft? What difficulties might such an action present?
- What security measures might prevent a situation like this one from happening? Are administrators aware of the irreducible risks?

PAPER CHASE: CANADA'S TAX RECORDS SWIPED, RETURNED
ASSOCIATED PRESS

TORONTO—The story had an almost happy ending, but certainly not for Revenue Minister Elmer Mackay, who had to tell Parliament that someone had swiped the tax records of everyone in Canada.

Tuesday, police questioned an employee of the government tax office about the theft of personal records on 16 million Canadians on Oct. 30.

Mackay disclosed the theft in Parliament on Monday, outraging opposition legislators, who suggested he find another job.

Three hours after Mackay's admission, the records were returned. But the theft still raised fears that terrorists or criminals may have copied the data to use for obtaining false birth certificates or passports or to file fraudulent claims for welfare or pensions.

The bundle of tax records, about the size of a lunch bucket, consisted of 2,000 acetate microfiche cards, transparent 4-by-6 inch plastic sheets on which thousands of pages of information are stored.

The data include names, addresses, birth dates, social insurance numbers, spouses' names and details of income.

Opposition New Democratic Party leader Ed Broadbent demanded that Prime Minister Brian Mulroney's Conservative government notify all taxpayers that their social security numbers may no longer be confidential.

Mackay and Health Minister Jake Epp said the government might consider changing the numbers.

Royal Canadian Mounted Police said a Toronto lawyer returned the records after Mackay reported the theft in the House of Commons.

Toronto newspapers said the lawyer was acting for the suspect from the Revenue Canada tax office, who has been under interrogation for five days.

A police spokesman would not speculate Tuesday on when charges might be brought, the motive for the theft or whether the documents had been copied.

"At the moment, we are considering it an active investigation," he said.

Inspector Tim Jay of the RCMP Toronto Commercial Crime Section said he expected the investigation would lead eventually to charges of theft or possession of stolen goods.

Mackay told Parliament he had ordered "an intensive review" of security, but he rejected calls for his resignation. The minister said he could not be responsible for every locked room and desk in his department.

Police said there was no sign of a break-in at the Toronto office of Revenue Canada, where officials spent nearly a week searching before they called police Nov. 4.

"The motivation might have been merely to do mischief or to damage the reputation of the department," Mackay told Parliament.

"Or the purpose might have been to secure lists of taxpayers for commercial or more nefarious purposes," he said. "Or it is conceivable that the intended use was to attempt to obtain money from the government by using the information for fraudulent purposes."

Source: The Associated Press, November 19, 1986.

VIGNETTE 3: THE ENTHUSIASTIC AGENCY

The New York State Department of Taxation and Finance has begun using its computerized records, and those of other agencies, to conduct an aggressive enforcement campaign against sales tax evaders. Within three years, the department's computer system is expected to be able to cross-check more than two hundred information sources in its quest to collect all the taxes owed in New York State. Explore the following questions in the context of the news article:

- Should information collected by one agency for one purpose be made routinely available to another agency for other purposes? Should general statewide standards for these exchanges be established? If so, how would they be determined? What would they be?

- What effort should be made to inform citizens who are registering their cars, for example, that the information they are obliged to provide to the Motor Vehicles Department will be shared with the Tax Department or the Social Services Department or some other agency?

- What responsibility does an agency have to verify the accuracy and currency of information it receives from another agency before using it? Should shared data be further exchanged at second or third hand?

- Most computer matching is conducted to "catch" abuse, eliminate duplication, and save money. Should different standards apply to sharing data that might provide some benefit? For example, what about a match of Subsidized School Lunch Records with Food Stamp Records in order to inform low-income families of an additional benefit for which they might be eligible?

STATE TAX-MAN MEANS BUSINESS OVER SALES TAX: MILLIONS BEING COLLECTED
BY NANCY HASS, BUSINESS WRITER

The thick black lettering on bright red stickers seal the doors of the store like a quarantine warning: "Seized for nonpayment of taxes."

The state tax-man means business these days; businesses that evade sales tax are the primary target of increased enforcement efforts.

"As far as I am concerned," said Arthur Gross, deputy commissioner for the Department of Taxation and Finance, "this kind of behavior should be treated as though it were a social disease."

During the past month, dozens of Capital District businesses—including a legislative hangout and a chain of sub shops—have been seized for non-payment of sales tax.

Two weeks ago, a car chase ended in the arrest of Meyer Dall, the former owner of Dall's Ltd. who was charged with falsifying the tax filings for the now-defunct Niskayuna clothes store. Tax officials say the arrest, which involved 14 felony counts, was the first of its kind in the region.

And they say it probably won't be the last.

Enforcement action like that, tax-reform legislation and increased voluntary compliance have "easily" helped the state pick up "a couple hundred million dollars" annually in revenue, some experts believe. About $100 million has been raised from motor fuel, and a "sizeable" increase has come from other sectors this year, these experts say.

Officials say aggressive enforcement isn't just a temporary operation. They say it's the first stage of a new system that will use a state-of-the-art computer network to catch and prosecute tax evaders.

"Right now, trying to identify such businesses is like finding a needle in a haystack," said Gross. "But after this system is in place, there will be hundreds more ways for us to find these people. The chances of getting caught will increase astronomically."

While the new computer linkage will help identify tax cheats across the board, officials say they are particularly interested in pursuing businesses that evade paying sales tax.

The nature of such a tax—called a "trust" tax because the public pays the vendor who is in turn entrusted with reimbursement to the state—makes violation a sore spot with officials.

"It's bad enough when an individual omits paying his fair share," said Gross, "but when it's a business(man) that pockets the money you gave him in good faith, that's really low."

The computer system, which should be in place within three years, will be the nation's most sophisticated means to track returns, according to Patrick J. Bulgaro, executive deputy commissioner for the department. The network will cross-reference more than 200 sources, says Bulgaro, allowing the mainframe computer to more efficiently choose returns for audits.

Soon, your Mercedes or that little hideaway at Lake George may betray you, Bulgaro says, if you've been underestimating your business revenues or haven't been filing at all.

The new computer will automatically cross-reference your return with your car registration or your property tax bill. Most importantly, the new system will standardize the exchange of information between the Internal Revenue Service and the state.

"What we've got on our side is that requesting an audit isn't as legally complicated as arresting someone," said Bulgaro. "If we are even a little perturbed about the outcome of the cross-references, then we can get an audit. If everything checks out, then we say 'thanks a lot, goodbye.' If it doesn't, well. . ."

Forget about registering assets in a relative's name, officials say, because those records can be checked automatically, too.

The computer, says Gross, will not replace human beings. Instead, it will streamline tedious functions, reduce error and free personnel to exercise judgment—the most crucial function of the department.

"The success of our operation depends on people making intelligent judgments," he said. "Now we can equip people better

to make more of those judgments so fewer violators slip through the system."

Gross acknowledges that the notion of a centralized computer is frightening to the public. The image of "Big Brother"—a metaphor explored by George Orwell in "1984" to describe an omnipresent intelligence which monitors behavior and disregards privacy—is imprinted on the collective memory, Gross says.

And, while huge strides in electronic information technology have facilitated tremendous advances in communication, the issue of security has grown from a nagging whimper to a roar across the country.

Last year, *Fortune* magazine called electronic security "the most disturbing issue posed by the advent of advanced technology."

"People are terrified the wrong person will have access to their records," said Gross, "and frankly, I don't think that's at all irrational."

"But the ability to make information available is outweighed by the responsibility to protect it."

Although Gross agrees with national analysts who say there is no sure way to seal off a computer system, he insists the department has planned rigid monitoring of access to records.

The message, he says, is constant vigilance—the same message that governs the department's policy on nabbing tax evaders.

Such vigilance is paying already, Gross says. Since the recent seizures, six business owners have approached the department voluntarily, paying more than $100,000 in liability—each mentioning the actions taken against the seized properties.

"Some people think the key to raising lost revenues is to put on more auditors," said Gross. "Well, it's true that raises success in a modest, measurable way."

"But, we're interested in raising revenues at a more ambitious rate. And the way to do that is to radically change taxpayer behavior. It means finding sexy, scary ways to show people what we can do."

Source: *The Times Union,* Albany, NY, October 26, 1986.

VIGNETTE 4: THE EXPLOITED COMPUTERIZED BENEFIT PROGRAM

Government agencies often administer benefit programs that regularly issue cash or reimburse claims for individual needs. The introduction of the computer into program administration has led to growing concern over the vulnerability of these programs to fraudulent use by employees. Federal investigations indicate that two-thirds of the employees who commit fraud are functional users, and one-third are data processing personnel. More than half the cases uncovered are detected by accident rather than through routine controls or special audits. Co-workers uncover twice as many cases as managers. The accompanying excerpt is from the statement of one employee who was discovered and prosecuted. Consider the following questions in light of the government benefit programs with which you are familiar:

- Most offices operate in an atmosphere of trust. How can an agency balance its need for security and maintain that important workplace ethic?
- What responsibility do information processing professionals have to educate agency management about the vulnerabilities of the agency's computer-supported benefit programs? What agencywide policies could be expected to reduce the risks of internal fraud?
- Research indicates that employees who commit fraud are likely to be young and, therefore, more comfortable with and knowledgeable about computer systems than their supervisors are. With workers' technical skills changing so rapidly, what responsibility does an agency have to keep supervisors abreast of workplace technology? What methods might it use to carry out this role?

EXCERPT FROM "A PERPETRATOR'S STORY"

My scheme went like this:

I would note the death of a beneficiary who had been receiving a monthly entitlement check. I would be alerted to the death because I would receive a computer message that a check had been returned with this notation, "Possible Death of Payee."

Next, the office would send out a letter to the beneficiary's address asking for information as to the beneficiary's status. We would receive a response confirming the death. I would then ascertain that there were no other possible claimants. I would then proceed with my scheme.

First, I would remove the entire case file from the office. I took it home and destroyed it.

Second, I would enter into the computer a message that the beneficiary had undergone a change in financial circumstance—a large number of medical bills, for example. I would make a retroactive benefit totalling less than $5,000. Anything under $5,000 I was authorized to process without another section's participation. In theory, two persons' computer access cards were necessary to create the benefit checks that I created by myself. However, there was no security regarding those cards, as the cards of other employees who may have been absent from the office, were just left lying around, totally unsecured. Additionally, each employee had a personal ID number to be used to log on to the computer when the access card was put in the terminal. I was able to steal another employee's ID number by standing behind them as they logged on. I simply watched their fingers as they typed their ID number.

Third, I would alter the beneficiary's address. Instead of sending the check to the beneficiary's home, I directed it to my address. However, because you needed two employees to complete such a transaction, I first used my own access card and ID to initiate the change and then I used another employee's card and ID to confirm the change. It was easy.

Fourth, I would terminate the beneficiary's case on the computer a month later. In six months, I knew the computer would erase all memory of the case and its history. That is why I call this a fool-proof scheme.

The checks would come to my house. I would sign the beneficiary's name, then endorse it myself and then deposit it in my personal account. I quit committing the crimes in November of 1981. Four months later I resigned, and about a year and a half later, the crimes were detected.

The mistake I made was that around the first of the year, I inadvertently misdated the date of a beneficiary's death. This, when caught in a computer led auditors to make a routine inquiry and they discovered several checks going to one address. It wasn't long before they realized that a violation may have occurred. The Secret Service was called in. My checking account was subpoenaed. Further inquiry established that the beneficiaries had all died earlier than I had listed them. The authorities put together a solid case against me.

Source: *Computer-related Fraud in Government Agencies: Perpetrator Interviews,* U.S. Department of Health and Human Services, May 1985.

Further Reflections

1. Chapter 5, "Information, Citizen, and State," discusses in some detail the competing demands on information managers both to provide public access to government data and to protect personal privacy. Melody Mallory (Vignette 1: The Concerned Citizen) became caught up in these competing demands.

a. Do you think the Freedom of Information Act contributed in any way to Melody's losing her job? Discuss your reasoning.

b. Were employees of the Lebanon County Child Abuse Hotline negligent in their responsibility to protect Melody's personal privacy? Do you believe Lebanon County had developed and was observing proper procedures with respect to releasing information on Hotline callers?

2. The stolen Canadian tax records (Vignette 2: The Theft of Information) were on microfiche cards. A large microcomputer with a good-sized hard disk could have downloaded the entire data file in machine-readable form in just a matter of minutes. Chapter 4 discusses securing mainframe systems and securing micro-based systems. The security of both types of systems appears to interact.

a. With this fact in mind, should the Canadian Tax Ministry ever consider allowing microcomputers to hook into its main databases? Should other agencies of government with confidential data allow microcomputers to be connected to their networks? Who in the organization should be responsible for making this decision?

b. Can you imagine any conceivable circumstance under which the Canadian Tax Ministry should allow a machine-readable disk or tape containing its master taxpayer file out of its possession? For example, should such information be released for purposes of cracking down on fraud via a computer match? If such a machine-readable file were to be released, should it be allowed to be copied? How should the Tax Ministry go about deciding on answers to these policy issues?

CASE STUDY 6

THE INFORMATION HISTORY OF THE OFFICE OF THE STATE TREASURER

Coauthored by John Peter Seagle

The Office of the State Treasurer is a hypothetical agency responsible for the full range of financial functions of a large state. It is headed by a state treasurer appointed by the governor, and its major operating divisions are headed by deputy state treasurers and, in the Audit Division, by the state auditor general. This case explores the recent history of OST, tracing its use of information processing across three decades. This information history is placed in the context of bureaucratic and electoral politics, public policy processes like budgeting and legislative activity, and the course of general technological innovation. The officers and the agency itself are fictional.

THE OFFICE OF THE STATE TREASURER (OST)

The Office of the State Treasurer (OST) was one of the first executive departments created after the state was established. Its head, the state treasurer, is appointed by and serves at the pleasure of the governor. The OST is responsible for the following functions:

- Receives funds (from taxes, fines, fees, federal government, etc.)
- Disburses funds (in payroll, retirement benefits, purchases and contracts, state aid to localities)

- Approves and monitors contracts of all state agencies
- Invests, borrows, and issues bonds on behalf of the public retirement systems and the state
- Audits other state agency expenditures and programs

The OST has carried out the first two basic responsibilities for many decades. In the past thirty years, however, like most agencies of government, it has grown substantially in size and scope. It was an early user of computers and has experienced several significant shifts in information technology. It has also taken on new functions and changed roles vis-à-vis other state agencies and the overall political structure.

Until the mid-twentieth century, OST was viewed as an accounting house for the state. It was not involved in making or changing state policies but served as in-house banker and accountant to the state and its operating agencies. As the state's population grew and the number of public programs it administered increased, the volume of work handled by OST grew as well: more people to pay, more accounts to set up, more program financial statements to audit. This increase in workload grew slowly at first and then with ever-increasing rapidity. By 1960, other agencies began to view OST as a stumbling block to program operations. Desirable programs were delayed, reduced or caused to fail, they believed, from strangulation by OST red tape. At about the same time computers began to appear on the scene.

THE OFFICE OF THE STATE TREASURER

The Hill Administration—1960

State Treasurer Winston Hill is sensitive to the criticism being leveled at his organization. Having entered state service from the banking community, he has kept a close eye on the changes taking place in that industry. Innovations in the private sector convinced him several years ago that OST needed to adopt computers in order to keep up with the increasing demands for service.[1]

The OST had used tabulating equipment and punched cards for check issuance starting right after the end of World War II. These were not nearly enough help. Tabulating machines were purchased after they were no longer the most cost-effective approach. Moreover, each new piece of tabulating equipment required additional staff positions, although at fairly low Civil Service grades. Those tabulating machine operators who were especially skilled at wiring control boards had been sent to vendor training programs to learn how to use computers. For several years, they had expected to apply their new skills on the job. But as the hoped-for computer

[1]For a chronology of the Office of the State Treasurer, see Appendix A.

purchases kept getting postponed at budget time, these operators left for jobs providing greater opportunity for advancement.

This year, after several years of proposals, pleadings; and justifications, three small business-oriented computers, costing several hundred thousand dollars each, were finally installed. Each was dedicated to serving the separate accounting needs of one of the large operating agencies. Specialized accounting programs were written in assembly language to serve each department.

Hill is pleased with the substantial increase in productivity that resulted from the computer installation. This is especially evident in the reduction of the many mechanical sorts required to reconcile checks and to post agency accounts. However, OST is now left with a surplus of lower-skilled tabulating machine personnel, and a shortage of people willing and able to learn about the new computers. Moreover, Civil Service classifications do not distinguish between the two kinds of activity, so computer programmers and operators are still all classified as tabulating machine operators. This problem, however, is certainly overshadowed by the improved operations the computer has introduced.

The Walker Administration, 1967–82

In 1967, a new governor took office and appointed a new treasurer with substantial political clout (see Figure OST.1). Charles Walker, another respected banker, wished to make the state a leader in applying new technology to increase productivity. Edward Fischer, a man with a great deal of experience in computing, was hired from private industry as the new deputy treasurer for Administration, and Anthony Ravello, another financial expert, became the new state auditor general.

With the ease often accorded a new administration, Walker and Fischer successfully started OST on the road to state-of-the-art computing. A large system development project was initiated which would produce a modern, efficient Financial Control System (FCS) for the agency. In 1968, large general-purpose computers were installed, and all OST processing was centralized into a single large computer center. New Civil Service titles had finally been established for computer programmers and systems analysts, and a large number of each were hired to develop programs that would enable the new computers to process all receipts and disbursements for OST. Those new staff with organizational as well as technical skills were informally titled "project management specialists," and although Civil Service did not recognize them as a new kind of professional, they developed a set of skills and responsibilities distinctly different from what others in the project were doing.

At the same time, the number of tabulating machine positions was reduced through attrition and position elimination. It was unfortunate,

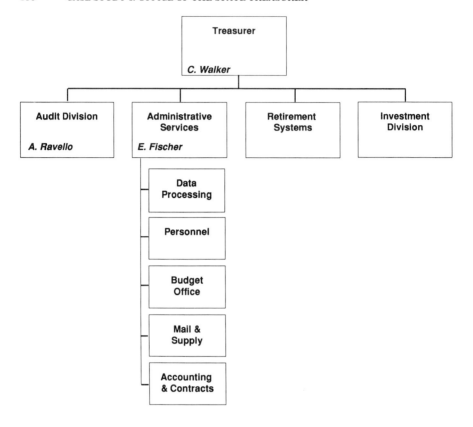

Total staff positions: 500

Figure OST.1   1967 Organizational Structure of the Office of the State Treasurer

however, that tab operators who had, in fact, been programming for several years were, despite formal protests, still being barred from taking exams in the programmer series.

The equipment was obtained through a private leasing company on a eight-year lease-purchase arrangement. The lease contained the usual clause allowing termination during any year that funds were not appropriated in the annual budget, but the treasurer obtained informal assurances from both the governor and legislative leaders that this would not happen. The leasing company gave the state a favorable rate based on that assurance, but it negotiated an arrangement in which the annual payments for the first three years of the lease were double those of the remaining five.

Optimistic about this entire endeavor, Walker relied on Fischer's computers to show a substantial cost reduction before the 1970 gubernatorial election. He turned to Ravello to boost OST's profile in the crusade for productivity.

In Ravello's opinion, the Audit Division had languished under the previous administration. Few of the public programs established in the past five years had been reviewed at all, and older ones had been audited at only the most minimally acceptable level. Auditees usually scoffed at OST reports that were issued up to a year after the review and often several years after the fact. Typically, the most critical findings had long been resolved, but newer and more important problems went uncovered. Ravello introduced planning and project control techniques into the Audit Division and assigned staff to systematically review new programmatic developments, legislative initiatives, and operational problems in the agencies. An OST audit began to mean something to the rest of the world even though the number of auditors increased only modestly.

By the time the 1970 election campaign was in full swing, Walker was grateful for Ravello's accomplishments. They were impressive enough to overshadow the fact that implementation of the highly advertised and generously funded new computer system was more than six months behind schedule. It seemed that many newly hired programmers lacked the necessary experience, and the veteran staff the supervisory skills, to get the job done on time. Large COBOL programming tasks were distributed among many programmers, causing many errors that had to be found and corrected. Convinced that delay was better than disaster, Walker abandoned his hope for a showcase system during 1970.

The eventual cutover to the new system, thankfully after the election, was still premature. Some checks were issued as much as six weeks late. Several important reports were even later. Public criticism was loud and painful. There were several internal investigations of OST's conversion to FCS as well as one conducted under the aegis of the State Budget Office. The internal studies made many recommendations for improvement in OST's project control and reporting mechanisms, but the SBO investigation concluded that the state should have some centralized computer expertise to serve all agencies and that major systems developments should be done by outside consultants. Thus an individual agency, such as OST, would benefit from the expertise of experienced professionals and would be spared the radical changes in the number and skills of its own personnel, which were inevitable as a major computer application went through the various stages of its development cycle. OST was, of course, not the only state organization going through these cycles, and so it was not surprising that in the 1972 state budget, an oversight organization was established within the State Budget Office itself.

The job at OST was eventually completed and, beginning around 1972, there was a brief period during which the SBO investigation proved prescient: there was not enough work to keep the programmers busy. The personnel complement was going through a cycle of boom and bust.

In 1972, a new director of Data Processing was promoted from within

OST. Peter Mann had learned well from experience. He was well liked in the agency and had earned the respect of the entire DP staff during the period of criticism over the implementation of FCS. The new computers were running smoothly but were already reaching the limits of capacity. Fortunately, lease payments had dropped to half the starting level, so OST was able to add storage capacity without increasing the level of its budget. The previously underemployed programmers were more than kept busy now revising applications to run more efficiently and taking advantage of new peripheral hardware purchases. These achievements gave Mann a feeling of satisfaction.

His experience, however, had not prepared him for some of the new problems his organization now faced. There were numerous changes to be made to applications in response to new reporting requirements mandated by the legislature and demanded by the changing needs of the other state agencies. With this activity, additional programmers had to be added until the programming staff exceeded the size of the staff used to develop the applications in the first place.

Before the end of 1973, although the lease had three years remaining, the computers were no longer able to keep up with OST's needs. There were numerous delays in providing services beyond the most essential ones. Paychecks came out on time, but little else did. Several scandals in procurement and construction by other agencies had led to mandates for stricter preauditing by OST's Audit Division. Computer support for these audits was slow in coming, so suppliers of goods and services faced long delays in receiving contractual payments. The legislature responded by making the state pay interest on late payments. Walker and Ravello directed their considerable displeasure toward Fischer, who in turn pressured Mann for a fast solution.

Mann explained how recent advances in storage technology made the OST computers essentially obsolete. Newer disk storage devices had been developed that provided much greater capacity at attractively low prices. Of greater importance, these devices allowed data to move to and from the computer at a much faster rate. Unfortunately, new storage devices could not be attached directly to the existing computers. It was time for an upgrade.

Convinced of the logic of the argument, Walker appealed to SBO for new computers but found little support for replacing equipment before the term of the lease was completed. Some new storage devices were authorized, however, and were installed with specialized equipment that connected them to the old computers. This and other patchwork solutions kept the technical staff at OST quite busy but did not provide the challenge and excitement that would attract and hold high-quality data processing professionals. Overworked and disgusted with being continually seen as "the problem," many of the best staff began to leave.

Finally, in 1974, OST was allowed to issue an RFP for new computers.

They were installed in 1975, one year before the end of the old lease. The new computers were obtained under a five-year lease-purchase through the same source as the previous equipment.

Because existing applications software was written largely in a standard version of COBOL, and because the new computers had "systems software" (language compilers, sorting programs, and control programs) similar to that in the older computers, conversion went fairly smoothly and operations proceeded without delays or interruptions for a couple of years.

In 1978, in order to better respond to requests for service, Mann placed certain major data collections under control of a database management system. This was a major conversion project but provided important benefits. Report programs could be written faster because they no longer required the inclusion of detailed data descriptions. The database system also allowed changes to be made in physical data storage without affecting application programs. Large data collections could be revised for faster access, yet specialized reporting programs could run largely unchanged. To manage this activity, a member of the systems programming staff was appointed "database administrator," and thus another new job title was informally invented to accommodate a new function.

Another innovation introduced by Mann was the use of structured methods for programming. Data processing staff members participated in the development of detailed programming procedures and standards for OST. As a result, the inevitable changes in newer application programs were easier to make. Soon after, structured methods for analysis and design of new systems were also adopted. In keeping with the latest thinking in the field of project management, strict "sign-off" steps were included in the development process, requiring users to verify that specifications were correct and being met. These methods led to an increase in programmer productivity of approximately 25 percent and made the resulting programs even easier to maintain.

In 1980, the five-year term of the lease ended, and OST owned the machines. However, the capacity of even these computers was being taxed by a growth in both the amount of work and the kinds of services required of the agency. Many other state agencies now used their own remote terminals to enter transactions directly into OST computers. The volume of queries about the status of transactions rose, and there was a great deal of "on-line" activity. As before, the equipment to handle much larger volumes was available at a price lower than that paid for the 1975 equipment. Walker sought permission to obtain hardware that would be sure to support an optimistic, although reasonable, forecast of demand for the next five years. The State Budget Office knew the governor wanted to project an image of austerity. The request was denied. It could wait another year.

Two years later, the request, now more urgent than ever, had still not been approved. Instead, OST was allowed a minimal upgrade of the main computers. But by 1983, the skyrocketing demand for routine processing left the OST systems staff despairing of any time at all to perform development work for their increasingly unhappy users.

The McConnell Administration, 1983–86

In early 1983, Adam McConnell took over as state treasurer (see Figure OST.2). The new auditor general, Jane Colby, combined Ravello's drive for effective internal management with a strong sense (shared by McConnell) that OST had great potential for an important policy-making role in the new administration. A new position, deputy treasurer for Operations, was created and filled by an experienced public administrator, Martin O'Keefe. After a quick reorganization, director of Data Processing, Peter Mann, reported to this new deputy rather than to the deputy for Administration.

Colby lost no time establishing a Program Analysis and Evaluation Unit in the Audit Division. The staff were sophisticated policy analysts and evaluation researchers, not traditional auditors and accountants. This group began a series of program audits whose goal was not the documentation of financial transactions or cash flows in state programs, but rather their effectiveness in achieving public policy purposes. Computerized information was an important starting point for these reviews, and sophisticated data analysis was an essential component of the evaluation process. Microcomputers began to appear throughout the unit. The traditional auditing function remained a large operation, but Colby successfully introduced microcomputers here as well, and she encouraged word processing and other forms of office automation to streamline operations in both parts of her organization. Little time passed before numerous requests for new FCS reports began arriving on O'Keefe's desk.

O'Keefe and Mann faced other demands as well. Users had often complained about the long development cycle of any applications that went beyond reporting of existing data. The rigid "sign-off" procedures forced them either to agree to specifications that they did not completely understand or to face unendurable delays. Once users saw a system in operation, they identified many helpful changes, but these then took long periods of time to implement. The database administrator had resisted adding to the database for several years, pointing out that the present system was stretched to its outer limits. As a result, many staff groups began to keep their own databases on microcomputers. Data were filed in the microcomputers of several groups, each with its own needs regarding form, accuracy, and currency. A few staff groups even kept data that duplicated what was already on the main OST database because they did not have a clear picture of what information actually resided there, nor were they confident that they could have access when they needed it. Colby, the most demanding and sophisticated of the users, became increasingly concerned that some of her man-

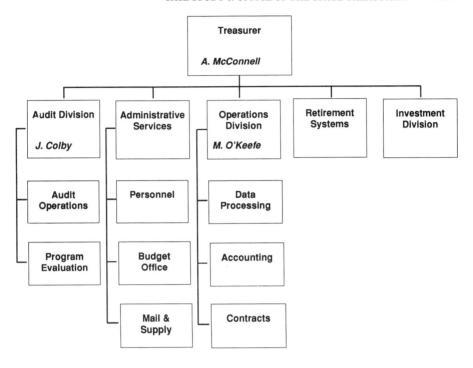

Total staff positions: 1,925

Figure OST.2   Organizational Structure of the Office of the State Treasurer at the Beginning of the McConnell Administration (1983)

dated auditing responsibilities were supported with information stored only on micros. This severely limited the value of that information for auditing and evaluating state programs—it could be augmented by or cross-matched with information in the mainframe database only with great difficulty and delay.

While these problems existed, Mann and his staff had many unheralded accomplishments to their credit. They had performed admirably through two major hardware changes, and as time went on more and more of the original COBOL programs were rewritten to meet the standards for structured programming and design. The database management software could be used within COBOL programs or on a stand-alone basis. That is, simple queries could be made of the data through the database management system alone. The data processing staff freely gave technical advice to purchasers of microcomputers within OST and made no attempt to control

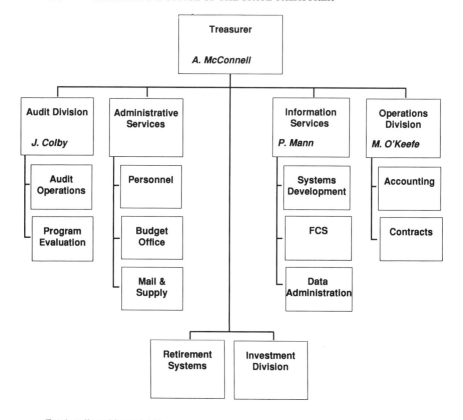

Total staff positions: 2,000

Figure OST.3   Organizational Structure of the Office of the State Treasurer at the Beginning of the McConnell Administration (1985)

their use or purchase. The database administrator had shown a genius for speeding up access to data, amazing other data processing professionals by the amount of work the medium-sized 1983 computers were able to handle. In recognition of the increasing importance of automated information systems to the agency, in 1985 Peter Mann, director of Data Processing, was appointed to the new position of deputy treasurer for Information Services, reporting directly to McConnell (see Figure OST.3). Mann's former boss, O'Keefe, was not pleased that the agency's data processing functions had been removed from his area of responsibility, but he had been unable to prevent it.

Shortly after the 1986 election, McConnell resigned as state treasurer to accept the chairmanship of one of the leading Wall Street investment houses.

Today

Reed Jones, formerly a member of the governor's personal staff, has been state treasurer for two weeks. He is familiar with the issues and strengths of OST from his tenure in the governor's office and, in fact, worked often and well with McConnell and his senior staff. He is determined to resolve the "systems" problem as one of his first items of business and so has sought the advice of people both inside and outside OST. Jones recognizes the pressing need to address the hardware limitations. He understands that more capacity is needed merely to keep up with the tasks OST is mandated to perform. He also knows that no problem involving information systems could have such a simple solution. Before his departure, McConnell had directed both Mann and an outside consultant to prepare advisory reports on the current situation. McConnell had also asked Colby for her assessment of the situation from the users' point of view. With the reports now in hand, Jones has spent the evening reviewing the results.

Mann urges an evolutionary approach. His key recommendation is for newer and larger machines made by the same company as the present computers. In this way, the capacity problem will be almost immediately resolved and the conversion effort, and its attendant problems, will be minimized. This approach builds on the organization's strengths: the experience of its staff, the known dimensions of existing applications. He argues eloquently that with these machines and a modest staff increase, the operational needs of OST will be met for the next several years.

The consultant report takes an entirely different position: convert all applications to a fourth-generation language (4GL), which has recently become available. OST's major systems could be reprogrammed in 4GL in a matter of months. Once the conversion is complete, revisions to these programs can quickly be made whenever needs change. New programs can quickly be developed in prototype versions. The users can then experiment with the prototypes and revise their specifications. Design, development, maintenance, and enhancements can all be streamlined. Unfortunately, the database management system in use by OST does not support any fourth-generation languages. The advantages of this proposal are so great, however, that in the consultant's professional opinion, they far outweigh the difficulties associated with a complete conversion of all programs and databases. Moreover, 4GL and its associated database system run on several brands of large computers, so any computer purchase can have the benefit of wide open competitive bidding. The consultant's firm has had substantial experience in making other conversions, and is anxious to perform this new kind of conversion for OST.

Colby's concerns were more oriented to staffing and functional issues. For the past several years, for example, OST had lost more than the typical number of what Colby liked to call "bridging" personnel: information users who had deliberately acquired a technical competence and had a good understanding of what the technology could provide, how to ask for what they wanted, how to get it, and, most important of all, how to use it. As such, these "bridges" were very valuable to the organization. Increasingly, though, the problem was that the systems in place were unable to unlock the needed data. Worse, since these staff members were neither purely technicians nor purely members of any other traditional occupation (like program specialists or accountants), they suffered at promotion time. Narrowly defined job descriptions prevented them from either qualifying for or scoring well on established exams. Meanwhile, they were often given greater responsibilities. Continued frustration had prompted too many of the brightest people to accept positions in the private sector, where their value was formally recognized and the compensation was substantially greater. Furthermore, within OST's professional DP community, a number of employees who had been with the agency since the mid-1960s were tied in to one existing technology and reportedly were not at all enthusiastic about moving to 4GL and a complete conversion of existing systems. Would one-time skills training be enough? In her words, "We have to expect to continuously retrain our workforce to take advantage of new technologies. Instead, we wait for problems and hope for after-the-fact training to correct them." In short, Colby saw an information-rich future blockaded by an unresponsive bureaucracy.

Then there is history to be considered. With their different experiences and perspectives, the three deputy treasurers and the state auditor general had seldom acted as a team. Worse, intra-agency rivalries sometimes spilled out into the open and impeded OST's operations and damaged its image. Jones felt sure that organizational issues as well as technological changes would need to be addressed.

Finally, Jones faced some nagging doubts about the 4GL software possibilities. Was it really superior to adding to the current system, at least for the next few years, and would it satisfy OST's increasing information needs brought on by expanded responsibilities? The system was so new that there were few existing examples of a successful conversion to examine. What if it turned out not to be very effective, despite the substantial costs? The governor's campaign slogan had been "Compassion and Competence," and it was clear that OST was expected to weigh in heavily on the Competence side of the equation. "Smooth-running," "businesslike," "up-to-date," and "reliable" were words the governor often used. She would be equally unhappy about a stormy conversion to a new system or continued deterioration of the old one.

Jones considers all these interacting pressures with growing concern. "Is this decision one of only hardware and software, or are organizational changes needed as well? And, as Colby tenaciously points out, what about all the information in these huge machines and their micro-sized counterparts? Are we making good use of any of it? The governor's term is only beginning. We have at least four years under her administration. Is it enough time to see results? Dare I plan out any further?"

THE ASSIGNMENT

1. What "life cycles" are at play in this case? Identify the cycles and describe how they relate to OST's information requirements.

2. What are the technical, organizational, and political implications of the various life cycles that you identified on the time period to be covered by Jones's plan? As stated in the case, Jones is considering four years as the time period to be covered in an OST information systems plan. Should he contemplate a different time period? Why? More important, what strategic goals should guide the development of OST's action plan?

3. What institutional changes in state government related to budgeting, legislative processes, personnel policies, etc., are needed to better meet changing demands?

Further Reflections

1. One major issue raised in this case involves the locus of policy making about information technology within an organization. This topic is discussed in more detail in Chapter 2, "Information Policy in the Public Sector." After reading Chapter 2, draft a brief paper summarizing how the locus of policy making has shifted in OST since 1960. Might Jones consider an organizational solution at this time? If so, what kind of reorganization would you recommend? How will this improve the situation Jones is now facing?

2. As discussed in Chapter 1, information management policy in the public sector emerges from the interaction of three points of view—information technology professionals, information users, and policy controllers. Consider for a moment the role of various control agencies in developing policies for the Office of the state treasurer.

a. Through the years, the State Budget Office has played a pivotal role with respect to policy development within OST. List the major interventions by budget since 1960. Discuss how these have facilitated or impeded the overall evolution of the agency. What factors should Jones consider in his present choices that might involve Budget? How could interventions by Budget at this point in time facilitate or impede his plans?

b. Civil Service has also played an important role in the OST case. Review the critical decisions that Civil Service has made since 1960 that may have impacted on OST. Discuss how actions by Civil Service might facilitate or impede the actions that Jones is anticipating. Should Jones take any special actions in his present dealings with Civil Service (such as request a reclassification of some sort)?

Appendix A

Chronology - Office of the State Treasurer

1960   - Installation of three small business-oriented computers
        - Winston Hill is State Treasurer

1966   - Gubernatorial election

1967   - Charles Walker appointed State Treasurer
        - Edward Fischer appointed Deputy Treasurer for Administration
        - Anthony Ravello appointed State Auditor General
        - Initiation of a modern Financial Control System (FCS)

1968   - Installation of large general-purpose computers; eight-year
          lease-purchase

1969   - FCS installed one year late

1970   - Gubernatorial election

1972   - Creation of oversight section in State Budget Office
        - Peter Mann promoted to position of Director of Data Processing
          reporting to Deputy for Administration

1974   - Gubernatorial election

1975   - Installation of new computers; five-year lease-purchase
          arrangement

1978   - Gubernatorial election
        - Some data collections put under the control of database
          management system

1982   - Gubernatorial election

1983   - Adam McConnell appointed State Treasurer
        - Jane Colby appointed State Auditor General; creates Program
          Analysis and Evaluation Unit in Audit Division
        - Martin O'Keefe appointed to new position of Deputy Treasurer for
          Operations
        - Mann and the DP Organization removed from Administrative
          Division and placed in Operations Division

1985   - Peter Mann appointed to new position of Deputy Treasurer for
          Information Services reporting directly to the State Treasurer

1986   - Gubernatorial election
        - McConnell requests advisory report on the future of OST's
          information systems from Mann and external consultant
        - McConnell requests Colby's assessment of current situation

1987   - Reed Jones appointed State Treasurer

CASE STUDY 7

INTEGRATED INFORMATION FOR POLICY MAKING: A SYSTEM FOR SERVICES TO PEOPLE WITH DISABILITIES

By Catherine Couse, New York State Council on Children and Families

A large state, under federal and state legislative mandates, must decide how to integrate its stores of information about people with disabilities and the services they receive from a variety of state agency programs. Operating agencies responsible for various segments of the client population, coordination and control agencies responsible for sound financial and policy decisions, and legislative representatives are all legitimately involved. Each has a different set of needs and a different solution to their mutual challenge.

BACKGROUND

State-sponsored services to people with disabilities are provided through a complicated system of programs of various sizes and intensity, authorized or administered by several state agencies. Services range from residential programs in institutional settings where most of a client's needs are met on the grounds of a facility to day services, including employment programs, where the goal is to assist a client to become a fully functioning member of the community. In some cases, the programs offered do not differ a great deal from agency to agency. Clients can gain access to the same program through more than one referral mechanism and, in certain instances, can be considered to be a client by more than one agency at the same time. This duplica-

197

tion in service is accompanied by a lack of certain *kinds* of services that are not presently provided by any of the agencies. The system has caused difficulty for planners and policy makers in their attempts to eliminate these gaps and overlaps, and to plan for the disabled population in a comprehensive way. Disabled people and their families have continuously advocated for a unified service system and have found sympathetic ears in both the current governor and a respected state senator.

Funding for disability services has always been limited, putting agencies in competition with one another for scarce resources. The resulting lack of cooperation between agencies is manifested in poor communication and an unwillingness to share information or otherwise assist one another in the planning process. A well-known fact underscores the severity of the situation: two of the commissioners of agencies involved in disability services have never sat together at the same table to discuss mutual service or planning issues.

A new federal law has recently been enacted that changes the requirements for reporting information on disabled individuals and the services they receive. The requirements are part of a new program that provides higher rates of federal reimbursement for disability services—in certain instances up to 75 percent of the cost of care. States are to report on the number of individuals being served as well as on units of service provided. The state could gain substantially under the new program if it can show that its historically high level of service *units* also represents a high rate of service *coverage* of the entire population of people with disabilities.

State Senator William Benecet, chairman of the Committee on Services to the Disabled, sees this legislation as a key lever in making the kinds of changes he has consistently urged in the the state's disability services programs. The senator has long been an advocate for service coordination, and he has tried in the past to convince the governor's staff and commissioners of the involved agencies that cooperation would work to their mutual advantage. Two years ago, he successfully negotiated a bill with the Administration and the General Assembly to create a Commission on Services to the Disabled (CSD). The CSD is a small coordinating agency whose function is to smooth out disagreements between the operating agencies, to identify gaps and overlaps in the present service system, and to coordinate the policies and activities of the agencies that provide services. The CSD began with an executive director and six professional staff. As its first initiative, the commission took on the considerable task of compiling a Budget for the Disabled, a document that presented for the first time in one place a description of the services available to the disabled population, and their associated costs. The production of this document gave staff at CSD some valuable experience and an opportunity to quickly become familiar with the policies and the important players in the service delivery system. The quality of their efforts also helped establish some credibility for the fledgling agency, which nevertheless continues to be eyed with some suspicion by the others. At present, federal grants and funding from private foundations have increased the size of CSD's staff to twenty.

Benecet is optimistic that the new federal financial incentives will provide the impetus for cooperation among the agencies which has heretofore been lacking. To this end, he sponsored a successful bill, the Disability Services and Information Act, which requires agencies involved in disability services to comply with the new reporting standards. The new state law calls for development of a computerized tracking system on disabled individuals that would combine information from the four state agencies currently involved in disability services. It is to be called the System for Services to Disabled Individuals (SSDI).

The senator has been frustrated over the years by the lack of coherent, reliable, and, above all, comprehensive information about the population needing services and about the services themselves. As the bill was being drafted and negotiated, Benecet's key staffer, Edward Fitzjerald, convinced him that a strategic database could be built to support the long-range, policy-oriented information needs that needed attention. Benecet therefore took the opportunity to expand upon the reporting requirements of the federal law and included language that outlined the content and uses of a new database that went well beyond simple tracking and reporting. Working with representatives from the governor's program staff and the State Budget Office, the senator's committee convincingly outlined the potential of the new database for use in planning, research, and policy making related to programs and services for people with disabilities. The requirements for the SSDI, therefore, include specific references to financial claims for services to individuals; historical records of services provided and agency actions; programwide trends, statistics, and management reports; and needs assessment data. (See Appendix A for text of the statute.)

Like many other federal laws, the new national disability services statute requires the designation of a single state agency to be the conduit for federal funds and the reporting agent at the state level. This requirement posed a major dilemma in naming the agency where the SSDI should be housed. The Department of Services to the Disabled (DSD), the lead agency in provision of services to this population, is known for its reluctance to share information or otherwise cooperate with other agencies in an area that it feels should be under its exclusive purview. The DSD does, however, have the largest data processing capability of any of the involved agencies and serves the largest number of clients. Initially, DSD opposed the development of the SSDI, arguing that each involved agency should take care of its own reporting to the federal government, and that there was no need to develop SSDI at all. However, once it became clear that neither the federal government nor Senator Benecet shared that interpretation, DSD lobbied for the SSDI to be housed there. DSD staff made their public argument on the basis of the agency's superior technical capabilities, but they also intimated that if the system were to be placed elsewhere, the degree of cooperation forthcoming from DSD would be minimal. Lacking persuasive counterarguments, the state law named DSD as the single state agency and the home of the SSDI.

AGENCIES INVOLVED IN PROVISION OF DISABILITY SERVICES

There are four agencies involved in provision of services to disabled people, all of which have been named in the legislation as participants in SSDI. The heads of all four agencies have been briefed by the governor's program director and have pledged their cooperation.

Department of Services to the Disabled (DSD)

DSD is the largest of the four agencies, serving fifteen thousand persons at any point in time in some type of residential or day program. DSD has a computerized tracking system and can identify each of the individuals in its care and the services they are receiving. The DSD system, however, has been in operation for twelve years and is not completely equipped to meet the requirements of SSDI. Its major failing is the lack of a historical tracking capability. Data are entered and maintained and reports are produced on a quarterly basis, with no built-in capability to link information about the same person between quarters.

A year prior to the passage of the SSDI legislation, DSD had requested and received funds to redesign its own system. Responsibility for the redesign fell to Dick Higgins, director of Information Services. Higgins is a veteran information technology professional, with twenty-five years experience in the field. He has traditional views on the uses of computerized data, and a strong belief in centralized processing and data ownership. It was with some reluctance that he contracted the work of developing the redesign to an outside consultant rather than taking on the job in-house. Higgins is pleased with the hardware component of the contract, having decided against a system with strong distributive processing capabilities and selected a system known for its processing speed against large files. Disagreements between Higgins and the consultant as to the exact requirements of the system, however, have caused the project to get off to a slow start.

In part, Higgins's problem is the lack of a clear idea on the part of agency users as to how the redesigned system should be used. This confusion, coupled with strong feelings on the part of the DSD commissioner that assessment data should not be entered into the system due to the dangers of "labeling," has resulted in continual revision of the data element dictionary and general system design. Communication between Higgins's data processing staff and program staff at DSD is poor. At present, the redesign of the DSD system is six months behind schedule.

Higgins has made little effort to further the development of SSDI, being understandably unhappy about having to worry over a new system in the middle of his redesign. He would nevertheless be very reluctant to send his data to another agency for input into the SSDI and has therefore not argued against housing the system. Higgins's approach has been to assign the work on SSDI to a junior member of his staff, who has been instructed to avoid commitments and to keep Higgins informed of any developments.

Division of Education for the Disabled (DED)

DED is the second-largest service provider, responsible for educational services to eight thousand disabled children and adults. DED programs are both residential and nonresidential and, in many instances, children and adults attend the same program. DED is administered in a decentralized fashion, having eight regional offices throughout the state with general oversight of the school programs in their respective geographic areas. The regional offices operate with some degree of autonomy. In keeping with this structure, the data processing capability of DED is microcomputer-based, with each regional office maintaining information on its own clients. Client information remains at the regional offices and is aggregated and reported, in keeping with the requirements of the DED central office, primarily for billing purposes. Although there are no individually identifiable records maintained at DED central office, an attempt is made to assign unique identifiers to clients in the micro-based files via a call-in system to DED central office, where a name search file is maintained.

Central office data processing, as well as the somewhat loose administration of data processing across regional offices, is the responsibility of Henry Mabley. Mabley, who operates under rather severe budgetary constraints, runs an efficient system that responds accurately to tightly defined requirements from the agency administration, most of which are outlined in statute. Mabley therefore makes no attempt to share data with other agencies, even though certain programs used by DED through purchase of service arrangements are also serving clients of DSD and the Office of Children's Services.

Office of Children's Services (OCS)

The population of disabled children is a small subset of the clients served by this agency. Its disability service programs are dwarfed by comparison with day care, foster care, teenage pregnancy, and drug education and prevention programs. In providing services to disabled children, OCS and DSD sometimes share information on individual cases, but at present there is no computerized mechanism for information sharing between these two agencies. Planners at the DSD have complained that the lack of information sharing between the two agencies causes problems in the planning of services for children once they have reached adulthood and are ready to move on to the programs administered by the DSD.

Attempts have been made at sharing information between these two agencies in the past but have not been given support by Higgins at DSD or Mary Lennon, his counterpart at OCS. Lennon, in addition to the research and statistics function, oversees a large data processing operation that includes several different systems containing information on a variety of children's services. Lennon is not as concerned with data ownership as is Higgins, but she is bound by confidentiality regulations that prohibit sharing of individual identifying information with any agency not specified in OSC's governing legislation as an authorized agency with rights to the data. Lennon's concern for the current fragmented system of services to children with disabilities has led her in the past to advocate for a change in legislation that would allow data to be shared between OCS and DSD. Lennon's efforts to improve services for disabled children through improved information sharing, however, have often taken a back seat to other issues concerning larger populations of children also served by OCS.

Department of Health Services (DHS)

DHS is responsible for medical and health-related services to disabled children under the age of two, to multiply-disabled adults who live in skilled nursing facilities, and to the elderly population residing in nursing homes. It also provides reimbursement to the other agencies for many of the medical expenses they incur for clients in their care.

DHS is a large department with a wide array of services and programs, and a complementary number of computerized tracking systems. While most health-related services information is maintained on large mainframes, each of the disabled populations served by the DHS is tracked on a different micro-based system. Vince Capacola, director of Data Processing for DHS, while nominally in charge of all data processing activities in his department, has taken a laissez-faire attitude toward the micro operations in his department, choosing to concentrate his energies on the larger mainframe operation used to support laboratory work and the monitoring of hospital systems around the state. Capacola has been approached about the SSDI but has stated that he does not see himself as a major player in an initiative of this kind.

THE PRESENT SITUATION

Eight months have passed since passage of the state's Disability Services and Information Act. Little progress has been made toward beginning the design of SSDI. Higgins has come under increasing pressure from Michael Dollery of the State Budget Office to move forward with the system design. Funds allocated in last year's budget for the design of SSDI were used up in the redesign of Higgins's own system, since Higgins was able to effectively argue that the implementation of SSDI was dependent on a successful DSD redesign. As the new fiscal year begins, Dollery is determined that this scenario will not be repeated.

Moreover, Senator Benecet has complained to the governor about the lack of progress toward SSDI implementation. In fact, to show how easily a competent professional could handle the task, he has forwarded a concept paper prepared by his senior staff adviser, Edward Fitzjerald, outlining certain design options for SSDI. Since the senator's support is needed for important elements of the governor's upcoming legislative agenda, Dollery has been given instructions, in no uncertain terms, to resolve the impasse. Feeling the heat of growing displeasure in the governor's office, Dollery has circulated Fitzjerald's paper for review and called an urgent meeting of the designated project coordinators of all the agencies named in legislation as participants in SSDI. Although not a named participant, the CSD staff were also asked to attend. Dollery begins by outlining the statutory obligations each agency is assigned under the act, and he points out that only twelve months remain before the expiration of the opportunity for higher federal reimbursement rates. The act's sponsors, the budget director, and the governor are not happy with the lack of progress toward implementing SSDI.

Higgins, alert to the possibility that the imminent fiscal deadline will encourage the others to stick by the investment already made in the DSD system, begins outlining the steps he sees as needed to move SSDI forward. Higgins's approach involves wrapping up the design of SSDI with work already under way on his own redesign. Higgins has looked into the existing technical situation often enough to know that all the agencies maintain and define data elements in different ways, in different file structures, and on different hardware. He begins to outline procedures whereby the other agencies would share their data with DSD.

Higgins, however, is barely able to begin presenting his ideas before the other agency representatives interrupt with certain issues of their own. As the discussion proceeds, it becomes clear that for a variety of reasons none of the other agencies are happy about providing data to DSD.

Mary Lennon of OCS begins by pointing out that while her agency agrees in principle with the concepts behind SSDI, and can see the benefit to the population of children "aging out" of the OCS system, confidentiality regulations prevent her from sharing any personally identifying information with either DSD or any of the other agencies named as SSDI participants. Lennon has checked with her agency's legal department and found no basis to support the idea that the SSDI legislation takes precedence over their own confidentiality requirements. Lennon's previous inclinations to advocate legislative changes to rationalize confidentiality restraints obviously do not translate into a willingness to become nothing more than a subsystem of the DSD redesign.

Henry Mabley of DED expresses philosophical support for SSDI but goes on to explain that he has no financial resources to put into the work required for him to provide data to DSD. In addition, Mabley points out, the regional structure of his reporting system means there is no central database in which the client service information needed by SSDI is maintained. Furthermore, Mabley has neither the staff nor the equipment to develop one. It is Mabley's position that the existing data processing set up at his agency, while not compatible with the goals of SSDI, is sufficient to meet his agency's own statutory requirements. He has no choice but to continue to look to his agency's own authorizing statute rather than the SSDI legislation for operational guidance.

Vince Capacola from DHS takes the position that, as is the case in other aspects of data processing in his department, the individuals who have responsibility for the databases containing information of interest to SSDI are essentially independent operators who, practically speaking, are under no obligation to report their information to him or anyone else in DHS, let alone to an outside agency such as DSD. Capacola is only willing to go so far as to provide the names of the individuals responsible for maintaining data on the three client populations of interest, each of which is maintained on a separate micro-based system.

Following a considerable amount of unproductive discussion, all agree to return to their agencies, review the situation with their respective commissioners, and to return in one week prepared to discuss alternative solutions.

After the meeting, Dollery holds a private conference with Marilyn Foster of CSD. Both of them express their concern with the plight of SSDI, and Dollery voices his suspicions that the participating agencies' primary concern is sharing data with another service provider agency—i.e., "the competition." Through her work on the Budget for the Disabled, Foster had developed good working relationships with agency staff. Subsequent conversations she has had with Lennon, Mabley, and Capacola confirm this suspicion. Dollery hopes that CSD, in its non-service-provider capacity, might be a more palatable negotiator among the participating agencies in coming to agreement on the design of SSDI.

Foster has certain concerns about taking over as lead agency in the design of SSDI. The CSD is not equipped from the standpoint of either personnel or budget to take on such an assignment. The CSD's work in compiling the Budget for the Disabled had made Foster all too familiar with the complexity of the service system SSDI was intended to capture, and at present the staff at CSD lack in-depth data processing experience. In addition, while fairly certain of her ability to work cooperatively with Lennon, Mabley, and Capacola, Foster is well acquainted with Higgins's proclivities to keep his data to himself. After all, the other agencies might have something to gain by cooperating. Higgins thinks he has everything to lose. Higgins had been difficult enough to work with in obtaining necessary information for the Budget for the Disabled. This new challenge might well be insurmountable. Foster also sees that, were the system to be housed somewhere other than DSD, the same kinds of confidentiality problems would pertain to Higgins sharing his data with another agency as they did with Lennon and OCS.

In his concept paper regarding the design of SSDI, Fitzjerald had raised the issue of the need for incentives for the agencies participating in the system, and he had suggested that each agency be given a data processing staff person to perform the tasks required for SSDI. Higgins had disagreed with this approach, suggesting that the other agencies should simply provide dumps of their data which would then be reformatted and input at DSD. Higgins preferred to have responsibility for all programming tasks related to SSDI, and for continuity and control purposes, to have the staff working on SSDI report to him. The other agencies had objected to this, preferring, as the information experts within their respective programs, to be responsible for any reformatting or manipulating of their own data.

Dollery feels the approach suggested by Fitzjerald is too costly, necessitating the addition of four full-time programmers for what is not likely to be a full-time task beyond the initial system design and implementation. On the other hand, Dollery is unwilling to provide any further SSDI funds to Higgins unless he can feel confident that there will be swift forward movement on the system design. Instead, Dollery offers Foster enough funding for two staff persons, to be given to CSD under a contractual arrangement with DSD. Foster and her staff will have six months to analyze the situation and make recommendations as to how the state should best proceed.

THE ASSIGNMENT

1. How should Foster proceed? Clearly, the presence of a legislative mandate does not guarantee cooperation. In fact, one of the major issues facing her is the result of legislation—multiple conflicting guidelines on confidentiality. How can SSDI be developed without changes in the law? Is the ultimate location of the system a factor in the equation? What principles for information security might overcome these objections?

2. Technology is both a barrier and a solution. SSDI is intended to give the state a comprehensive picture of a vulnerable population and the services it receives. The current constellation of information systems maintained by the separate agencies, however, mitigate against that result. Yet, they cannot simply be scrapped—they support ongoing, necessary, and expensive service programs. What are Foster's options for dealing with them? What should SSDI look like and where should it be housed?

3. How should Foster approach the political barriers to development of the system? What incentives can be offered to the agencies to cooperate in joint system development? How can Foster capitalize on the support of both Dollery and Benecet in bringing about a successful system implementation?

Further Reflections

1. Chapter 2, "Information Policy in the Public Sector," asserts that sound government information management policies combine four perspectives—the technology itself, economics, organizational factors, and political considerations. Reread the discussion in Chapter 2.

As her staff assistant, draft a memo to Foster that outlines her options from the four perspectives presented in Chapter 2. For each perspective, summarize the salient issues contributing to her decision and make a recommendation concerning what she should do. If the recommended actions differ when analyzed from each of the four separate perspectives, attempt to resolve these differences by creating a recommended action that blends the best from each.

2. Chapter 5 describes a number of procedures commonly being implemented by government agencies that are challenging how information managers think about personal privacy. Foremost among these procedures are computer matching, front-end verification, and computer profiling. SSDI is technically quite similar to a large-scale and ongoing computer matching project. Discuss how SSDI is the same as and different from computer matching projects as discussed in Chapter 5.

Appendix A

Partial Text of the Statewide Disability Services and Information Act

Section 4. System of Services to Disabled Individuals.

4.1. System objectives. The state, under the authority of the single state agency, shall design, develop, and maintain an automated information system capable of

a. documenting all financial claims to be made by the state to the federal government with respect to services to any disabled person;

b. compiling and maintaining a cumulative historical record of information with respect to state agency actions taken on behalf of each disabled individual in receipt of services;

c. producing regular and special reports of issues and trends to enhance the program planning capabilities of the state agencies, the governor and the legislature;

d. supporting analysis and assessment of the aggregate service needs of the state's disabled population and its access to services;

e. maintaining an interagency statistical information base to allow prompt, accurate responses to information requests from state agencies, the governor and the legislature.

4.2 Participating agencies. Services provided by the following agencies to disabled persons residing within the state shall be recorded in the system:

a. the department of services to the disabled;

b. the department of health services;

c. the division of education for the disabled;

d. the office of children's services.

4.3 Individual records. Each disabled person who receives services from any of the agencies listed in section 4.2 of this section shall be uniquely identified in the system in a manner which assures confidential treatment of personal information and which assures nonduplication of individual records.

CASE STUDY 8

A POLICY MAKER'S DATABASE: THE STATUS OF CHILDREN

A strategic long-range policy initiative requires not only good, reliable information but information from a variety of sources. Several approaches and technologies are possible—but all require that data be shared for a common purpose. The "right" choice is never clear. It depends on the subject matter, the priority of the initiative, the organizational and managerial skill of the institutional players, the political commitment of elected leaders. The richest stores of government information are collected to support program operations. These databases are usually custom-designed and highly detailed. They are not built to support policy analysis or research but to administer programs. Some other kind of database, perhaps drawn from these operational sources, is needed for this purpose. The key complicating feature of a research database like the one discussed here is its ability to support analyses that cut across traditional program and organizational boundaries.

INTRODUCTION

Concerned by the sobering results of the last census, a number of scholarly studies since, and especially by face-to-face experiences during his campaign, newly elected Governor James Akers has decided that the overriding "people" theme for his administration must be the endangered status of children. Demographers warn that the numbers of children and youth are declining relative to older age groups. At the same time, children are increasingly growing up in poverty, in single-parent homes, and in deteriorating communities. These are particularly acute problems for minority children. In general, fewer and fewer households have children present, suggesting that fewer adults are concerned with their needs. Drug abuse is threatening an entire generation whose educational attainment for the first time in history may not even match, much less exceed, that of its parents.

For a time the warnings were taken as provocative reports from scholarly research centers. But today, examples abound in every community: entry-level workers are harder to find and less able than in earlier generations. Every family, regardless of its economic status, knows of a child involved in drugs or suicide. Governor Akers maintains eloquently that these problems need attention now, in every community, and has committed the state's authority and resources to the campaign.

THE CURRENT SITUATION

A retreat of key executive branch officials has been scheduled to discuss this initiative. One topic on the agenda is the need for ongoing information that describes, tracks, and supports analysis of the status of children. While agency heads discuss themes, subthemes, and program initiatives, selected executives from a number of agencies are devoting their time to conceptualizing an information base. Four people in the group have come prepared with specific proposals.

THE PLAYERS AND THEIR PROPOSALS

Phillip Williamson, Director of the Management
Improvement Group, State Office of Budget
and Finance

Williamson is a young, dynamic, recently arrived administrator. He was brought into state government by the new Budget and Finance director, an experienced insurance company CEO, who is very business-oriented and a close personal adviser to the governor. Williamson was a vice president in the same insurance firm before being recruited to OBF by the director.

Williamson's Proposal: A Person-oriented Database. Williamson begins by pointing out that all children known to state agencies have Social Security numbers (SSNs) by age five. Most have them at even younger ages. These numbers are listed on their parents' tax returns and on all applications for any form of public assistance. The database he proposes could be constructed from existing files initially and could be built over time to add records for new births. An initial effort would involve a series of computer matches among agencies to test the idea, gather information about patterns, and decide on the comprehensiveness of the individual record. It's a tried and true technology, does not require any new data collection for children already involved in any state-sponsored program, and is a straightforward use of operating information.

Williamson realizes that the confidentiality requirements of such a system must be high. But he argues that billions of personal records are already being maintained and matched by both government and businesses everywhere in the nation. It is foolish to deny that this exists, and equally foolish to refuse to take advantage of these files and technologies when so much is at stake. He also knows that legislative authorization, particularly to use tax records, will be needed. However, this has been done in the past—as long as the reason is compelling, and reasonable safeguards are built in. A person-oriented system has many advantages: comprehensiveness, ability to understand the patterns of childhood experiences by looking at the histories of individual real children, and enough information to suggest intervention in specific cases or in individual programs that show warning indicators of a failed social support system.

Charlene DiLello, Staff Director, the Status of Children Commission

DiLello is a respected veteran of a national policy research center. She is known for the high quality and insight of her work and has served on advisory boards for several federal commissions on family and educational policy. The commission is brand new and needs to make a place for itself in the constellation of state government organizations. Its official mission is to increase awareness and understanding of children's issues throughout the state—within government, the business community, and the general public.

DiLello's Proposal: A Longitudinal Tracking System.   A rolling sample of 0–12 year-olds would be selected and rolled forward each year, adding new sample cases selected from children born in the preceding year and dropping those who "age out" of the study. This group would serve as a bellwether of the experiences and conditions of the entire childhood population in the state. They would be tracked at regular intervals, and information would be gathered through interviews, surveys, and computer matches of agency information systems.

DiLello argues that only carefully controlled and professionally conducted research will give results that can reliably be used in the policy-making process. Moreover, the commission, with its bipartisan membership appointed by both the governor and the legislative leaders, has no agenda to serve outside of this single policy initiative. Since it operates no programs, it can be trusted to be evenhanded in its evaluations. While, admittedly, it will take time to show results, DiLello lectures on the critical need for information to be reliable if it is to support something so important as the future human resources of the state.

The commission, she argues, is the right place for this effort. Everyone knows that, unfortunately, after the first blush of this initiative fades, operating agencies will turn to more-pressing daily responsibilities. Worse, if their financial resources become scarce, research projects will probably be the first thing to go. This effort needs to be located in a place where it will not be forced to compete with crisis-prone operations for visibility and support.

Charles Wing, Research Director, Department of Family and Children's Services

Wing is a five-year veteran of the agency who survived the change in administration and is eager to show just how much good research can add to good program operations and policy making. Wing represents an agency that is considered the central source of services and programs for children. It has a great deal of information of its own but has generally been unsuccessful in getting related agencies to routinely share their program information. Since DFCS is often the last stop in a family's decline, Wing has long advocated that information about the more "normal" circumstances of a child's life must be brought into the picture if the state is to ever design effective preventive programs or bolster healthy environments.

Wing's Proposal: A Geographic Database.   Wing advocates a recent and growing new technology—a geographic database of both demographic and program information drawn from all the agencies that have data on the circumstances and status of children. He proposes that the database be built initially in a series of layers. In each layer, data would be aggregated at the lowest geographic level available in existing records systems (consistent, of course, with confidentiality standards). In some instances, this would be at the level of a county, in others, census tracts or zip codes. By displaying this information in overlaying maps, it becomes possible to see graphically the intersection of population and program characteristics—it is a powerful analytical tool.

This kind of information system would offer policy makers the distinct advantage of being able to see existing cross-program patterns at the substate level. Since most program data is already aggregated regularly for statistical reporting purposes, it would take little additional effort to load it into a geographic system. Wing recently cajoled some assistance from the state tax office that operates a large geographic system for property assessments, and he has come armed with some convincing map outputs on foster care. With them he shows that communities that are matched on a set of demographic variables have widely different rates of foster care placements and recidivism. Such information should target the communities at either end of the spectrum for special attention. What makes them fail? What makes them succeed? In a time when funds for programming always seem to be shrinking in proportion to the size of the problems they are to solve, an ability to hone in on this kind of experience would be invaluable. How much more powerful these maps could be, he contends, if they also selectively displayed other information such as housing patterns, mental health characteristics, patterns of drug use, and school attendance records.

Wing wants to see a geographic system built in his agency. It avoids the confidentiality problems, gives fast results, and has synergistic qualities that none of the other proposals can match.

Marianne Moreau, Deputy Commissioner for Research, Planning, and Information Services, Department of Education

Moreau is the most experienced state official in the group. She has come up through the ranks as a planner and has always worked in the field of education. Moreau feels strongly that public service programs are so complex, and their problems so many-faceted, that only subject-area experts are competent to interpret them. Moreau is not alone in this. She represents the feelings of most agencies in which children represent only a part of a larger programmatic mission (e.g., health, mental health, etc.).

Moreau's Proposal: A Planned Series of Agency-based Research Reports.
Moreau begins by explaining that every agency has had bad experiences when uninterpreted information has been used by nonexperts. The conclusions inevitably find their way into the press, and the agency spends more time defending itself and trying to explain what's wrong with the reported data than it would conducting and disseminating good solid research of its own.

She envisions a well-supported, thoroughly-thought-out research series in which agency-based researchers treat critical issues with all the expertise and experience the organization has to offer. This idea has no confidentiality problems, requires no special technologies or big-ticket information systems, and, above all, makes the best use of deep wells of program knowledge resident within the agencies. It takes a huge subject, "the status of children," and breaks it into manageable bites—"educational attainment of inner-city youth," "trends in adolescent pregnancies," etc.

Moreau believes strongly in government's responsibility to inform. She doesn't see how sharing batches of raw data can match the production of "real" information in the form of carefully written reports that give context and interpretation in addition to simple facts.

THE ASSIGNMENT

The governor's special assistant for Children's Affairs, Katherine Manning, is chairing this session and is open to all ideas. She is, however, a shrewd judge of bureaucratic politics and a good policy analyst herself. She is aware of the broad outlines of each of the positions that will be discussed. But what questions should she pose to each of the parties present to further explore their proposals? By what criteria should they be evaluated?

You are Manning's assistant. She has asked you to prepare a detailed script summarizing how she should approach each of the presenters at the meeting. Detail for her the strengths and weaknesses of each proposal, evaluating them in terms of technical feasibility, organizational impact, and ability to get the job done.

Finally, give Manning one or several integrative proposals that, in your opinion, meld the best of each of the four agency proposals. For each proposal you sketch, give her your opinion of who will support and who will oppose it and how she might handle these objections in the meeting. Manning will use your suggestions as she guides the discussion.

Further Reflections

1. Chapter 5, "Information, Citizen, and State," examines in more detail the issue of personal privacy. After reviewing the contents of Chapter 5, draft a memo to Manning outlining for her the privacy issues inherent in each of the four proposals.

However, when privacy conflicts with another important policy goal (such as improving the status of children across the state), compromises can usually be constructed that respect both issues. For each of the privacy issues you have identified for Manning, also recommend compromises that might allow the information system to move forward.

2. Chapters 2 and 3 discuss a number of policy issues related to government information management, especially organizational ones. Several times those chapters suggest that new organizational forms are brought into existence to meet the challenges posed by modern information technologies. The Status of Children Commission may be just such an entity, custom-made to be the home for a policy-oriented database. On the other hand, the Status of Children Commission may not have the needed organizational capacity to implement such a system and may engender conflict with more established agencies.

Draft a memo to Manning discussing where the lead for this new policy-oriented information system should be located. Explicitly discuss the implications of placing this new analytic capability in a relatively new organization with a cross-cutting perspective versus putting it into a more established organization with more substantial operating responsibilities.

SELECTED
BIBLIOGRAPHY

ALTER, ALLAN E. The Art of the State. *CIO* 2(2): 28–39, November 1988.

ATKINS, WILLIAM. Jesse James at the Terminal. *Harvard Business Review* (63)4: 82–87, July–August 1985.

BELL, DANIEL. *The Coming of Post-Industrial Society.* New York: Basic Books, 1973.

BIGELOW, ROBERT P. *Symposium on Computers in Law and Society,* 76 Wash.U.Q. 527 (1977).

BOORSTIN, DANIEL J. *The Republic of Technology.* New York: Harper & Row, 1978.

BOZEMAN, BARRY. *Public Management and Policy Analysis.* New York: St. Martin's Press, 1979.

BOZEMAN, BARRY, and STUART BRETSCHNEIDER. Public Management Information Systems: Theory and Prescription. *Public Administration Review* 46(SI): 475–87, November 1986.

BREATH, C. M., and B. IVES. Competitive Information Systems in Support of Pricing. *MIS Quarterly:* 85–93, March 1986.

BURNHAM, DAVID. *The Rise of the Computer State.* New York: Vintage Books Division of Random House, 1984.

BURNHAM, DAVID. Ruling Pressures IRS to Modify Its Ways Significantly. *Times Union.* Albany: December 13, 1987: B-6.

CASH, JAMES I., JR., and BENN R. KONSYNSKI. IS Redraws Competitive Boundaries. *Harvard Business Review* 63 (2): 134–42, March–April 1985.

CAUDLE, SHARON L. *Federal Information Resources Management: Bridging Vision and Action.* Academy Studies, National Academy of Public Administration, June 1987.

CHANDLER, ALFRED D., JR., *The Visible Hand.* Cambridge, MA: Belnap Press of Harvard University Press, 1977.

CHEH, MARY M. Government Control of Private Ideas. *Striking a Balance: National Security and Scientific Freedom,* Harold C. Relyea, ed. Washington: American Association for the Advancement of Science, May 1985.

CLEMONS, ERIC K., and F. WARREN McFARLAN. Telecom: Hook Up or Lose Out. *Harvard Business Review* 64(4): 91–97, July–August 1986.

CLEVELAND, HARLAN. Government Is Information (But Not Vice Versa). *Public Administration Review* 46(6): 605-7, November-December 1986.

CLEVELAND, HARLAN. *The Knowledge Executive: Leadership in an Information Society.* New York: E. P. Dutton, 1985. 261 pp. Reviewed in *Public Administration Review* 46(6): 673-74, November-December 1986.

CLEVELAND, HARLAN. The Twilight of Hierarchy: Speculations on the Global Information Society. *Public Administration Review* 45(1): 185-95, January-February 1985.

CLOUSE, GARY. *The Constitutional Right to Withhold Private Information,* 77 N.W.Univ.L.Rev. 537 (1982).

COOPER, PHILLIP J. Acquisition, Use, and Dissemination of Information: A Consideration and Critique of the Public Law Perspective. *Administrative Law Review* 33(Winter 1981): 81-107.

COOPER, PHILLIP J. The Supreme Court, the First Amendment, and Freedom of Information. *Public Administration Review* 46(6): 622-28, November-December 1986.

CROSS, HAROLD L. *The People's Right to Know.* New York: Columbia University Press, 1953.

DANZIGER, JAMES. Computer and Local Government and the Litany of EDP. *Public Administration Review* 36(1): 28-37, January 1977.

DANZIGER, JAMES, et al. *Computers and Politics: High Technology in American Local Government.* New York: Columbia University Press, 1982.

DAVIES, THOMAS R., and WILLIAM M. HALE. Implementing a Policy and Planning Process for Managing State Use of Information Technology Resources. *Public Administration Review* 46(SI): 516-21, November 1986.

DEARSTYNE, BRUCE W. Saving Electronic Records. *State Government News,* Council of State Governments, 31(10): 23, October 1988.

DEITZ, JAMES. *Federal Government Computer Data Sharing and the Threat to Privacy.* 61 U.Det.J.Urb.L. 605 (1977).

DIZARD, WILSON. *The Coming Information Age.* Second Edition. New York: Longman, 1985.

EIN-DOR, PHILLIP, and ELI SEGEV. Organizational Context and the Success of Management Information Systems. *Management Science* 24(10): 1065-77, June 1978.

ELLUL, JACQUES. *The Technological Society.* Translated by John Wilkinson. New York: Alfred A. Knopf, 1964.

FEINBERG, LOTTE E. Managing the Freedom of Information Act and Federal Information Policy. *Public Administration Review* 46(6): 615-21, November-December 1986.

GIBSON, CYRUS F., and THOMAS H. DAVENPORT. Systems Change: Managing Organizational and Behavioral Impact. *Information Strategy: The Executive's Journal* (Fall 1985): 23-27.

GLUCK, FREDERICK W., and RICHARD N. FOSTER. Managing Technological Change: A Box of Cigars for Brad. *Harvard Business Review* 53(5): 139-50, September-October 1975.

GORR, WILPEN L. Use of Special Event Data in Government Information Systems. *Public Administration Review* 46(SI): 532-39, November 1986.

GORRY, ANTHONY, and MICHAEL S. SCOTT MORTON. A Framework for Management Information Systems. *Sloan Management Review* 13(Fall 1971): 55-70.

GURWITT, ROB. Computers: New Ways to Govern. *Governing* 1(8): 34-42, May 1988.

HADDEN, SUSAN G. Intelligent Advisory Systems for Managing and Disseminating Information. *Public Administration Review* 46(SI): 572-78, November 1986.

HEAPHEY, JAMES, and ROBERT CROWLEY. Standardizing Welfare Management: The State versus the Counties. *New York Case Studies in Public Management—ER008.* Albany, NY: Rockefeller Institute of Government, 1984.

HERNON, PETER, and CHARLES R. MCCLURE. *Federal Information Policies in the 1980s: Conflicts and Issues.* Norwood, NJ: Ablex Publishing Corporation, 1987.

HORTON, FOREST W. *Information Resources Management.* Englewood Cliffs, NJ: Prentice Hall, 1985.

HORTON, FOREST W., JR. *Information Resources Management: Concept and Cases.* Cleveland: Association for Systems Management, 1979.

HORTON, FOREST W., and DONALD A. MARCHAND, eds. *Information Management in Public Administration.* Arlington, VA: Information Resources Press, 1982.

HORTON, FOREST W., ed. *Understanding US Information Policy: The Infostructure Handbook.* Volume 1, The Information Policy Primer. Washington: Information Industry Association, 1982.

IVES, BLAKE, and G. P. LEARMONTH. The Information System as a Competitive Weapon. *Communications of the ACM* (December 1984): 1193-1201.

IVES, BLAKE, SCOTT HAMILTON, and GORDON DAVIS. A Framework for Research in Computer-based Management Information Systems. *Management Science* 39(September 1980): 910–34.

KANTER, ROSABETH MOSS. *The Change Masters.* New York: Simon & Schuster, 1983.

KANTER, ROSABETH MOSS. The Middle Manager as Innovator. *Harvard Business Review*, 60(4): 95–105, July–August 1982.

KEEN, PETER G. W., and MICHAEL S. SCOTT MORTON. *Decision Support Systems: An Organizational Perspective.* Reading, MA: Addison-Wesley, 1978.

KEEN, PETER G. W., and LYNDA A. WOODMAN. What to Do with All Those Micros. *Harvard Business Review* (62)5: 142–250, September–October 1984.

KELLY, MARCIA M. Telecommuting: The Next Workplace Revolution. *Information Strategy: The Executive's Journal* (Winter 1986): 20–23.

KIEL, L. DOUGLAS. Information Systems Education in Masters Programs in Public Affairs and Administration. *Public Administration Review* 46(SI): 590–94, November 1986.

KIRCHNER, JAKE. Privacy—A History of Computer Matching in the Federal Government. *Computerworld* 15(December 14, 1981).

KOTTER, JOHN P., and LEONARD A. SCHLESINGER. Choosing Strategies for Change. *Harvard Business Review* (57)2: 106–14, March–April 1979.

KRAEMER, KENNETH L., and JAMES DANZIGER. Computers and Control in the Work Environment. *Public Administration Review* 44 (1): 32–42, January–February 1984.

KRAEMER, KENNETH L., and JOHN LESLIE KING. Computers and the Constitution: A Helpful, Harmful, or Harmless Relationship? *Public Administration Review*, 47(1): 93–105, January–February 1987.

KRAEMER, KENNETH L., and JOHN LESLIE KING. Computing and Public Organizations. *Public Administration Review*, 46 (SI): 488–96, November 1986.

KRAEMER, KENNETH L., and JAMES PERRY. The Federal Push to Bring Computer Applications to Local Government. *Public Administration Review* 39(May 1979): 260–70.

KRAEMER, KENNETH L., et al. *The Management of Computers.* New York: Columbia University Press, 1981.

LAUDON, KENNETH C. *Computers and Bureaucratic Reform.* New York: John Wiley, 1974.

LAUDON, KENNETH C. *Dossier Society.* New York: Columbia University Press, 1986.

LAWRENCE, PAUL R. How to Deal with Resistance to Change. *Harvard Business Review* (January–February 1969): 4–13.

Legislative History of the Privacy Act. U.S. Code Congressional and Administrative News. 93rd Congress, 2nd Session, 1974.

LUCAS, HENRY. Performance and Use of an Information System. *Management Science* 21(April 1975): 908–19.

MAGEE, JOHN F. What Information Technology Has in Store for Managers. *Sloan Management Review* (Winter 1985): 45–49.

Management's Newest Star: Meet the Chief Information Officer. *Business Week* (October 13, 1986): 160–64, 170, 172.

Massachusetts Secretary of State. Public Records Division. *Report of the First National Conference on Issues Concerning Computerized Records.* Boston, 1987.

MCCAFFREY, DAVID P., and RONALD H. MILLER. Improving Regulatory Information: New York's Transition to Environmental Fees. *Public Administration Review* 46(1): 75–83, January–February 1986.

MCCLURE, CHARLES. Managing Public Information. *State Government News,* Council of State Governments 31(10): 14–16, October 1988.

MCFARLAN, F. WARREN. Information Technology Changes the Way You Compete. *Harvard Business Review* 62(3): 98–103, May–June 1984.

MCFARLAN, F. WARREN, and JAMES L. MCKENNEY. *Corporate Information Systems Management: The Issues Facing Senior Management.* Richard D. Irwin, 1983.

MCFARLAN, F. WARREN, and JAMES L. MCKENNEY. The Information Archipelago—Maps and Bridges. *Harvard Business Review* 60 (5): 109, September–October 1982.

MCFARLAN, F. WARREN, JAMES L. MCKENNEY, and PHILIP PYBURN. The Information Archipelago—Plotting a Course. *Harvard Business Review*, 61(1): 145–56, January–February 1983.

MCGOWAN, ROBERT P., and GARY A. LOMBARDO. Decision Support Systems in State Government: Promises and Pitfalls. *Public Administration Review* 46(SI): 579–83, November 1986.

MEYER, N. DEAN and MARY E. BOONE. *The Information Edge.* New York: McGraw-Hill, 1987.

MILLAR, VICTOR E. Decision-oriented Information. *Datamation* (January 1984): 159.

MILLER, ARTHUR. *Personal Privacy in the Computer Age: The Challenge of a New Technology in an Information-oriented Society.* 67 Mich.L.Rev. 1091 (1969).

MINTZBERG, H. *Impediments to the Use of Management Information.* New York: National Association of Accountants, 1975.

MOODY, H. GERALD. Optical Storage: Mass Storage with Mass Appeal? *Information Strategy: The Executive's Journal* (Summer 1986): 44–46.

MOODY, H. GERALD. Voice Recognition: At the Threshold. *Information Strategy: The Executive's Journal* (Summer 1985): 40–42.

MOORE, JEFFREY. Business Schools Find a Theory of Information Technology is Elusive. *Chronicle of Higher Education,* July 30, 1986.

NAISBITT, JOHN. *Megatrends.* New York: Warner Books, 1982.

National Association of Schools of Public Affairs and Administration, Ad Hoc Committee on Computers in Public Management Education. Curriculum Recommendations for Public Management Education. *Public Administration Review* 46(SI) (November 1986): 595–602.

NEWLAND, CHESTER A. Public Management Information Systems—Editor's Note. *Public Administration Review* 46(SI): 474, November 1986.

NOLAN, RICHARD L. Managing Information Systems by Committee. *Harvard Business Review* 60(4): 72–79, July–August 1982.

NOLAN, RICHARD L. Managing the Crises in Data Processing. *Harvard Business Review,* 57(2): 81–93, March–April 1979.

O'BRIEN, DAVID. *The Public's Right to Know.* New York: Praeger, 1981.

OLSON, MARGRETHE, and NORMAN CHERVANY. The Relationship between Organizational Characteristics and the Structure of the Information Services Function. *MIS Quarterly* 4(June 1980): 57–67.

OVERMAN, E. SAM, and DON F. SIMANTON. Iron Triangles and Issue Networks of Information Policy. *Public Administration Review* 46(SI): 584–89, November 1986.

PARSONS, GREGORY L. Information Technology: A New Competitive Weapon. *Sloan Management Review* (Fall 1983): 3.

PERRY, JAMES, and KENNETH KRAEMER, eds. *Public Management: Public and Private Perspectives.* Palo Alto: Mayfield Publishing Co., 1983.

PORTER, MICHAEL E. *Competitive Advantage.* New York: Free Press, 1985.

PORTER, MICHAEL E. *Competitive Strategy.* New York: Free Press, 1980.

PORTER, MICHAEL E. How Competitive Forces Shape Strategy. *Harvard Business Review* (March–April 1979): 137.

PORTER, MICHAEL E., and VICTOR E. MILLAR. How Information Gives You Competitive Advantage. *Harvard Business Review* 63(4): 149, July–August 1985.

Privacy Protection Study Commission. *Personal Privacy in an Information Society.* Washington, DC: Government Printing Office, 1977.

PROSSER, WILLIAM. *Privacy.* 48 Calif.L.Rev. (1960).

QUARTERMAN, JOHN S., and JOSIAH C. HOSKINS. Notable Computer Networks. *Communications of the AMC,* 29(10): 932–71, October 1986.

QUINN, ROBERT E. Impacts of a Computerized Information System on the Integration and Coordination of Human Services. *Public Administration Review,* 36(2), 1976.

QUINN, ROBERT E., and KIM CAMERON. Organizational Life Cycles and Shifting Criteria of Effectiveness: Some Preliminary Evidence. *Management Science.* (29): 33–51 1983.

QUINN, ROBERT E., and JOHN ROHRBAUGH. A Spatial Model of Effectiveness Criteria: Toward a Competing Values Approach to Organizational Analysis. *Management Science* 29(3): 363–77, 1983.

R&D Group Plugs Info Master Plans for Local Gov't. *Government Computer News* (March 28, 1986): 14–19.

REGAN, PRISCILLA. Privacy, Government Information and Technology. *Public Administration Review* 46(6): 629–34, November–December 1986.

RELYEA, HAROLD C. Access to Government Information in the Information Age. *Public Administration Review* 46(6): 635–39, November–December 1986.

RELYEA, HAROLD, and LOTTE FEINBERG, eds. *Symposium: Toward a Government Information Policy—FOIA at Twenty. Public Administration Review* 46(6): 603–39, November–December 1986.

ROCKART, JOHN F., and ADAM D. CRESCENZI. Engaging Top Management in Information Technology. *Sloan Management Review* (Summer 1984): 3–16.

ROCKART, JOHN F., and L. S. FLANNERY. The Management of End User Computing. *Communications of the ACM* (October 1983): 776–84.

ROCKART, JOHN F., and M. E. TRACY. The CEO Goes On-Line. *Harvard Business Review* 60 (1): 82–88, January–February 1982.

ROCKART, JOHN F., and CHRISTINE V. BULLEN, eds. *The Rise of Managerial Computing: The Best of the Center for Information Systems Research, Sloan School of Management*, MIT. Homewood, IL: Dow-Jones-Irwin, 1986.

RUBIN, BARRY M. Information Systems for Public Management: Design and Implementation. *Public Administration Review* 46(SI): 540–552, November 1986.

SHANGRAW, RALPH F., JR. How Public Managers Use Information: An Experiment Examining Choices of Computer and Printed Information. *Public Administration Review* 46(SI): 506–15, November 1986.

SIMMONS, AL. New York's Info Forum. *Government Technology Magazine* 1(4): July–August 1988.

STEVENS, JOHN M., and JOSEPHINE M. LAPLANTE. Factors Associated with Financial Decision Support Systems in State Government: An Empirical Exploration. *Public Administration Review* 46(SI): 522–31, November 1986.

STOKEY, EDITH, and RICHARD ZECKHAUSER. *A Primer for Policy Analysis.* New York: W.W. Norton, 1978.

STONE, NIDIA. InfoFind: A Practical Tool for Managing Information. *Information Management Review*, (Spring) 1988, 39–46.

SYNNOTT, WILLIAM R., and WILLIAM H. GRUBER. *Information Resource Management.* New York: John Wiley, 1981.

TIEN, JAMES M., and JAMES A. MCCLURE. Enhancing the Effectiveness of Computers in Public Organizations through Appropriate Use of Technology. *Public Administration Review* 46(SI): 553–62, November 1986.

TOREGAS, COSTIS. People, Services, and Technology. *State Government News*, Council of State Governments (31)10: 8–9, October 1988.

U.S. Congress. House. Hearings Before a Subcommittee of the Committee on Government Operations. *The Computer and Invasion of Privacy.* 89th Congress. 2nd Session. Washington, DC: Government Printing Office, 1966.

U.S. Congress. House. Hearings of a Subcommittee of the Committee on Government Operations. *Oversight of the Privacy Act.* 98th Congress. 1st Session. Washington, DC: Government Printing Office, 1983.

U.S. Congress. Office of Technology Assessment. *Federal Agency Information Technology: Electronic Record Systems and Individual Privacy.* 1986.

U.S. Congress. Office of Technology Assessment. *Informing the Nation, Federal Dissemination in an Electronic Age.* October 1988.

U.S. Congress. Office of Technology Assessment. *Federal Government Information Technology: Management, Security, and Congressional Oversight.* 1986.

U.S. Congress. Office of Technology Assessment. *Federal Government Information Technology: Electronic Surveillance and Civil Liberties.* Washington, DC: Government Printing Office, 1985.

U.S. Congress. Senate. Subcommittee of the Committee on the Judiciary. *Government Dossier: An Inventory of Government Information About Individuals.* Washington, DC: Government Printing Office, 1967.

U.S. Department of Health, Education and Welfare. *Records, Computers and the Rights of Citizens.* Washington, DC: Government Printing Office, 1973.

U.S. General Services Administration. Information Resources Management Service. *Computer Obsolescence: Federal Government and Private Sector.* 1987.

University of the State of New York, State Education Department, and State Archives and Records Administration. *A Strategic Plan for Managing and Preserving Electronic Records in New York State Government: Final Report of the Special Media Records Project.* August 1988.

WALLACE, WILLIAM A., and MICHAEL W. HURLEY. Expert Systems as Decision Aids for Public Managers: An Assessment of the Technology and Prototyping as a Design Strategy. *Public Administration Review* 46(SI): 563–71, November 1986.

WECHSLER, BARTON, and ROBERT W. BACKOFF. Policy Making and Administration in State Agencies: Strategic Management Approaches. *Public Administration Review* 46(4): 321–27, July–August, 1986.

WEISS, JANET A., JUDITH E. GRUBER, and ROBERT H. CARVER. Reflections on Value: Policy Makers

Evaluate Federal Information Systems. *Public Administration Review* 46(SI): 497–505, November 1986.

WESTIN, ALAN F. *Information Technology in a Democracy.* Cambridge: Harvard University Press, 1971.

WESTIN, ALAN. F. *Privacy and Freedom.* New York: Atheneum, 1967.

WESTIN, ALAN F., and Michael A. Baker. *Databanks in a Free Society.* New York: Quadrangle Books, 1972.

WHISTLER, THOMAS L. *The Impact of Computers on Organizations.* New York: Praeger 1970.

WYMAN, JOHN. Technology Myopia—The Need to Think Strategically about Technology. *Sloan Management review* 26(4): 59–64, Summer 1985.

ZUBOFF, SHOSHANA. *In the Age of the Smart Machine.* New York: Basic Books, 1988.

ZUBOFF, SHOSHANA. New Worlds of Computer-mediated Work. *Harvard Business Review* 60(5): 142–52, September–October 1982.

INDEX